CARVING SANTAS
with Special Interests

Ron Ransom

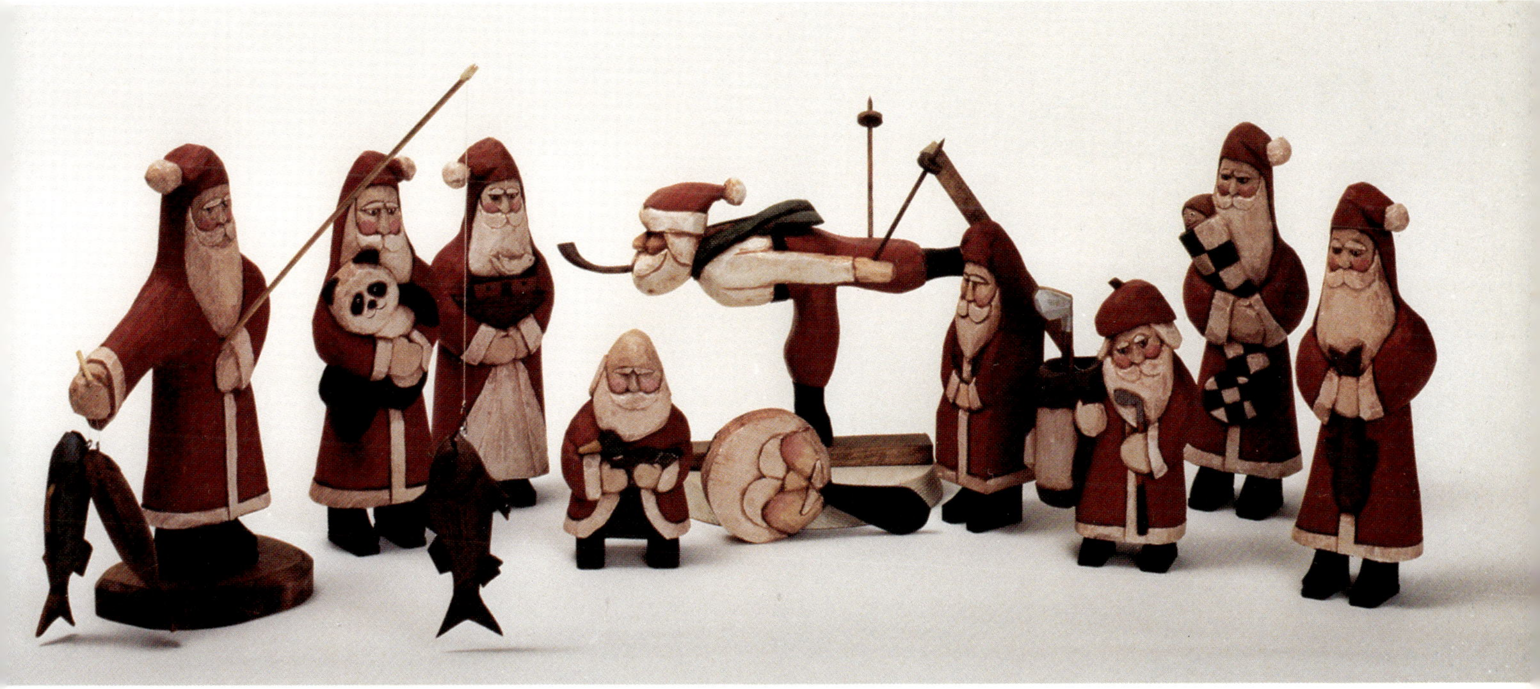

Photography by George A. Clark

I0792579

Schiffer Publishing Ltd

1469 Morstein Road, West Chester, Pennsylvania 19380

Dedication

To my sons, Randy and Scott, who are very special chips off the old block and to my brother, Hugh, who gave me my first knife and sex education. I've done more with the knife.

Published by Schiffer Publishing, Ltd.
1469 Morstein Road
West Chester, Pennsylvania 19380
Please write for a free catalog.
This book may be purchased from the publisher.
Please include $2.00 postage.
Try your bookstore first.

We are interested in hearing from authors
with book ideas on related subjects.

Library of Congress Catalog Number: 91-65655.

Printed in the United States of America.
ISBN: 0-88740-328-X

Foreword

I have to admit that I am a 60 year old Ransom Groupie. And I suppose a proper Foreword is usually done by such as a publisher, art critic, or academician. Well, not this time. For this, his third book on the subject, you get a retread who has found his nitch in woodcarving.

I am unabashedly for Ron Ransom and all he stands for. Things like Liberty, Motherhood, Freedom, Church, and the right of every adult to whittle. Of course the sophisticated among us call it wood carving, but when you come right down to it, it's whittlin'. The tools might be a little sharper or bigger, but it's still whittlin'. Just like we used to do when we were kids. And every bit as much fun.

Ah, the sheer joy of it, of picking up a piece of pine and a favorite knife, and actually breathing a new life into that wood. All my grown-up years I've longed to do this again, just as I used to do as a kid. All these years of pushing a typewriter and stringing words together; it was fun, but, inside, what I really wanted was a piece of wood, a penknife, and a little time just to sit and whittle.

There are only a few guys like Ron Ransom who have realized that life isn't total dedication to the work ethic. And that we, as adults, deserve time to recreate. He's done it, he took the time, and in the process he has created a simple beauty that has brought joy and happiness to all those thousands who have been exposed to his carvings, his books, his teachings, and his wit.

For here is the essence of relaxation coupled with productivity. I mean, where else would you find a grown man whittlin' such characters as Santa in his Jams, Mrs. Santa (who looks more like Jonathan Winters in drag), Santa with a banner, and this tall, thin dude with a long, thin Christmas list—all characters from Ron's second book, *Angel Carving*. Here's a hobby that is not only fun to do, but spreads endless cheer and happiness. Goodness knows, in this world of instant communications, we need some cheer.

So, if you're like me and enjoy wood carving, grab a knife and a chunk of basswood or pine, and get with it. Ransom is turning out new ideas so fast he's using up all the good stuff. We gotta hustle just to catch up.

D.R. Norris
Melrose, Massachusetts
Journalist—retired.
Artist—retired.
Stock marketer—retired.
Carver of Santa Clauses—active, at last.

Contents

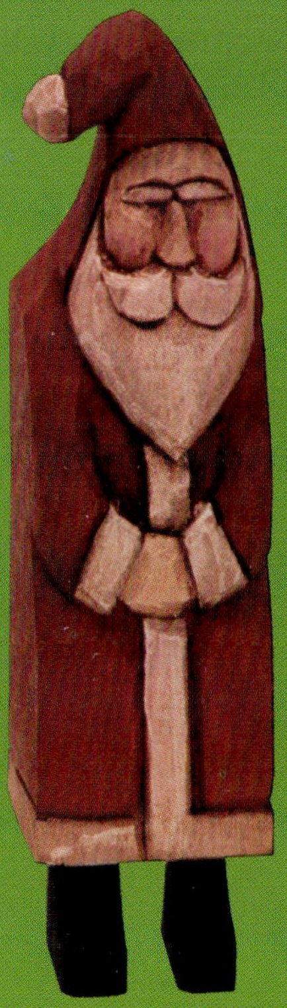

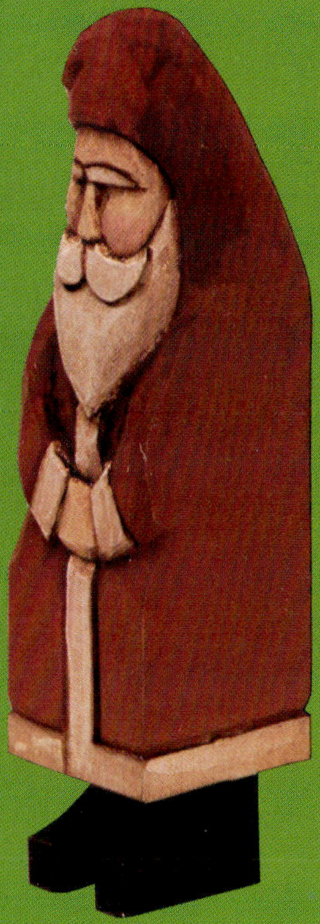

These are good examples of bad examples. New carvers sometimes have a problem getting their Santa rounded. The one above looks like he was trapped in a chimney and assumed the square shape. I use him in classes to emphasize the square look. The other example is what I call the frying pan face. Try to get the face area as egg-shaped as possible before you start cutting.

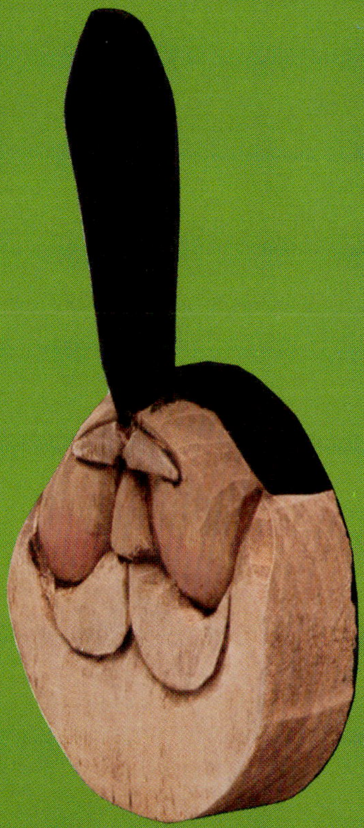

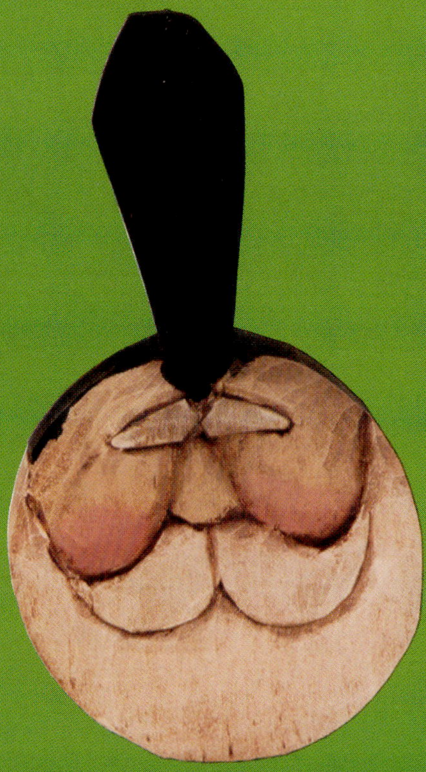

Introduction

I am a firm believer in "if it ain't broke, don't fix it." In this, my third book, I want to go a little further into Santa carving. Your letters and calls, and of course, periodic prodding from my publisher, have encouraged me to share additional ideas.

I have heard from many of you who have begun to make a few bucks carving and selling Santas, and even more who are doing it for your own enjoyment.

The market for Santas seems to be growing. I feel this is partly due to the fact that most collectors only put them out during the holiday season and don't get tired of seeing them. I also think a greater love and understanding of wood carving is taking place. New clubs are being established all over and the publicity seems to be reaching the right people.

The Southeastern Woodcarvers had their first show here in my hometown of Marietta, Georgia, last June and we plan to make it an annual event. We had over one hundred exhibitors and vendors from all over the country. For our first show we thought the crowds were good.

Anyway, back to the book. I've found that people with special interests enjoy Santas that show that special interest. There are very few people who have not collected. I still have some marbles from my childhood and my wife has a great collection of little antique cows. The collectibles and special interest items shown in this, my third book, have either been special to me or someone I know.

I hope these designs stimulate you to new heights in carving and creating Santas.

As in the past, I welcome your letters, phone calls and visits. Send any questions or comments to Ron Ransom, Box 4101, Marietta, GA 30061.

Please send a stamped, self-addressed envelope.

Ron Ransom, 1991

I realized that the women who do not carve would like something to do while the hubby or boyfriend is carving Ransom Santas.

A company here in Marietta, Georgia, created a cross stitch book inspired by designs from my first two books. If you have a significant other who might enjoy stitching while you're carving, check with your local needlework store. The book is called *Folk-Art Trimmings*. My friend, Kris Lyden, of Winter Park, Florida did the cross stitch pillows for my wife and me.

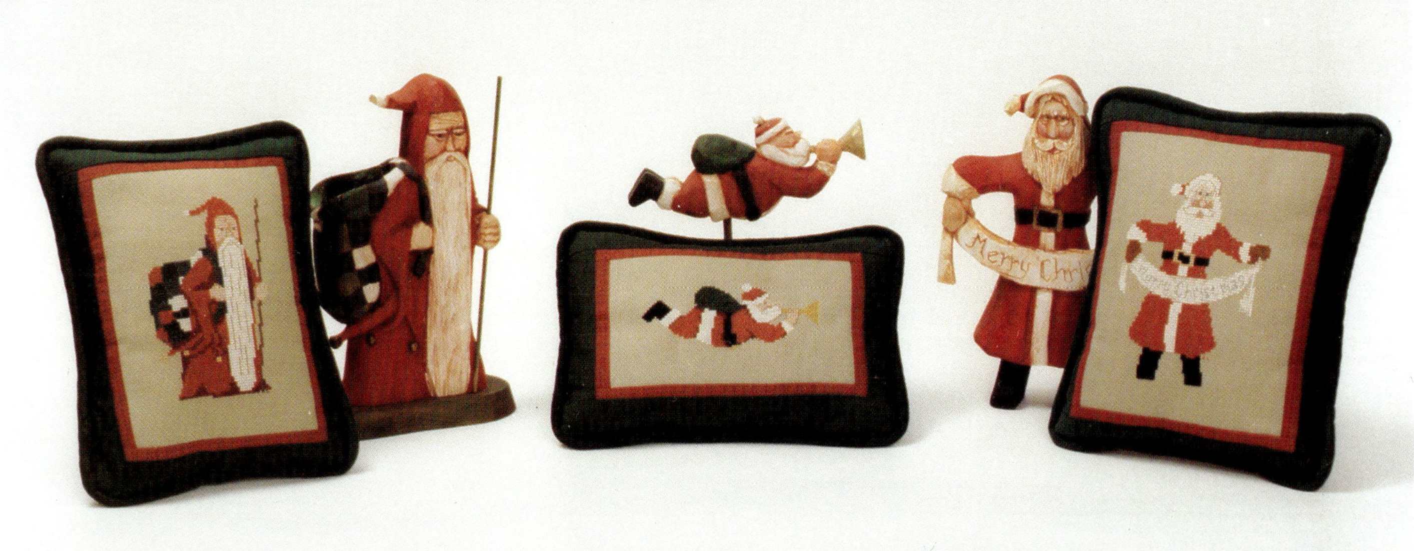

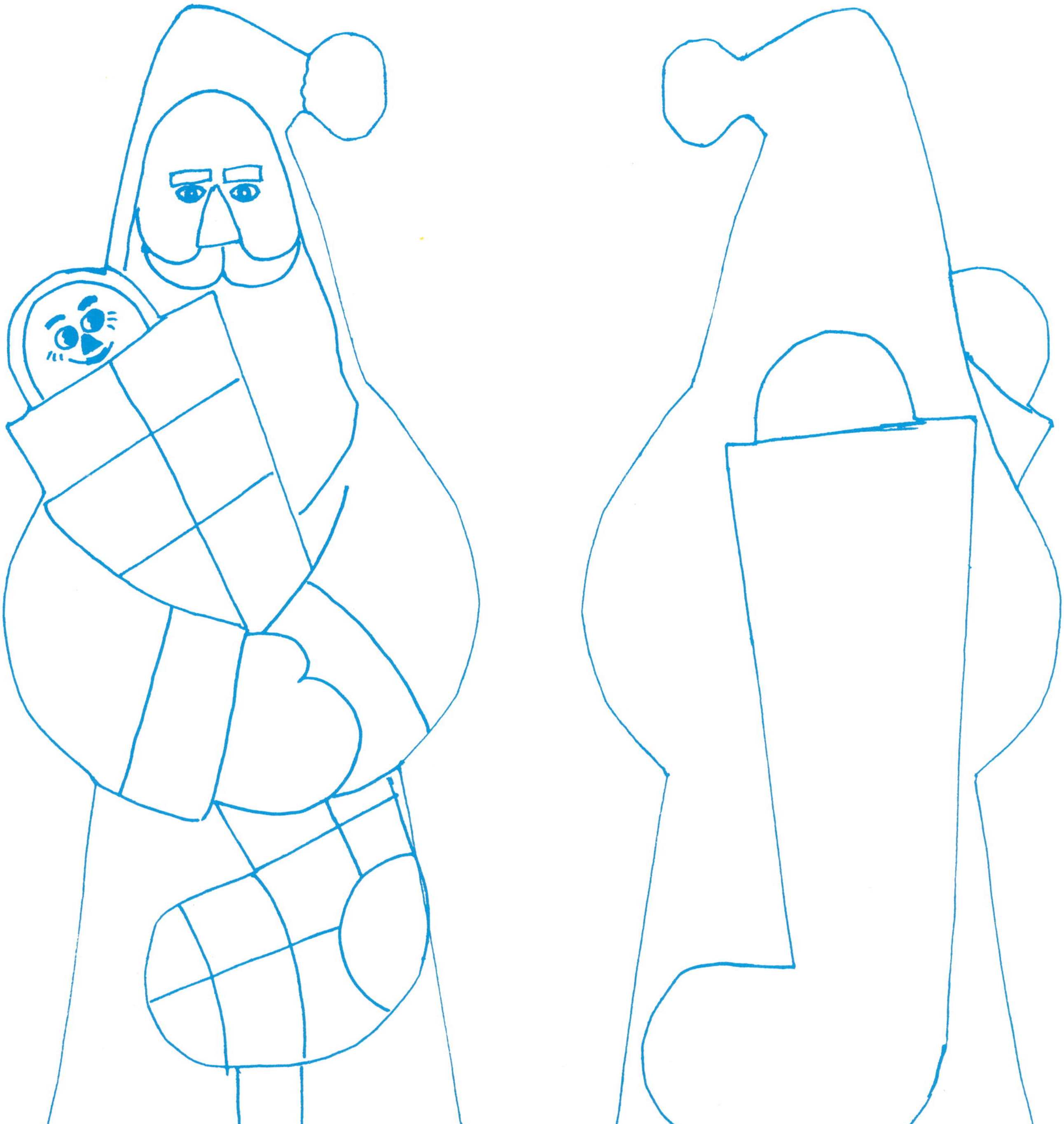

Santa With Stocking

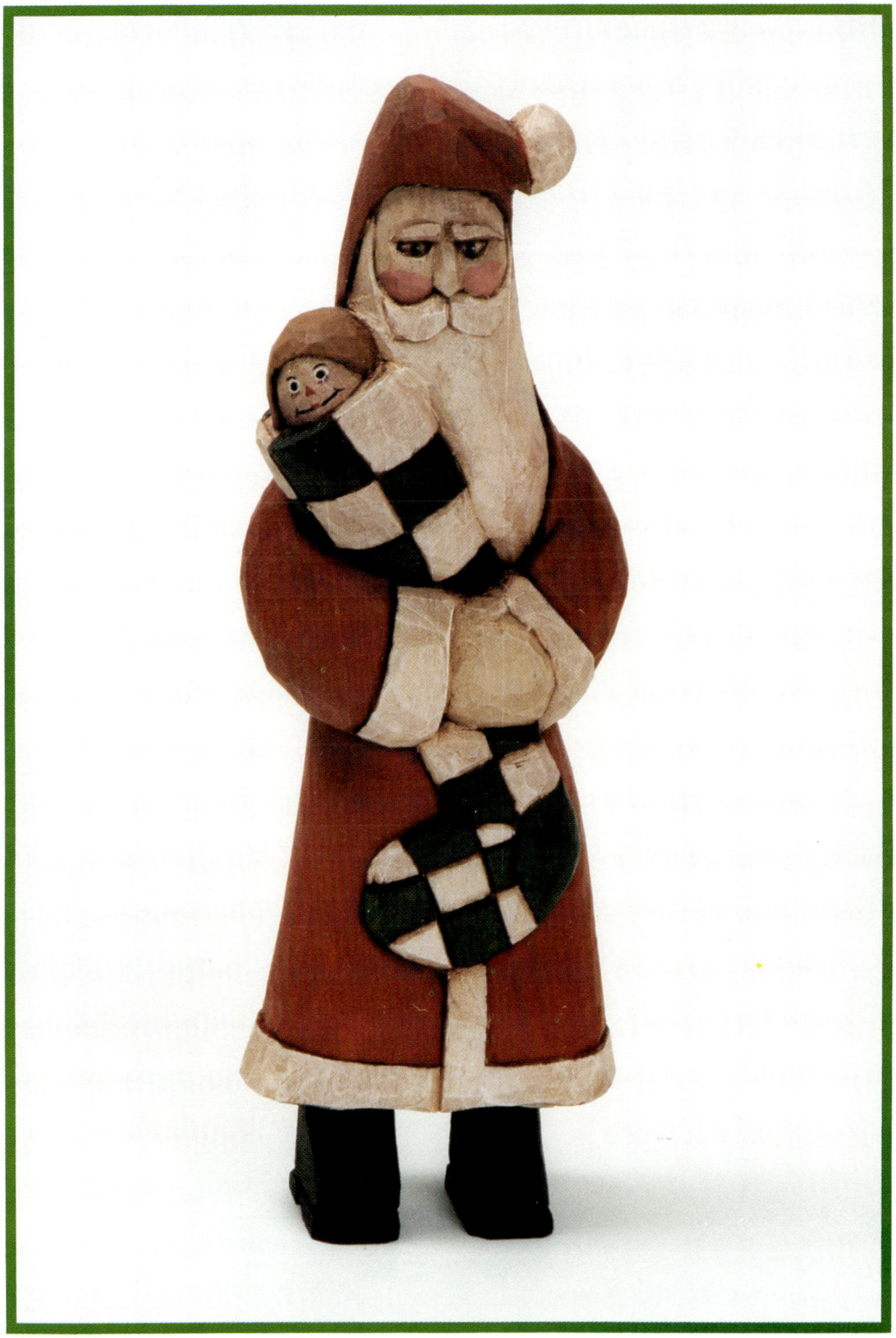

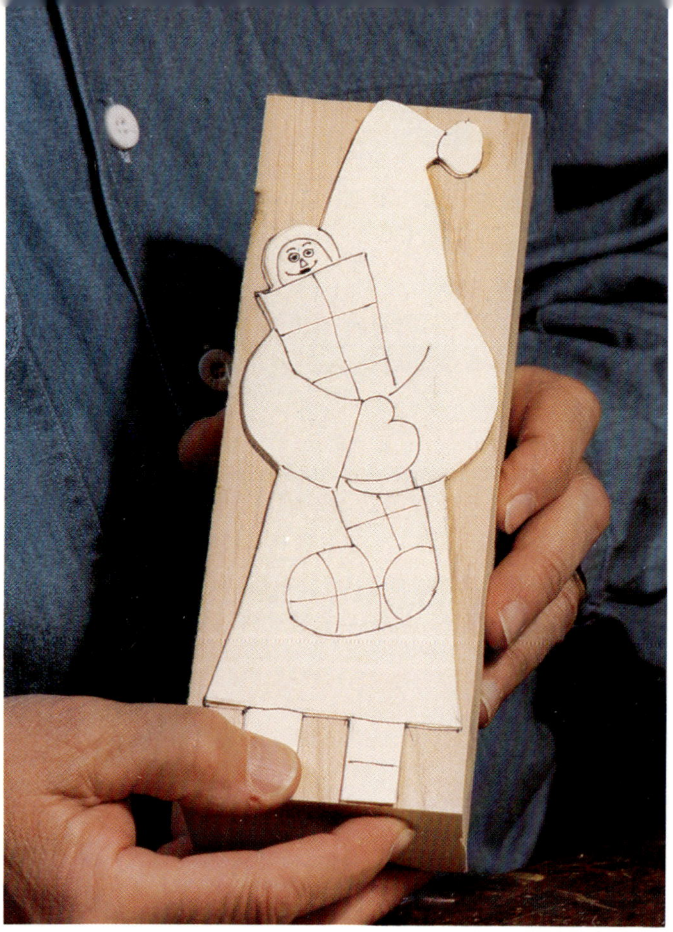

Trace the pattern on a basswood block 1¾" thick, 9" high, and 3¼" wide.

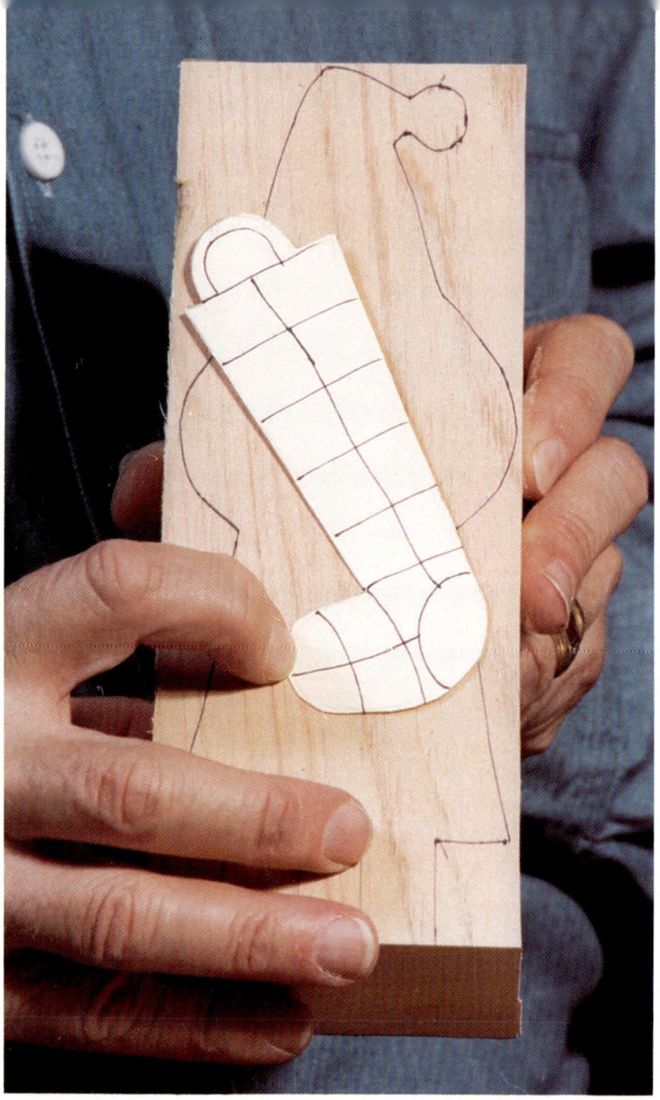

Unless otherwise specified, all wood is 1¾" thick. I cut the stocking pattern out to help position it on the Santa.

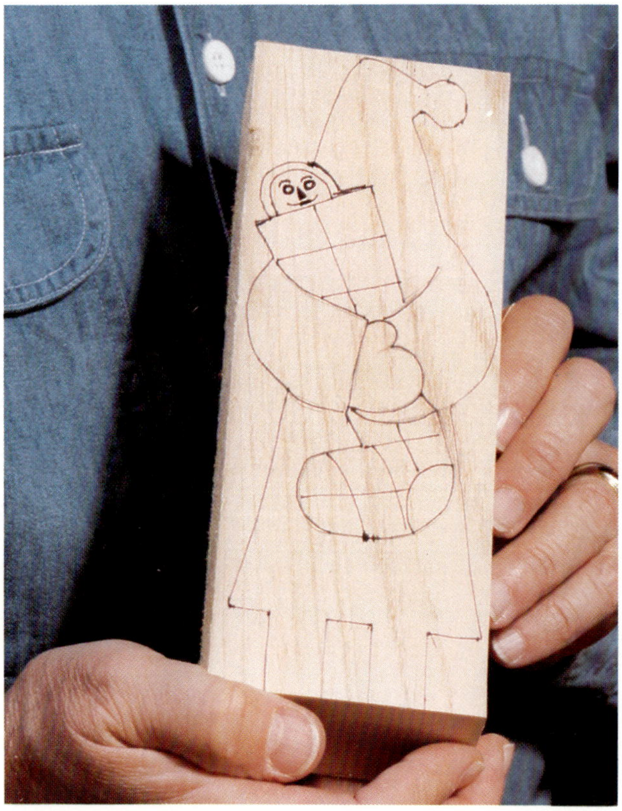

The pattern is ready to cut.

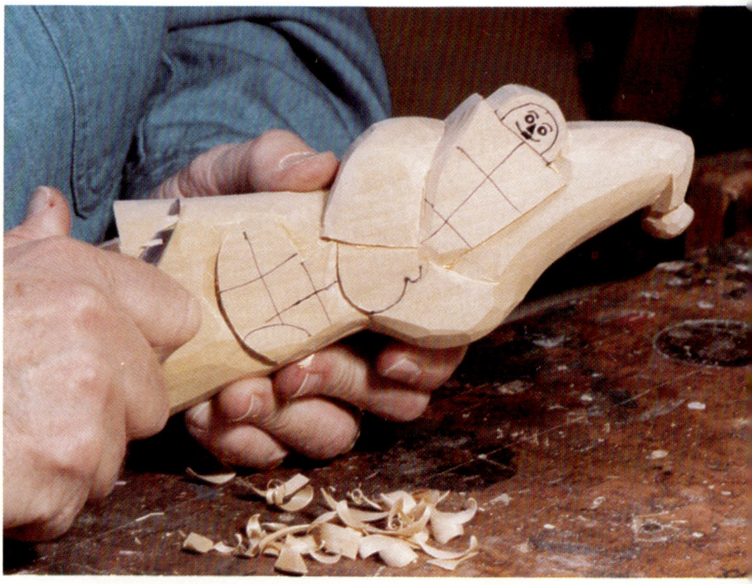

After carefully cutting, begin to round and shape. Remember the example of the square Santa.

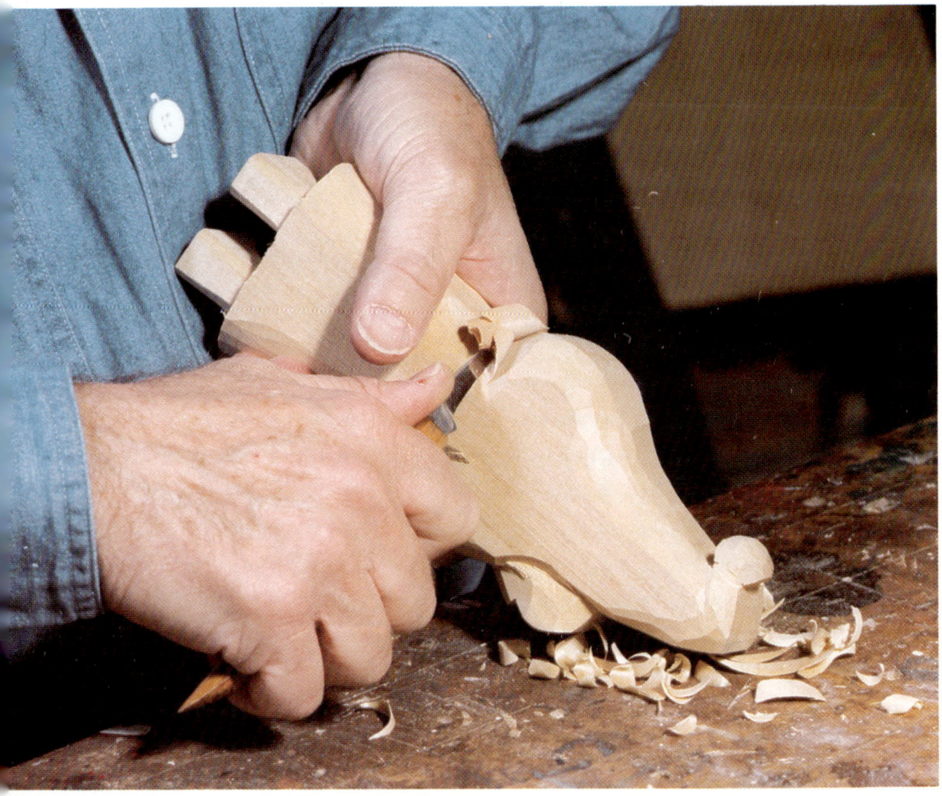

Continue to round. Notice the roundness of the left arm. Round the ball on the hood. Don't worry if you cut it off. It will look O.K. without the ball.

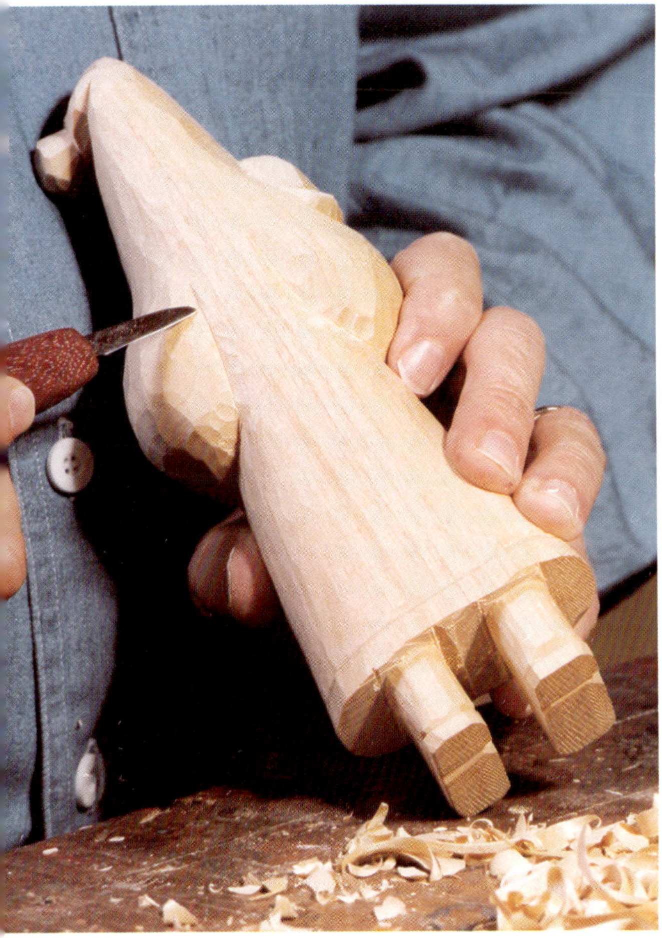

I've gone into detail with back carving a little further on.

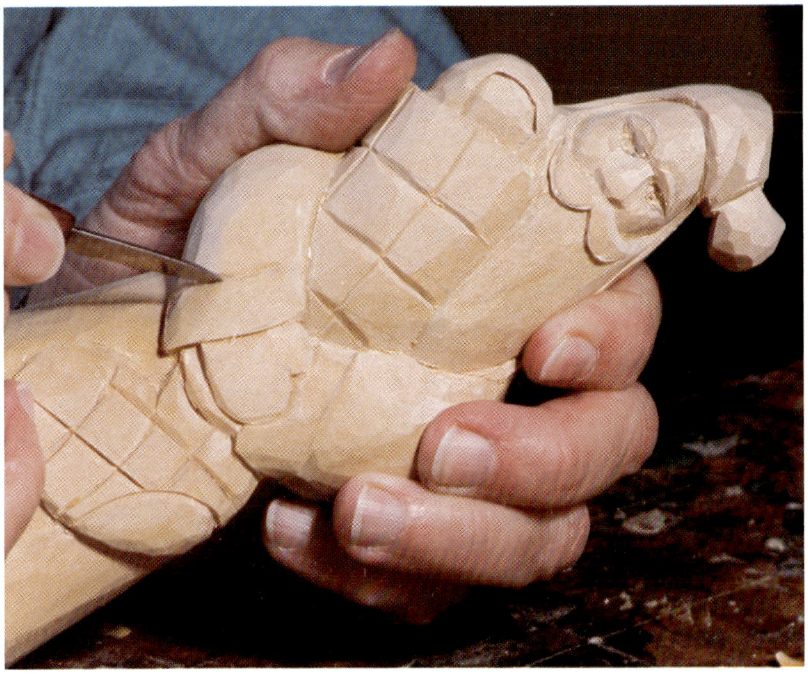

I have started incising lines.

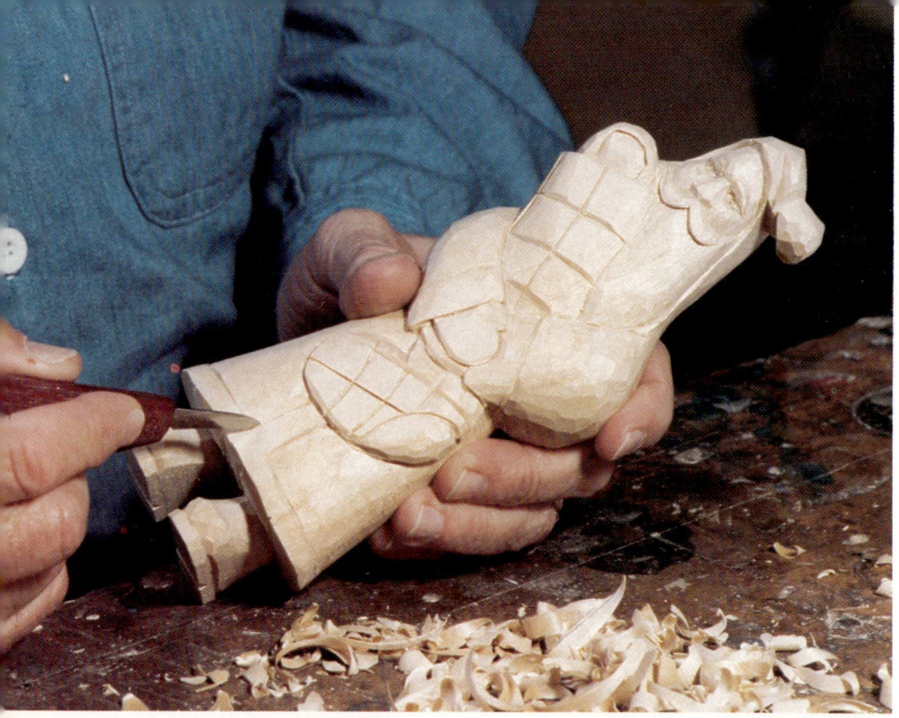

Don't be concerned with cutting too deeply with your incising.

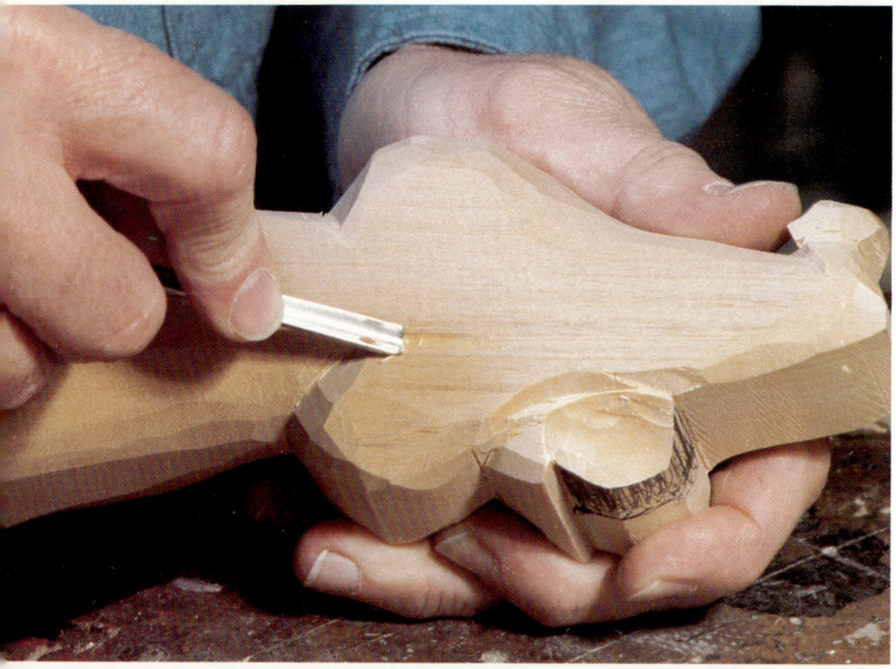

From the mail I received after "Santa Carving" was published, I found I assumed too much about backs. I hope these photos will help. Make a good groove with a gouge or by making a series of V-cuts and rounding the edges of these cuts.

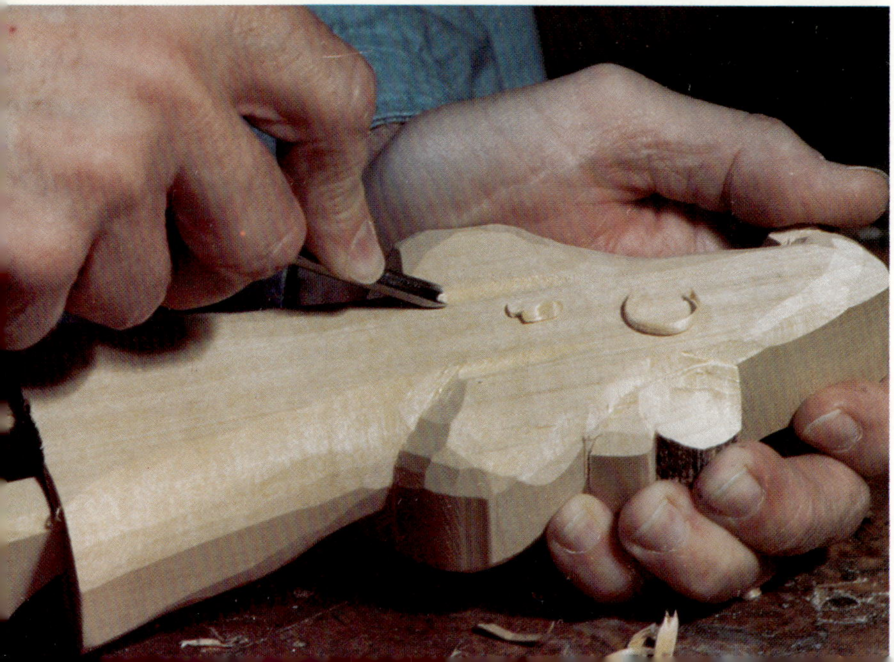

Do the other arms in the same way.

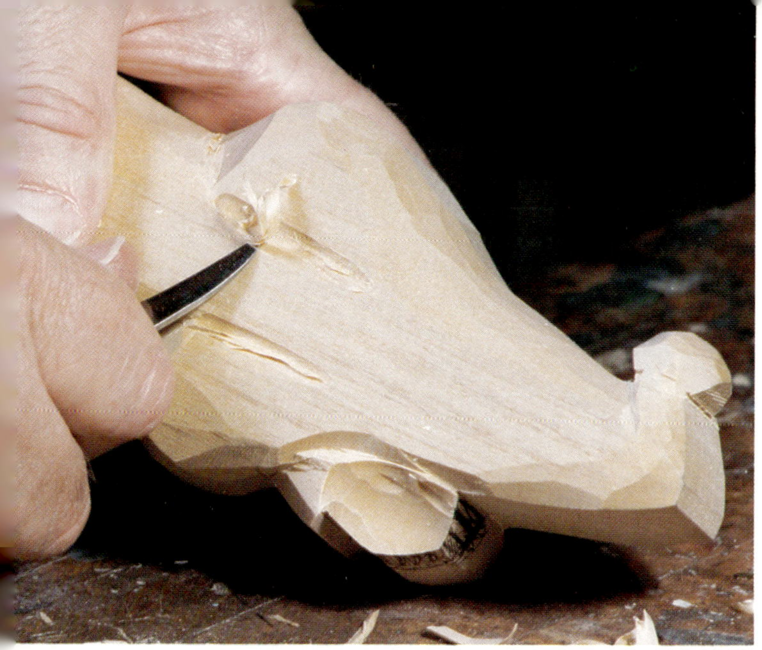

Even with the gouge you will need to round some of the edges that remain.

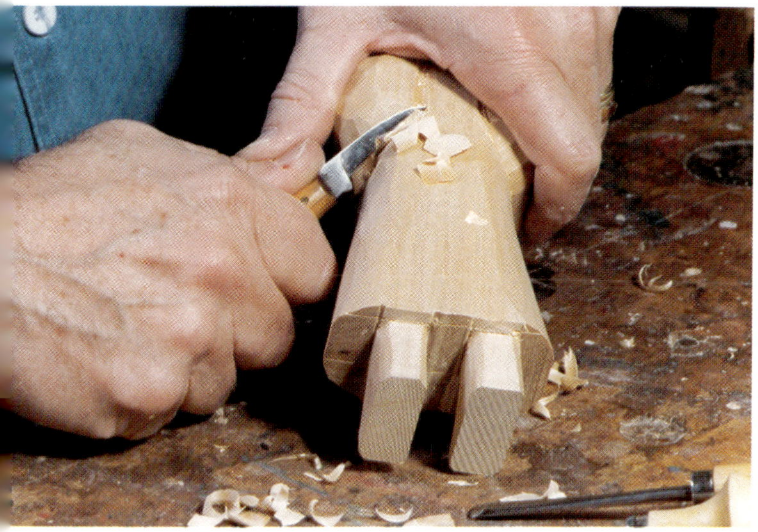

Round the underside with your knife.

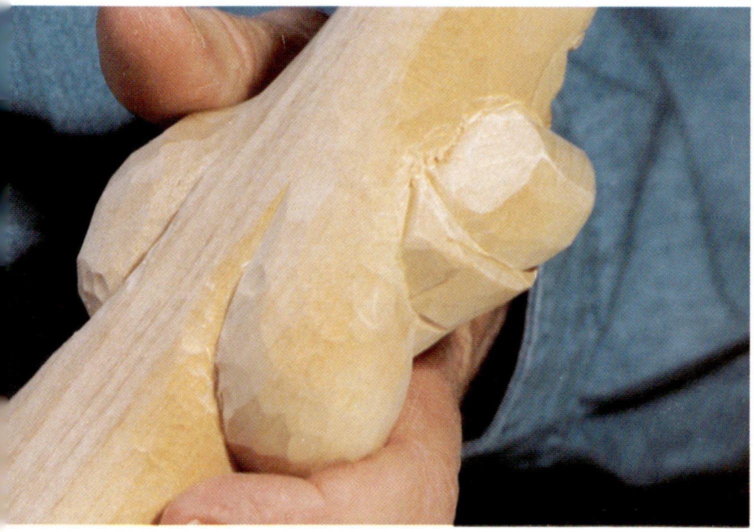

The backside of the arms should look something like this.

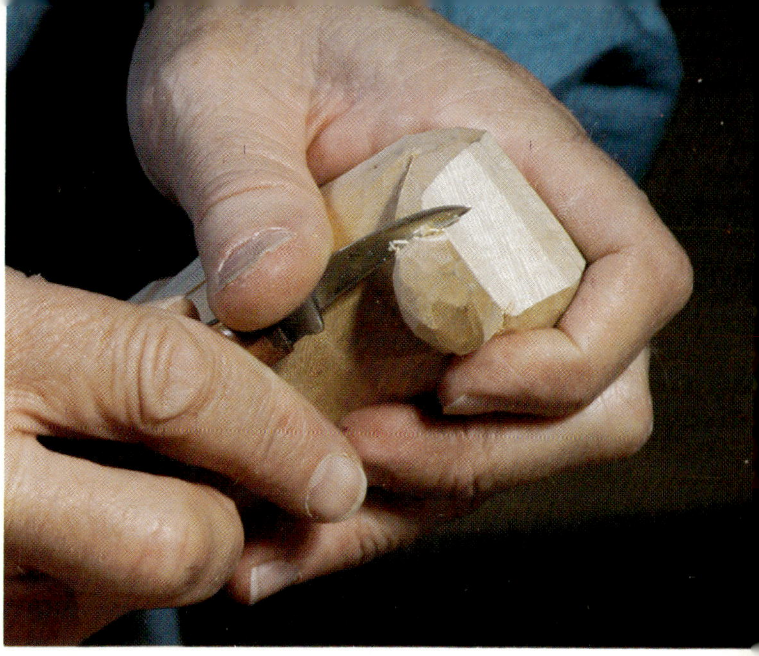

To shape the ball on the hood you will need to make several V-cuts. If you did a good job sawing, you will just have to round off some corners.

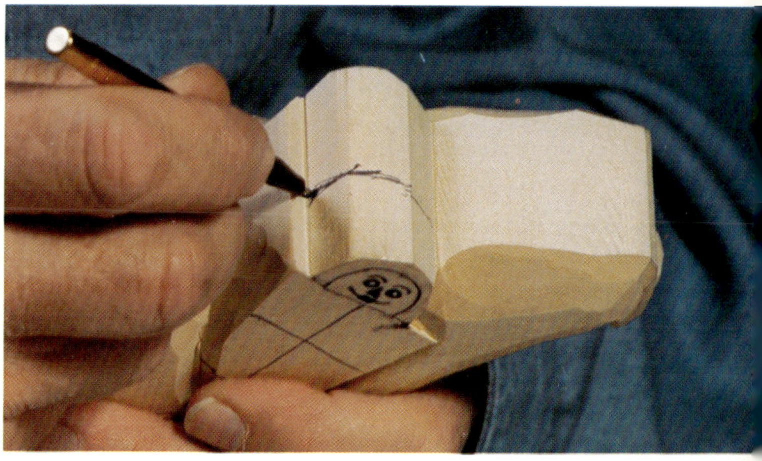

Here I'm drawing a line so I will know how much waste to remove from the doll's head.

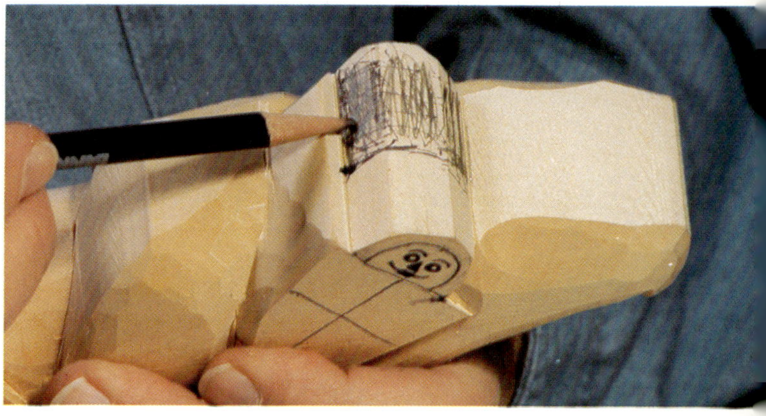

I've blackened it so you can see how much to remove. A felt tip pen works better than a pencil. This darkening of an area probably would be a help to new carvers.

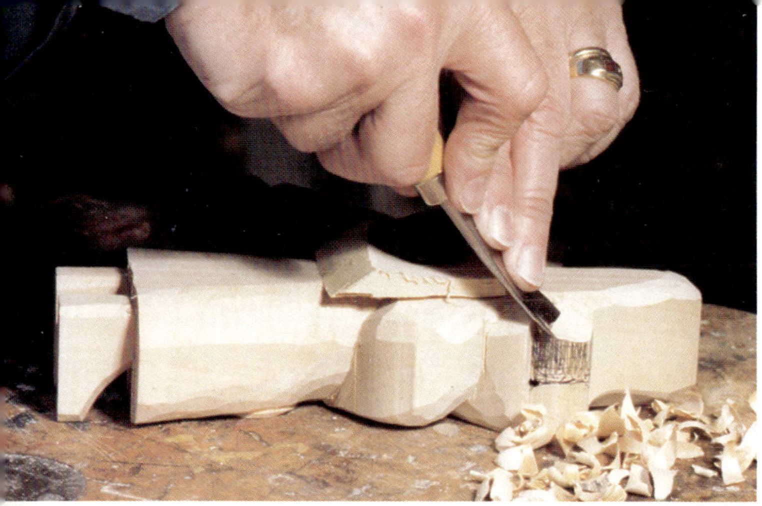

I've wedged the piece on my work bench with a scrap to protect the surface. Now, I can use both hands.

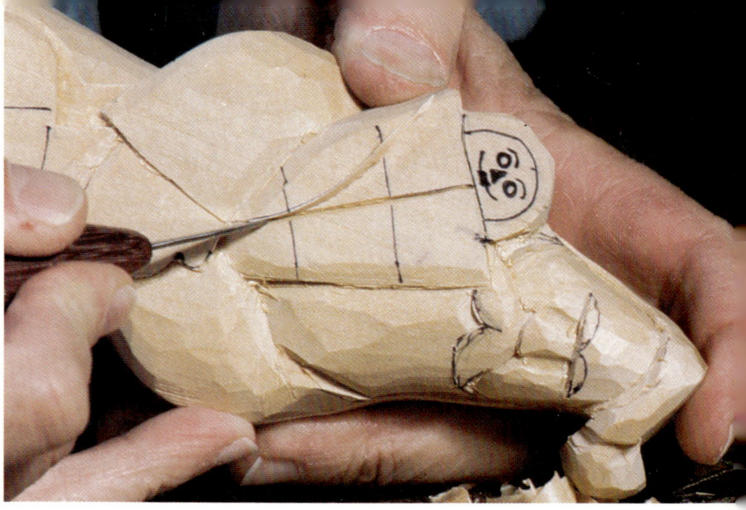

Here you can see the little sliver I'm taking out.

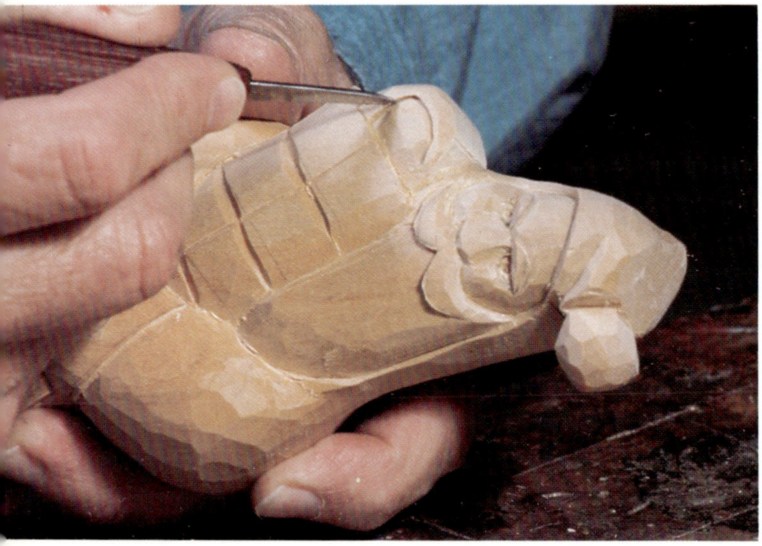

In rounding the doll's face, I trimmed off the lines. It's no problem to draw the face back on.

I've found that it's easier when I get to the painting phase if I cut out the lines on the checkered stocking. If you can do it without cutting the lines, good for you. It will look just as good.

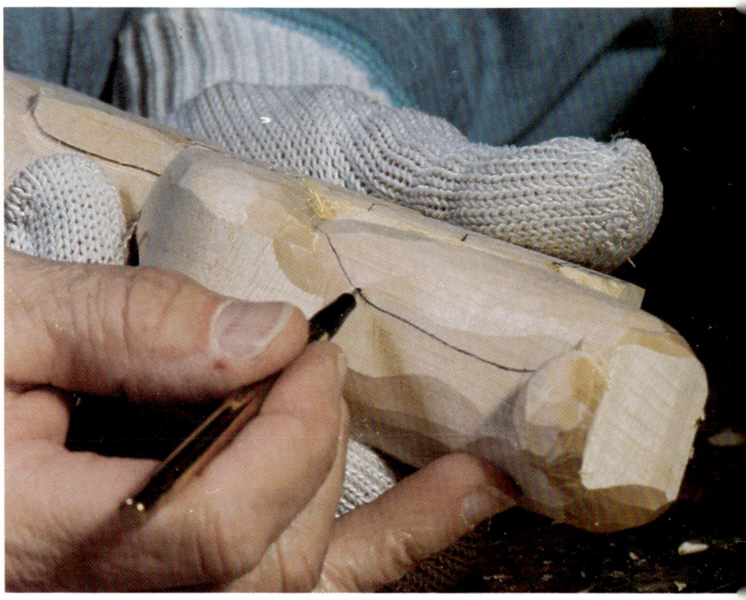

I'm dangerous with a felt tip pen. I've put on a meat cutter's glove to protect me from the sharp pen. Seriously, if you're squeamish about cutting yourself, these gloves are available from your better woodcarving supply catalogs. I'm drawing the line where the face will go.

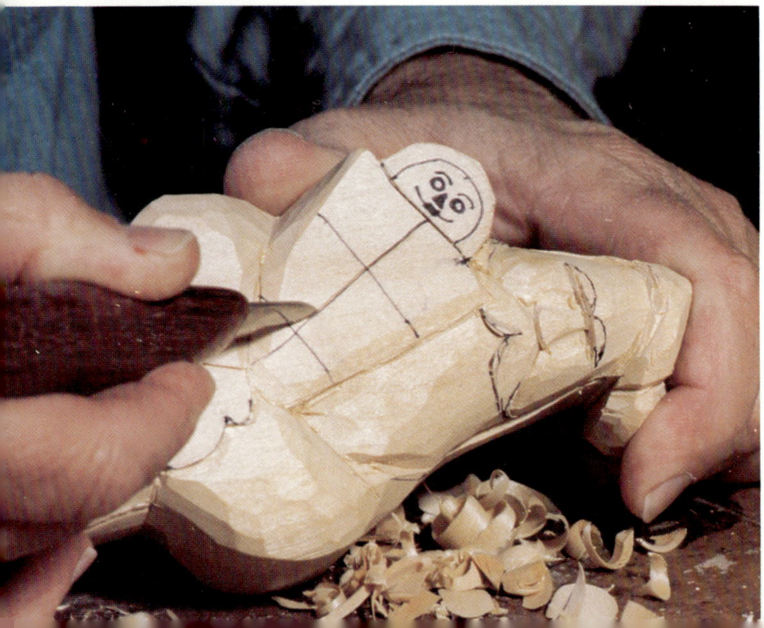

Incise a deep line around the mark. Don't worry about going too deep.

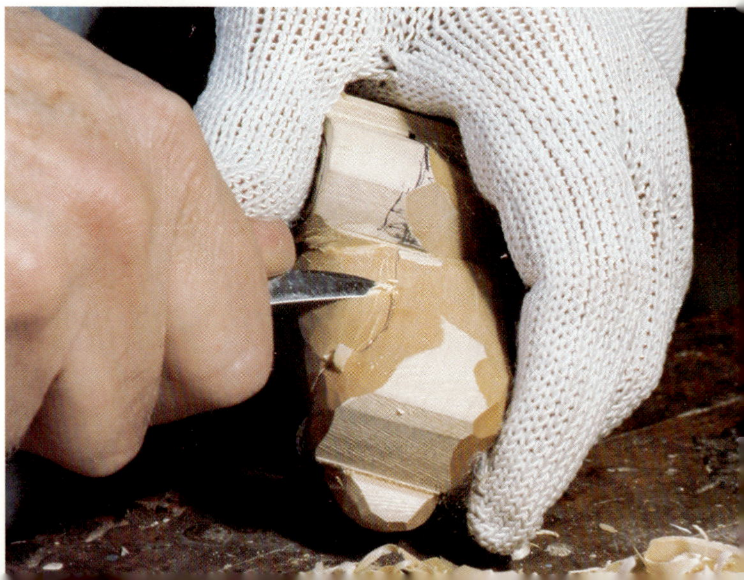

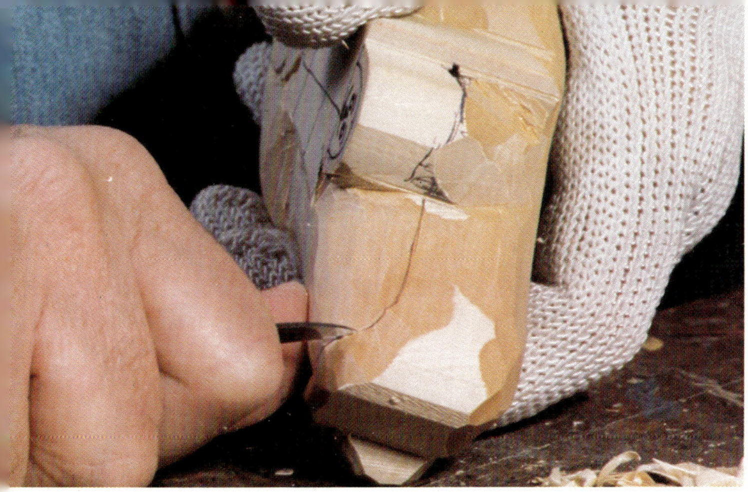

Take it slow and easy. Speed will come with each carving you complete.

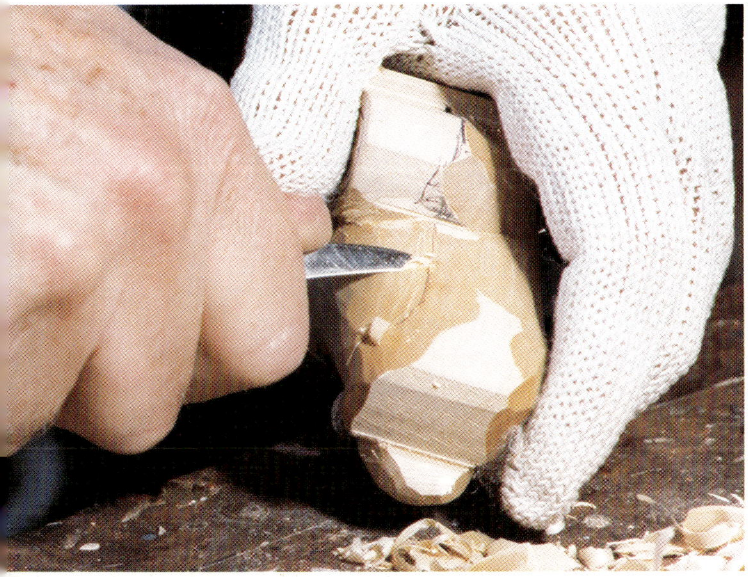

After you have incised the pen line, cut back into the incision and begin rounding the face.

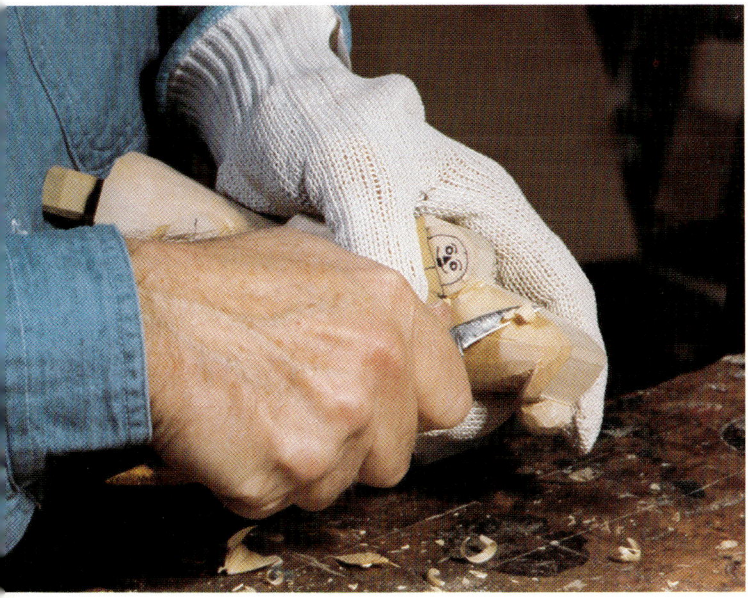

Continue to round. Remember the frying pan Santa.

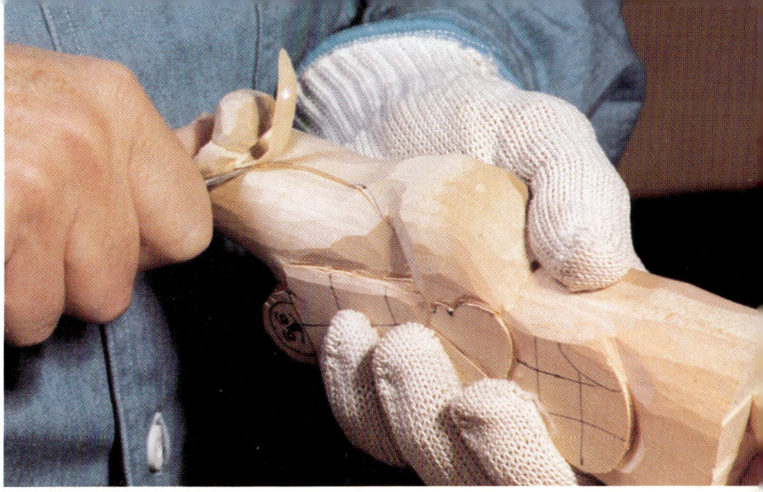

You want the face area to be as egg-shaped as you can get it.

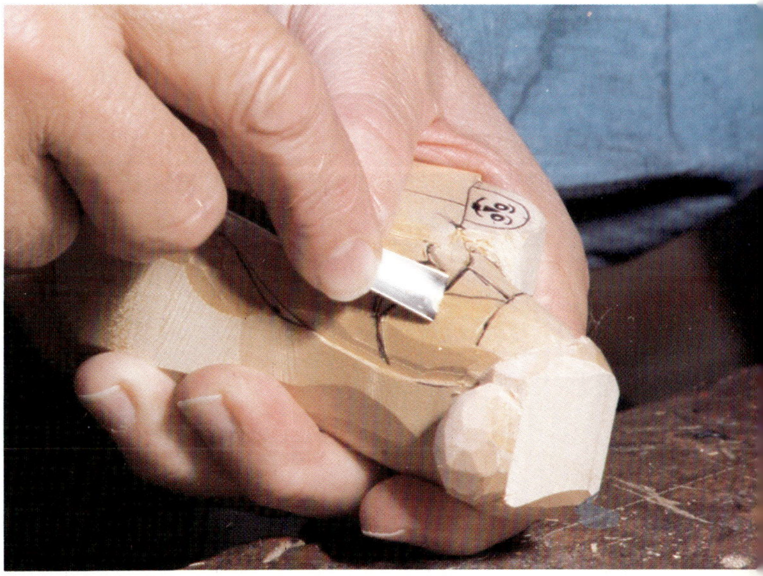

With a #7 gouge, trim on each side of the nose where the nose and cheek join. This gives it a smoother look. I still use a knife a great deal to do the nose. With practice it won't look like a little pyramid.

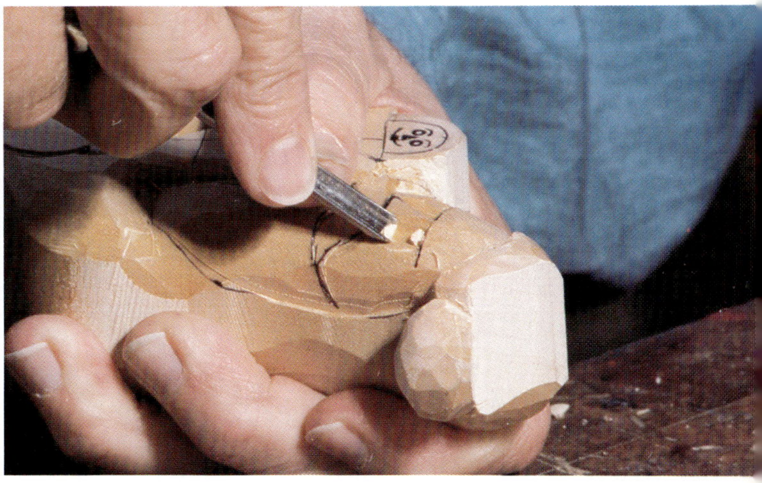

Come back with a #6 gouge and make a deeper cut. Don't worry about cutting too deep. The nose should be prominent.

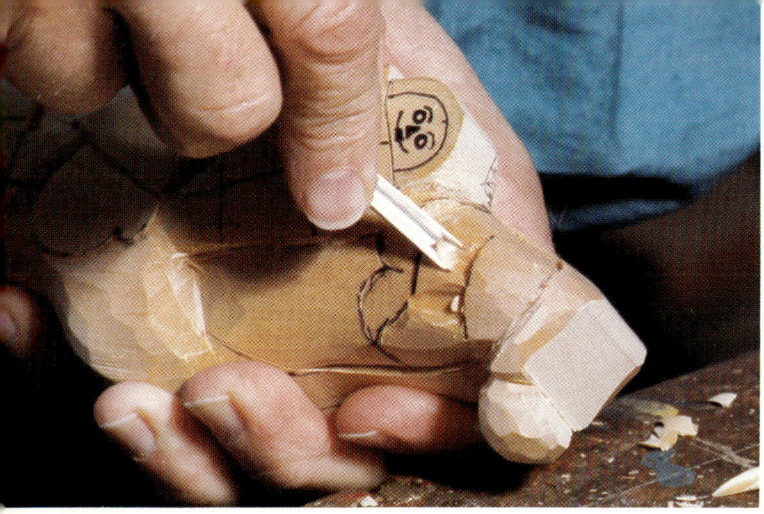

Now, do the left side of the nose. You may want to practice on a scrap before you try the nose on your finished Santa.

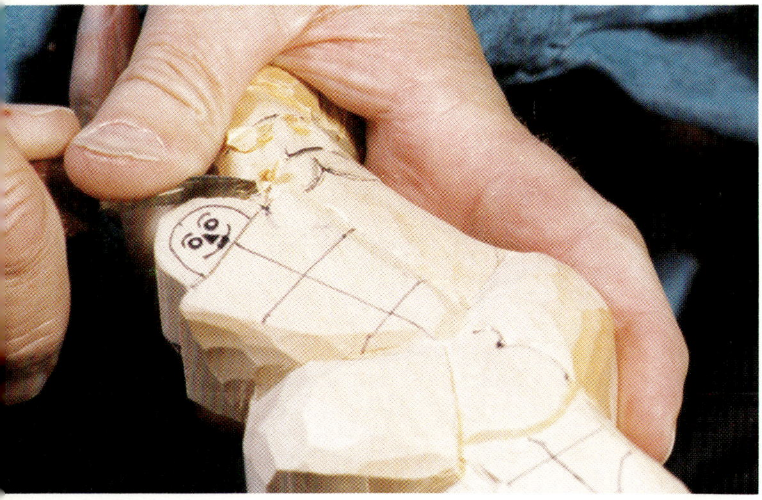

Blend the beard into the doll's head.

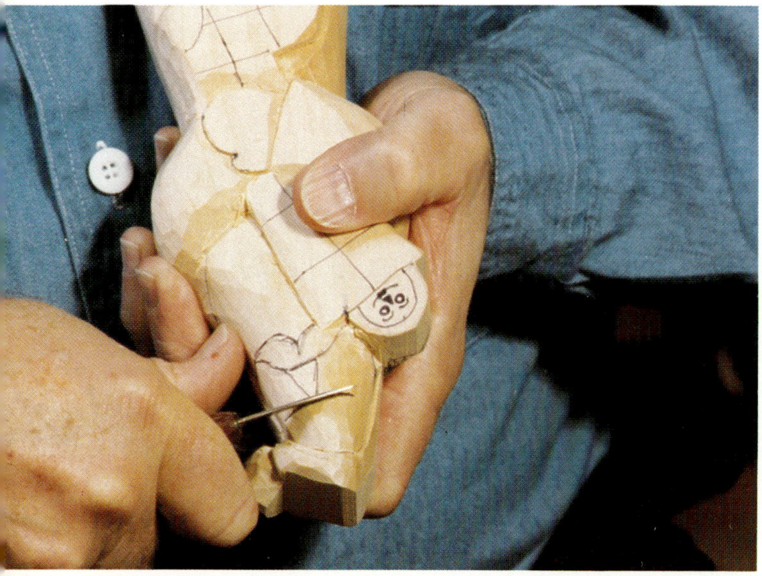

Make a deep horizontal cut along the top of the eye sockets. This is a stop cut. As you can see from the next photo, you will take a nice little chunk.

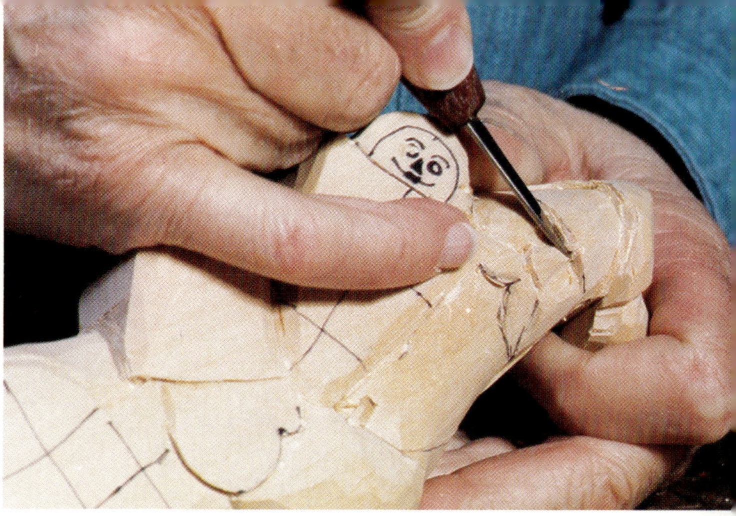

Smooth the top of the cut. I've watched Harold Enlow and Claude Bolton do eyes. They are wizards with gouges. I think one reason is that they know how to sharpen the durn things.

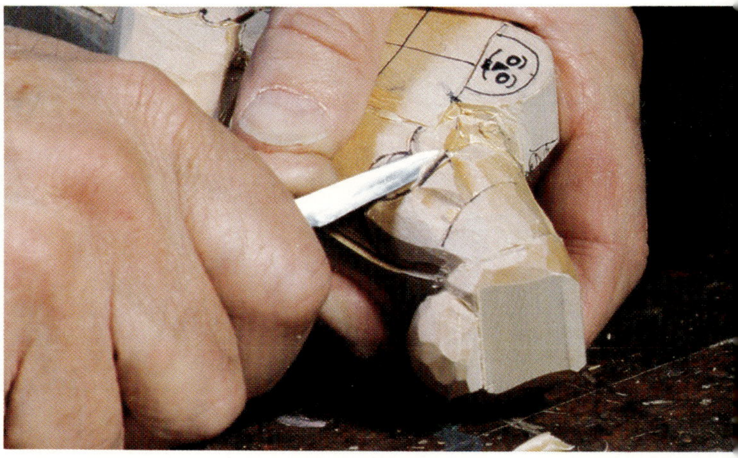

Round the moustache up to the stop cut you made for the nose.

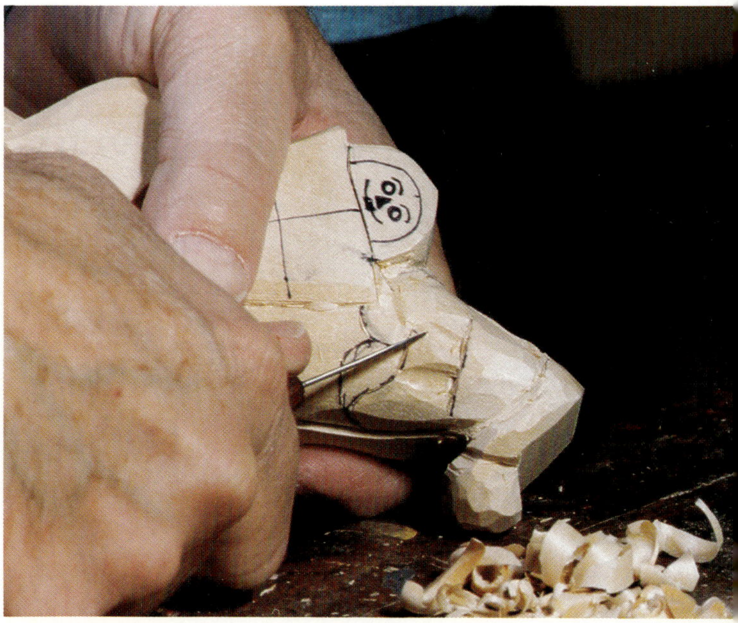

I've found it helps to cut a little angle on each side of the nose.

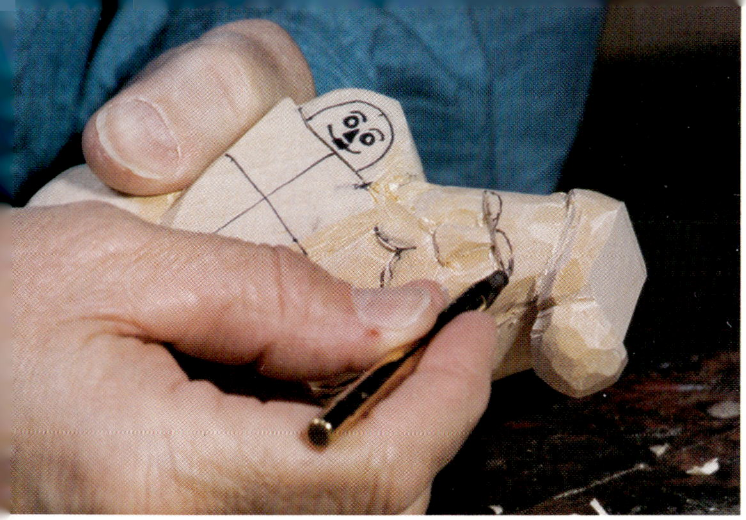

Draw the eyebrows back in. Be very careful when incising and cutting them in. They can be painted on.

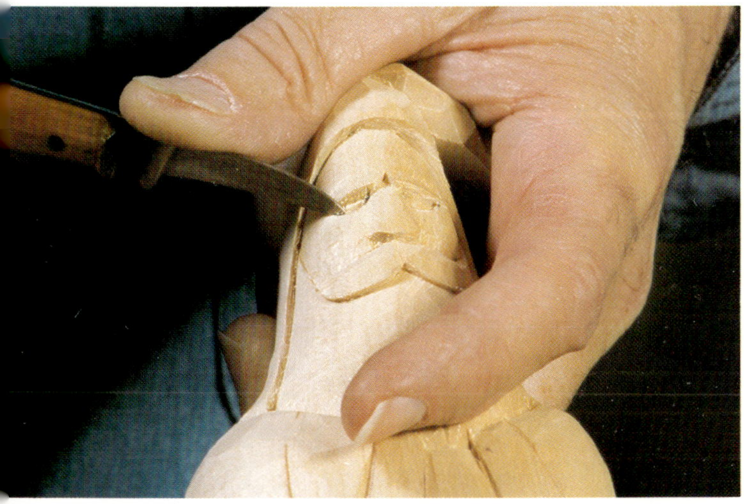

Incise a half circle for the eye. Cut deeper into each side of the eye.

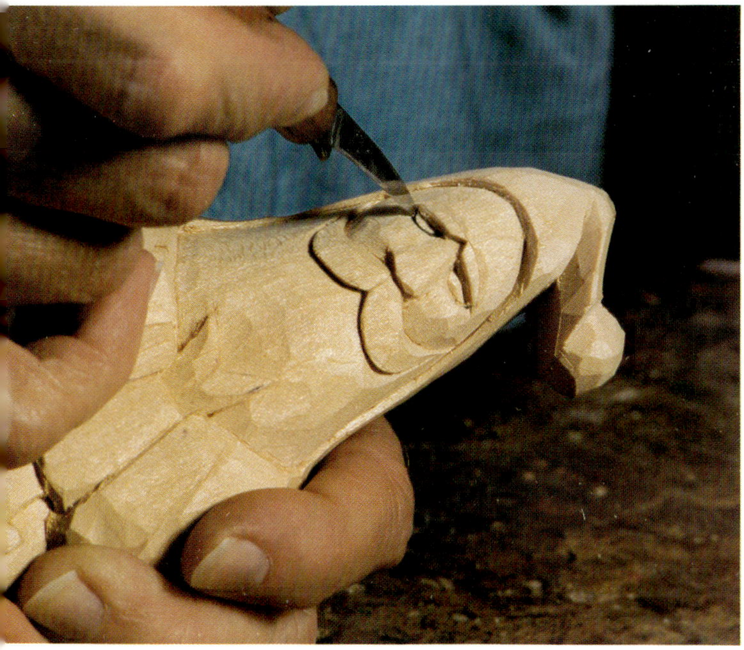

Trim the eye out, making it as oval as possible.

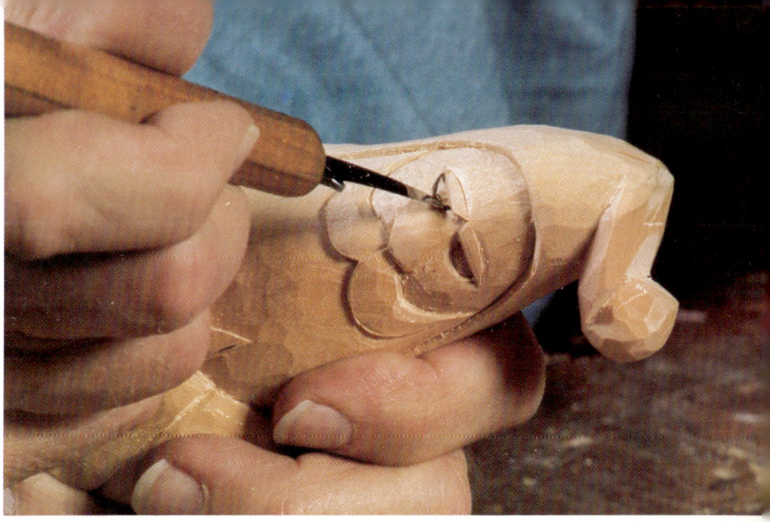

Cut the right corner.

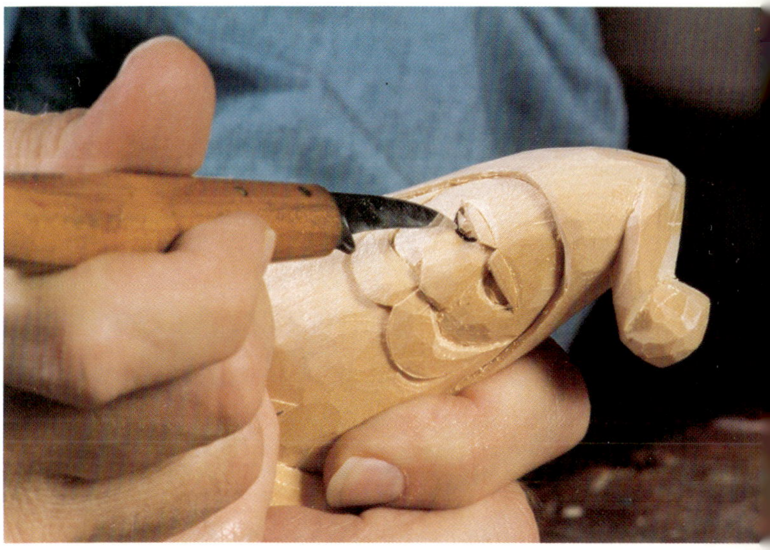

Since it will be painted, make the eye smooth.

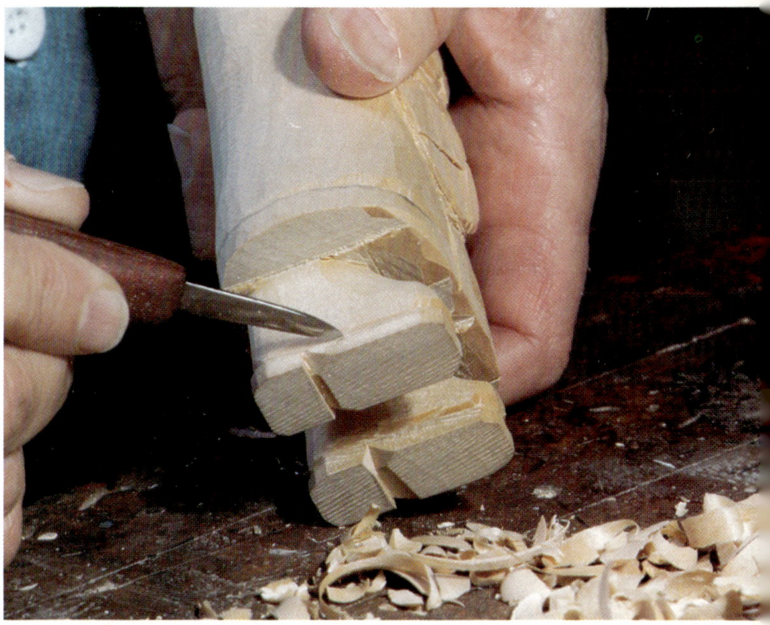

Although I haven't had any complaints about my plain boots, I've decided to cut in the soles. It does look a little better.

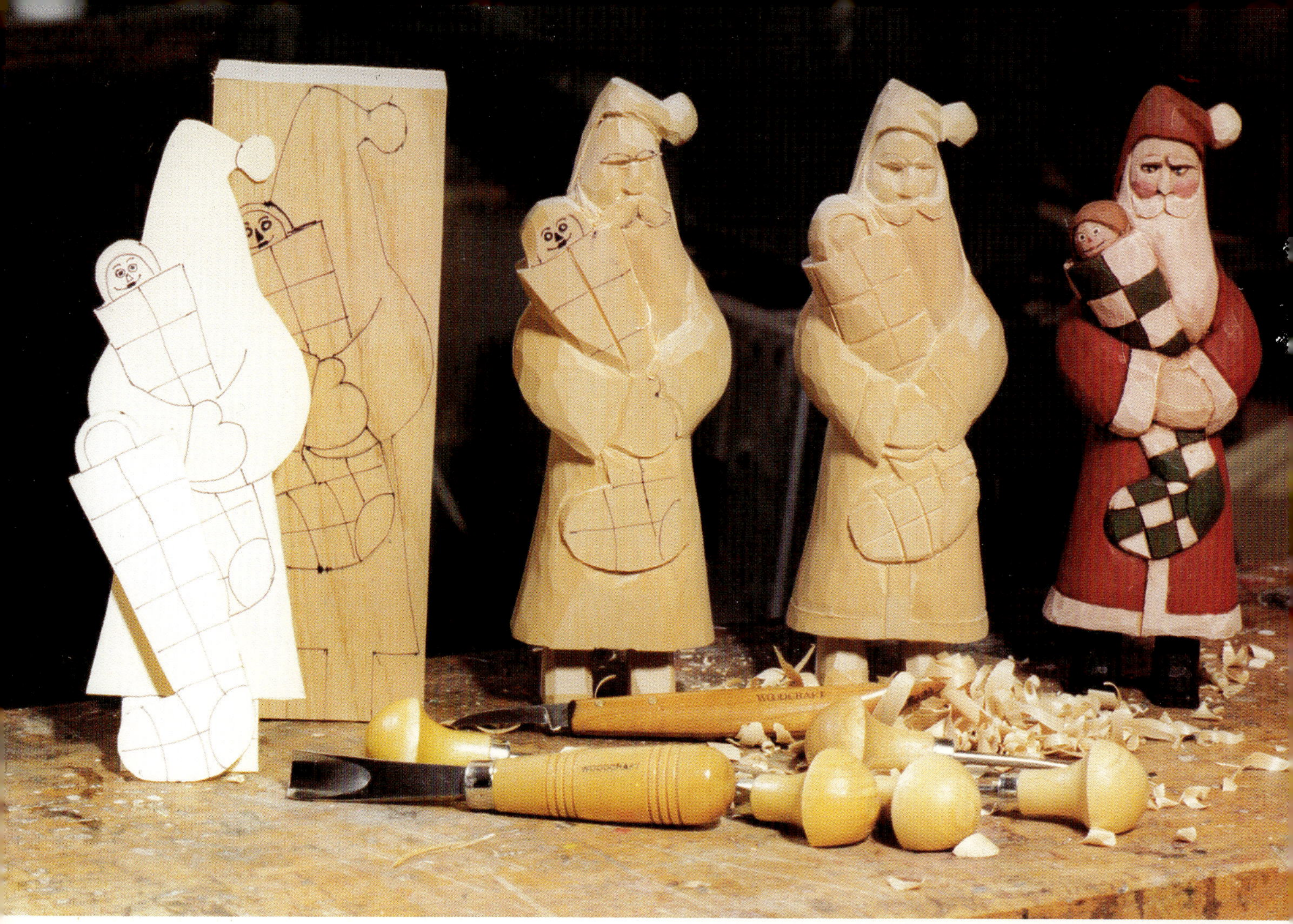

These are the different stages of the Stocking Santa.

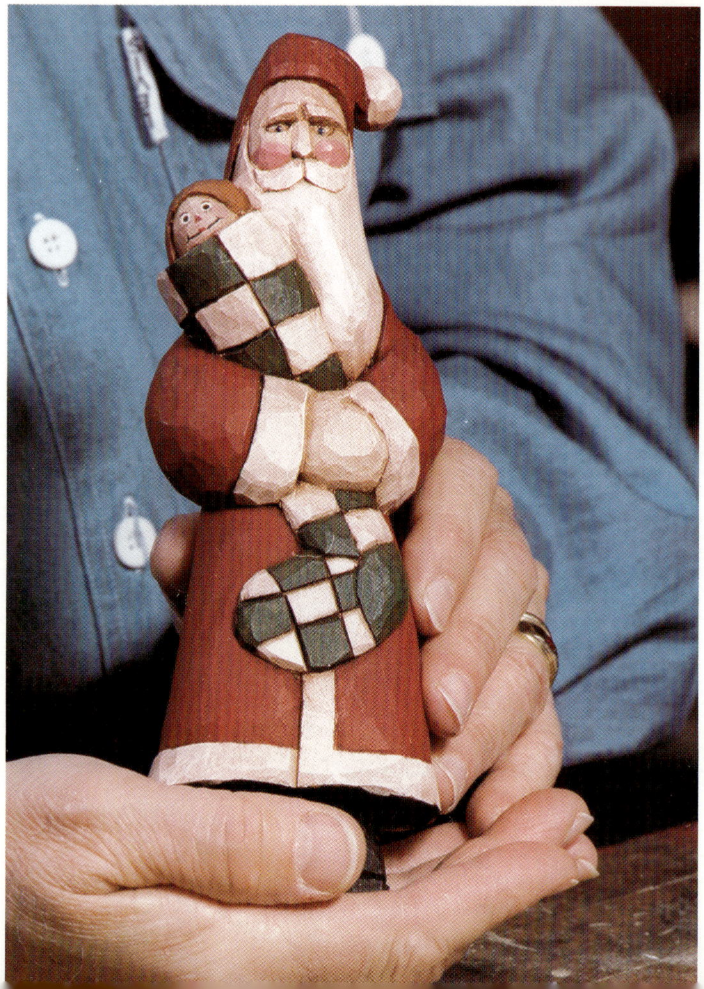

The finished Stocking Santa.

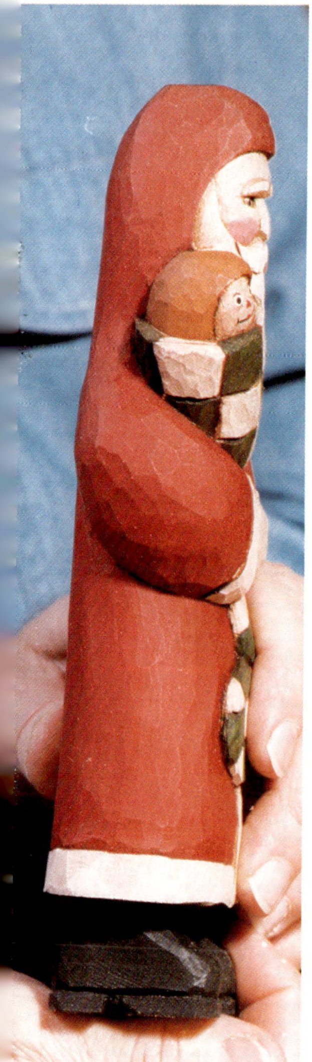

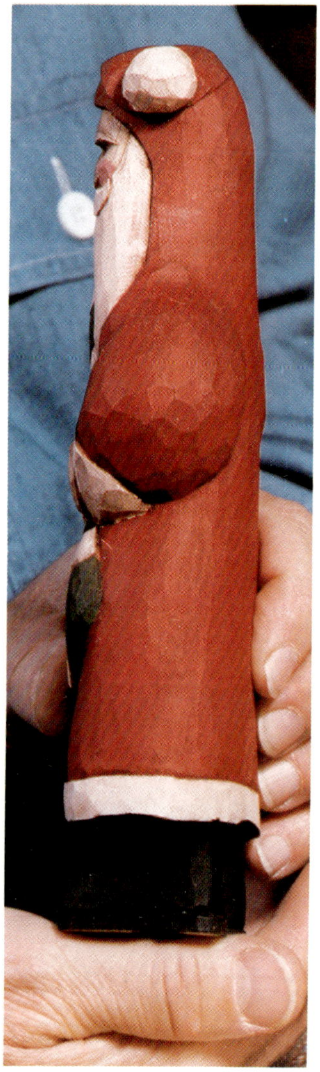

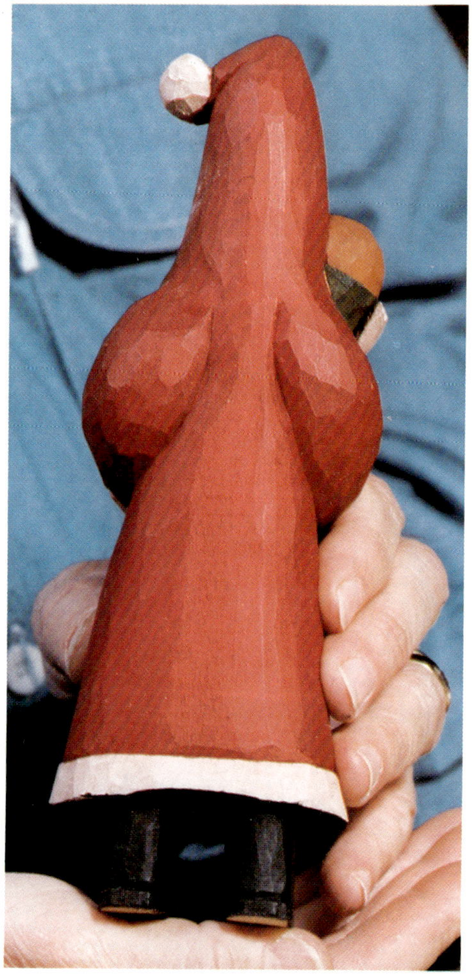

Many of you who are friends from *Santa Carving* and *Angel Carving & Other Favorites* have asked for additional views.

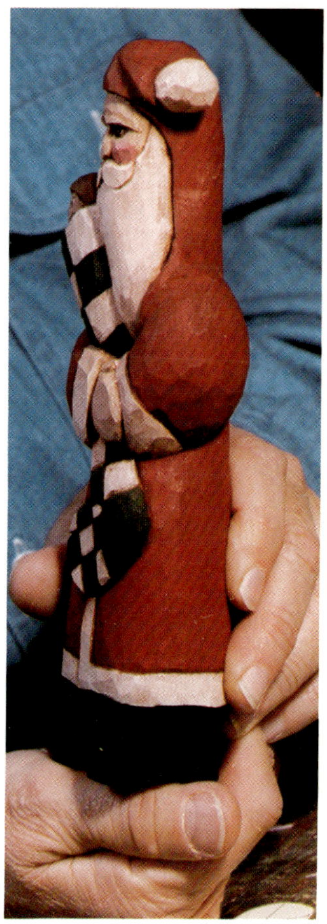

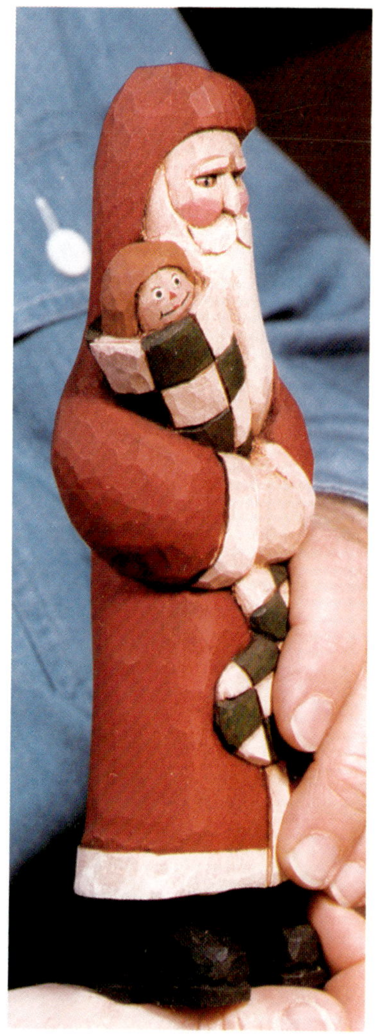

I hope these help.

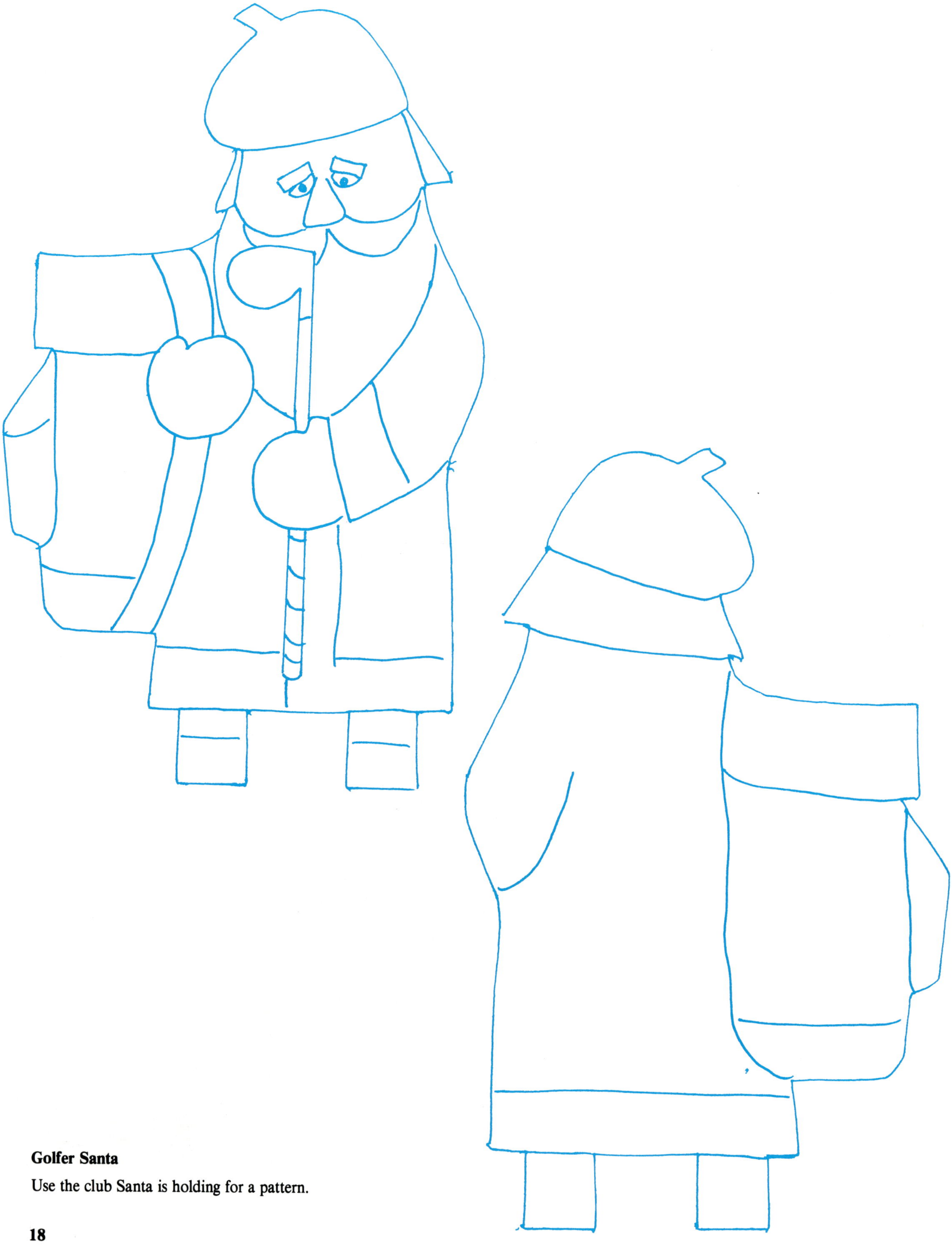

Golfer Santa

Use the club Santa is holding for a pattern.

Golfer Santa

Golf is growing faster than courses can be built. I have been collecting old golf clubs for several years and the Calamity Jane Putter is a real treasure. This is the type that the great golfer, Bobby Jones, used in winning the Grand Slam.

I believe the Golfer Santa will be very popular. However, if you are a novice carver you might want to practice on some of the other Santas before trying this one.

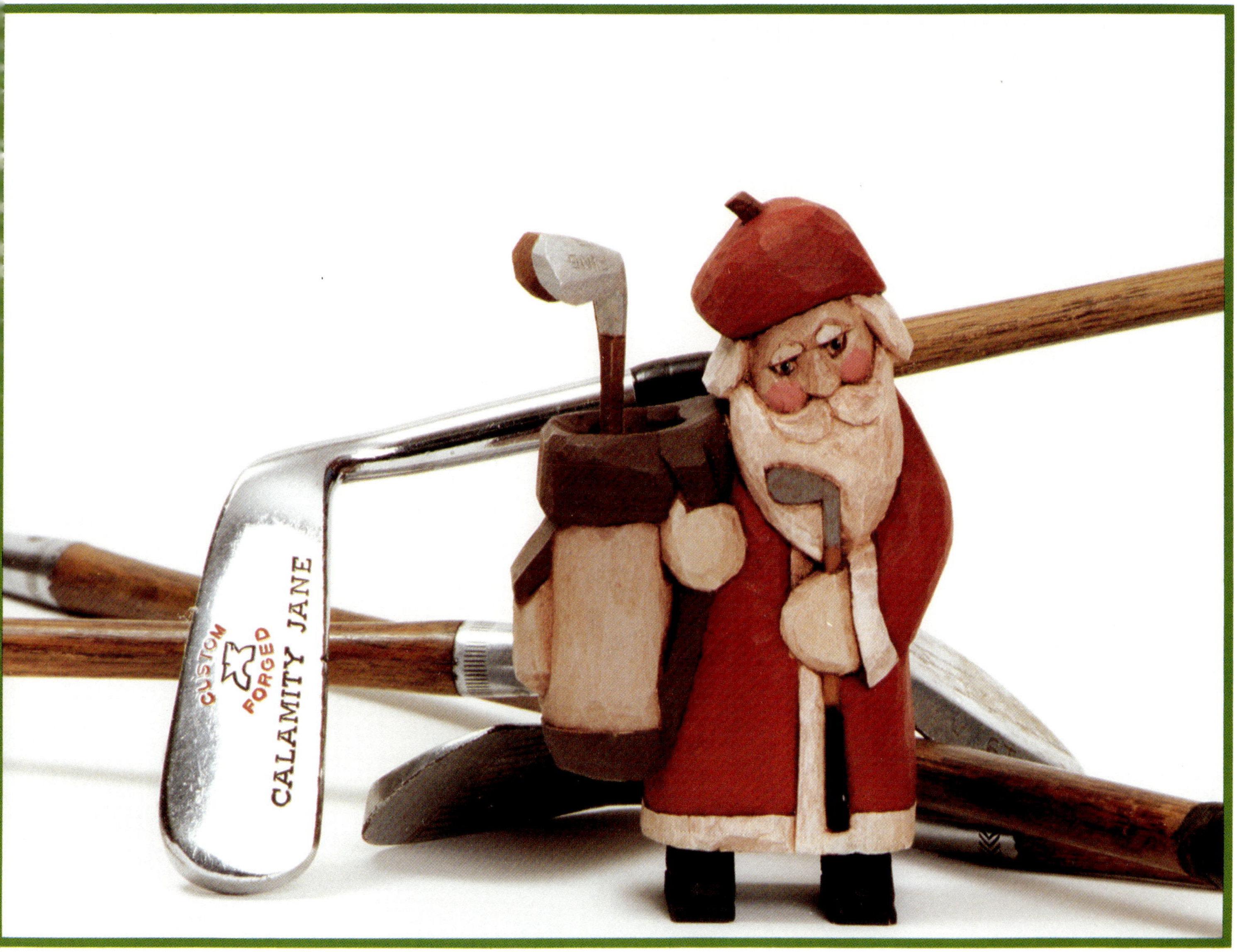

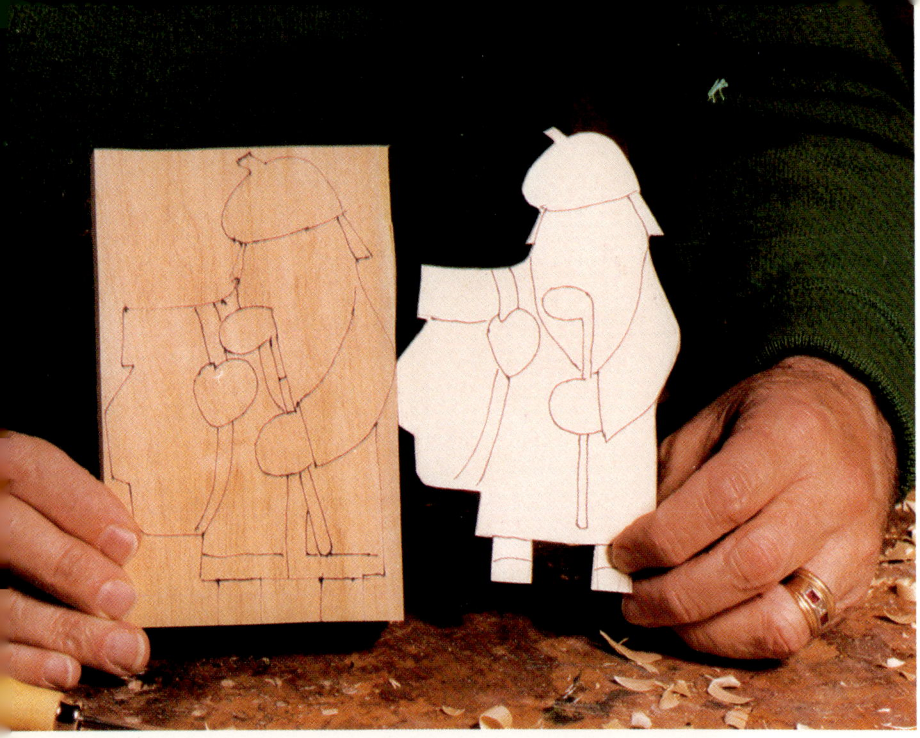

In my position as parks and recreation director, I'm heavily involved in golf. I don't play worth a toot, but I love it. I'm sure in the off-season Santa must play. This block is 4" wide, 6⅜" high, and 1¾" thick.

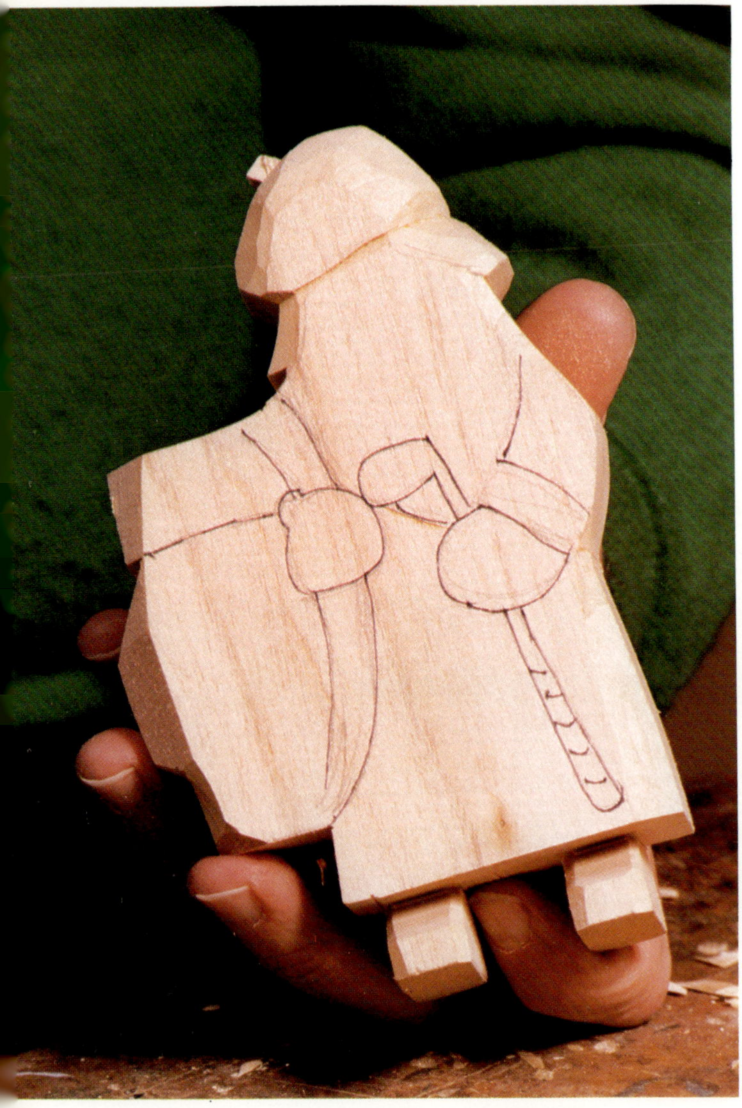

The golfer is cut out and I started rounding his beret.

My granddaughter, Meredith, can't decide if she wants to be a dancer, teacher, or a woodcarver. I've told her she can be all three.

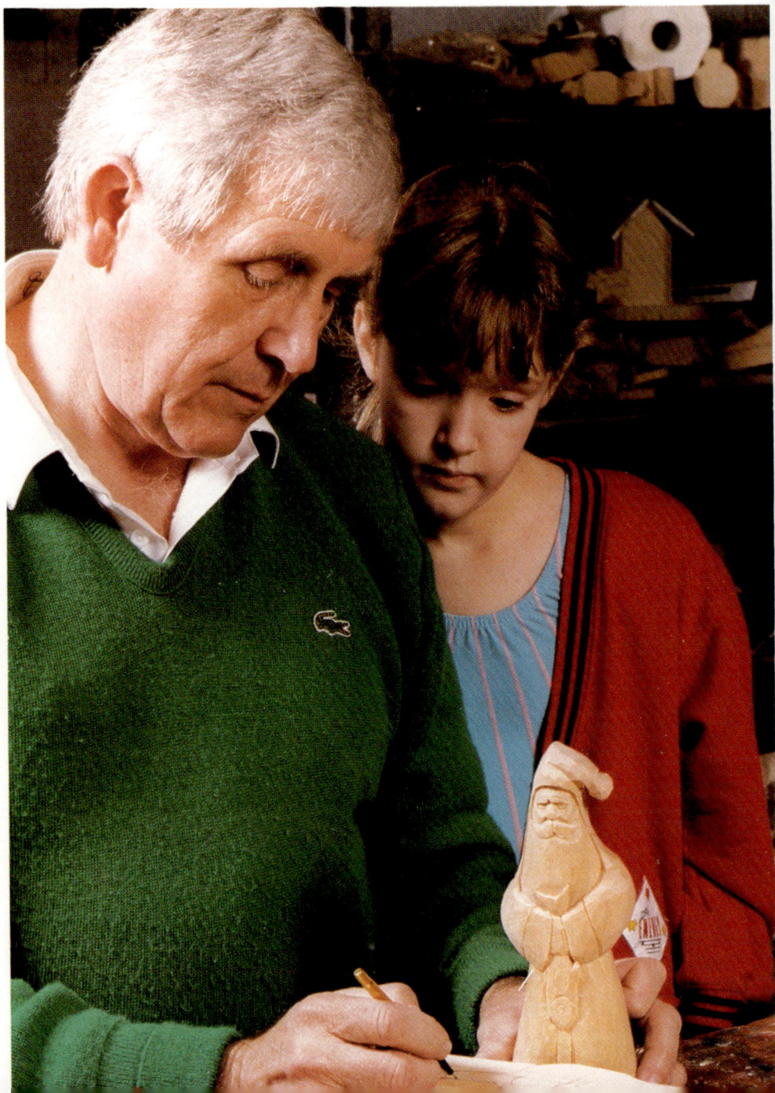

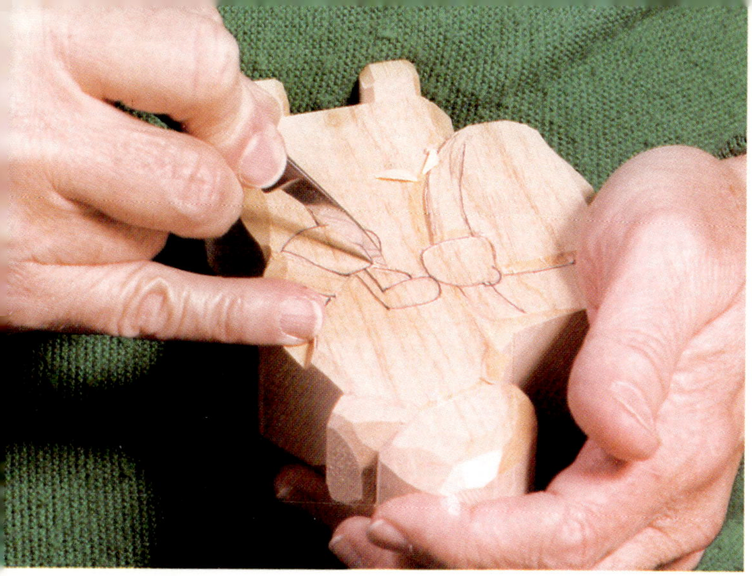

Deeply incise all your dark lines.

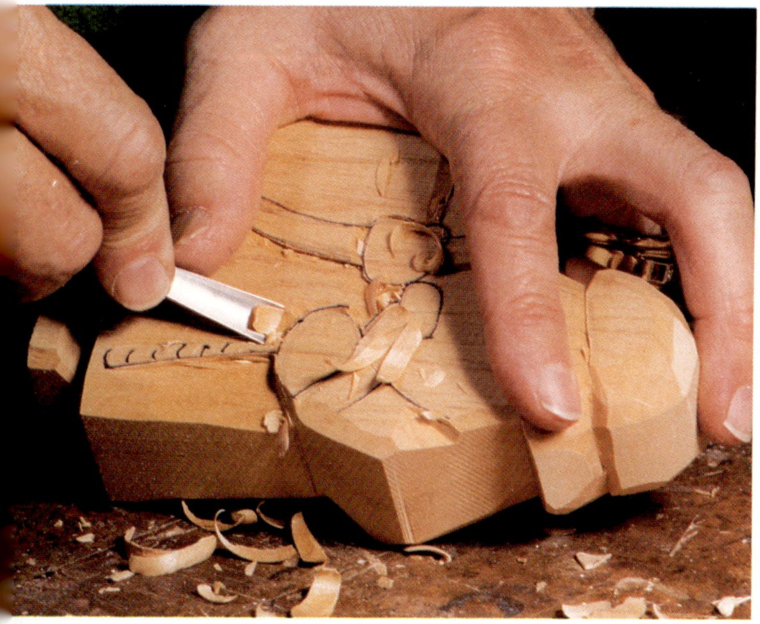

I use a #6 and a #7 gouge to remove waste.

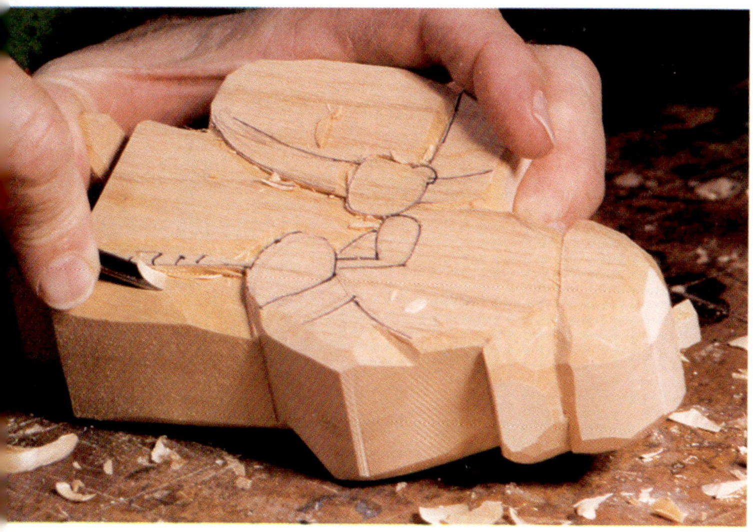

Continue removing waste on the golf club shaft.

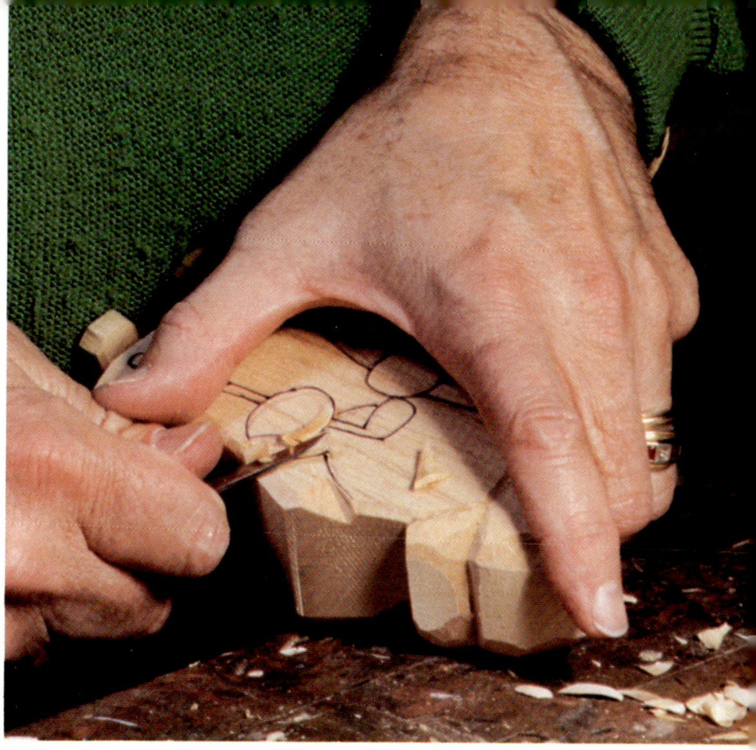

Continue to round and shape.

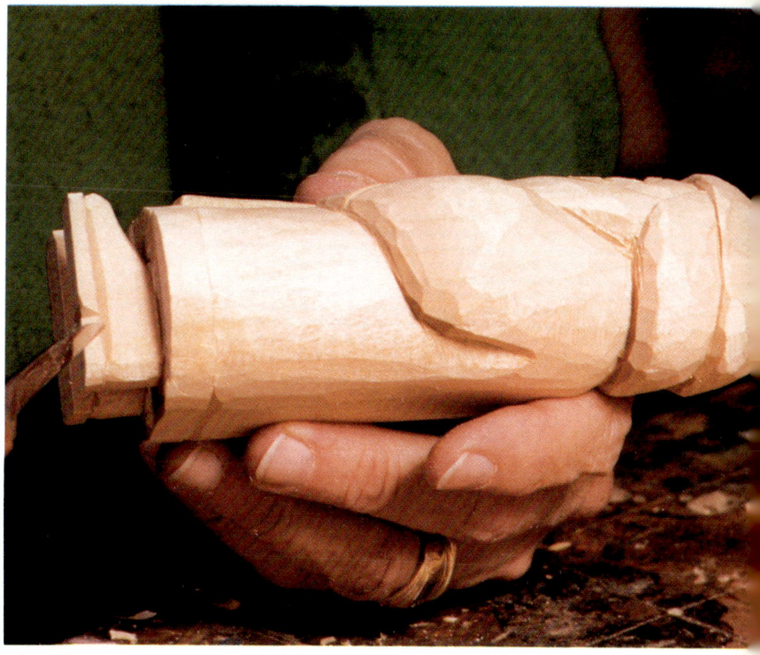

The left side of the golfer should start looking something like this. I'm showing that I have put heels and soles on the shoes. If you have the time and the inclination, drill a few holes and put in some tiny dowels for spikes. I had neither the time nor the inclination.

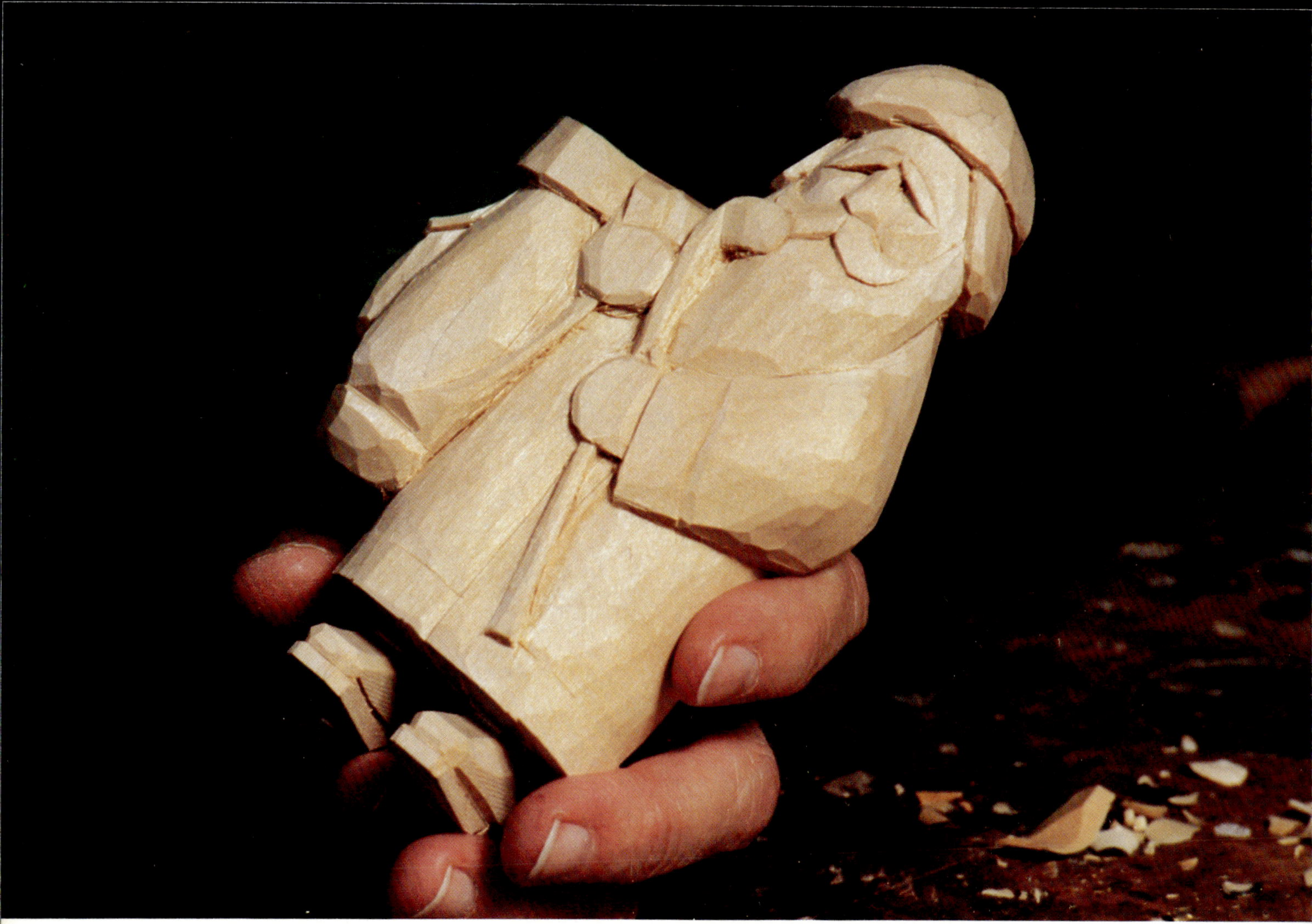

Your Santa should begin to look something like this.

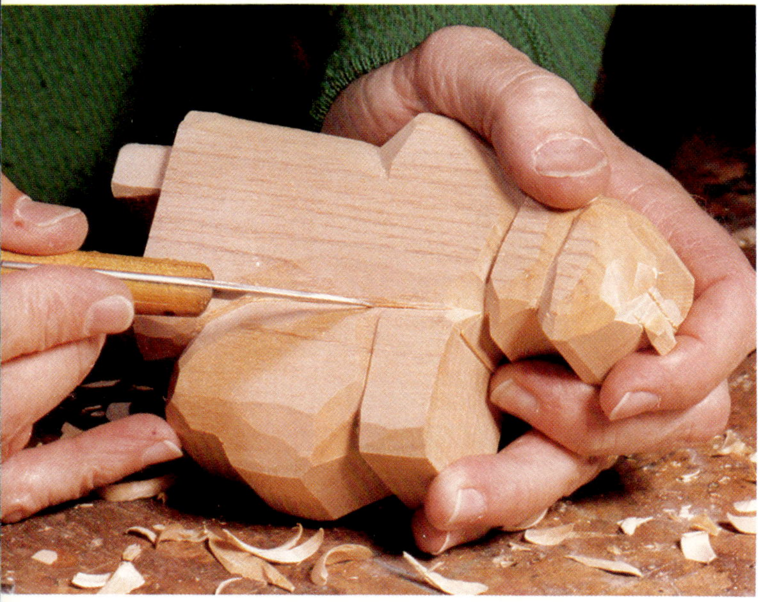

Take out a nice chunk between the bag and the back. That doo-hickey that sticks out of the beret can be replaced with a small dowel if you accidentally cut it off.

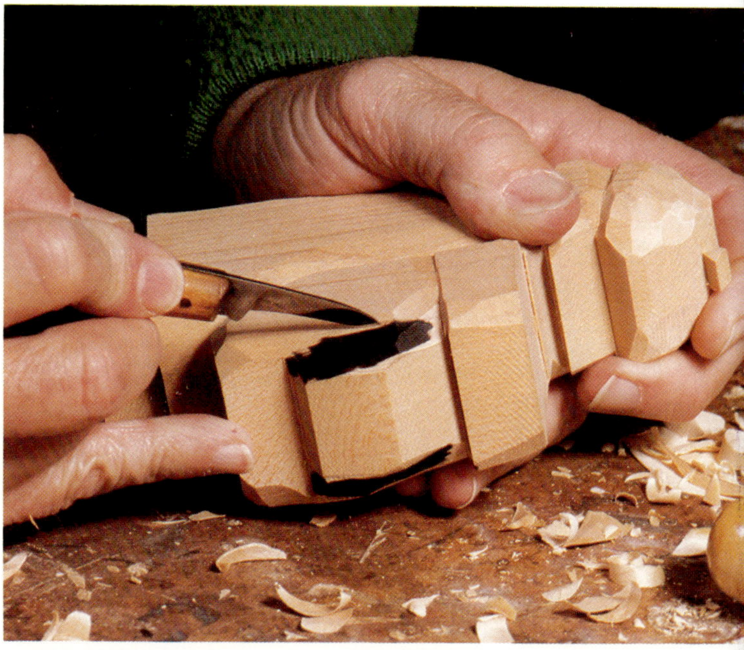

I've blackened the area around the golf bag pouch that needs to come out. Make a deep cut on the side and...

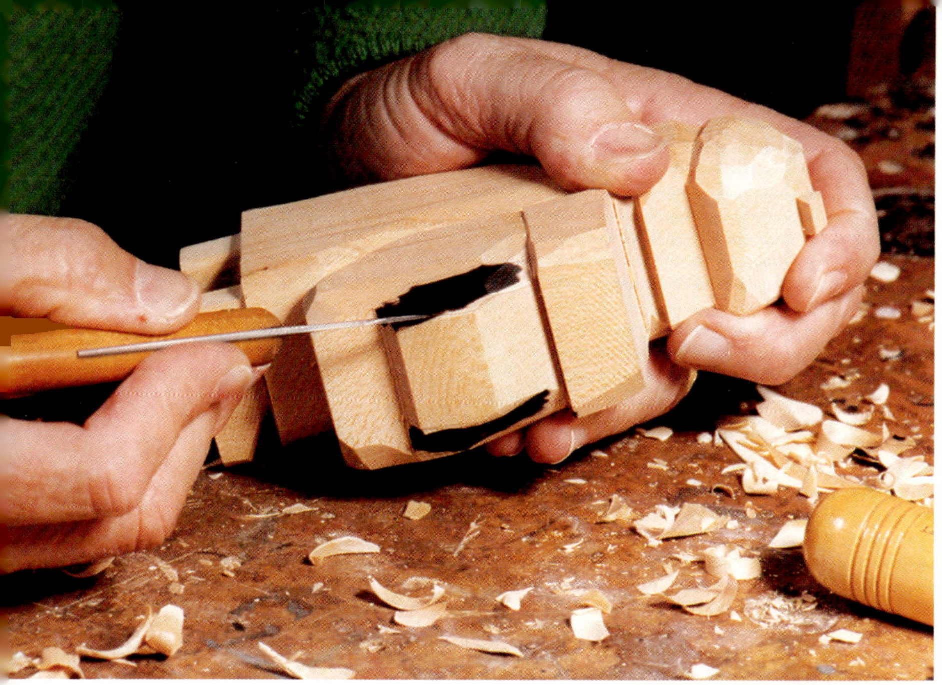

on the top. I've also cut a little detail into the bag.

Use your gouge or knife to clean out around the pouch.

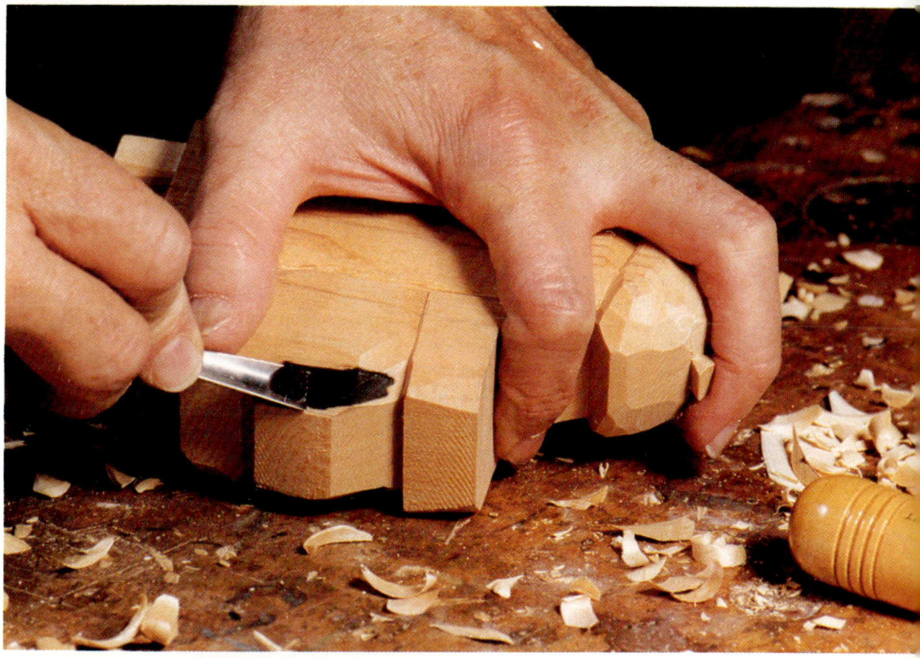

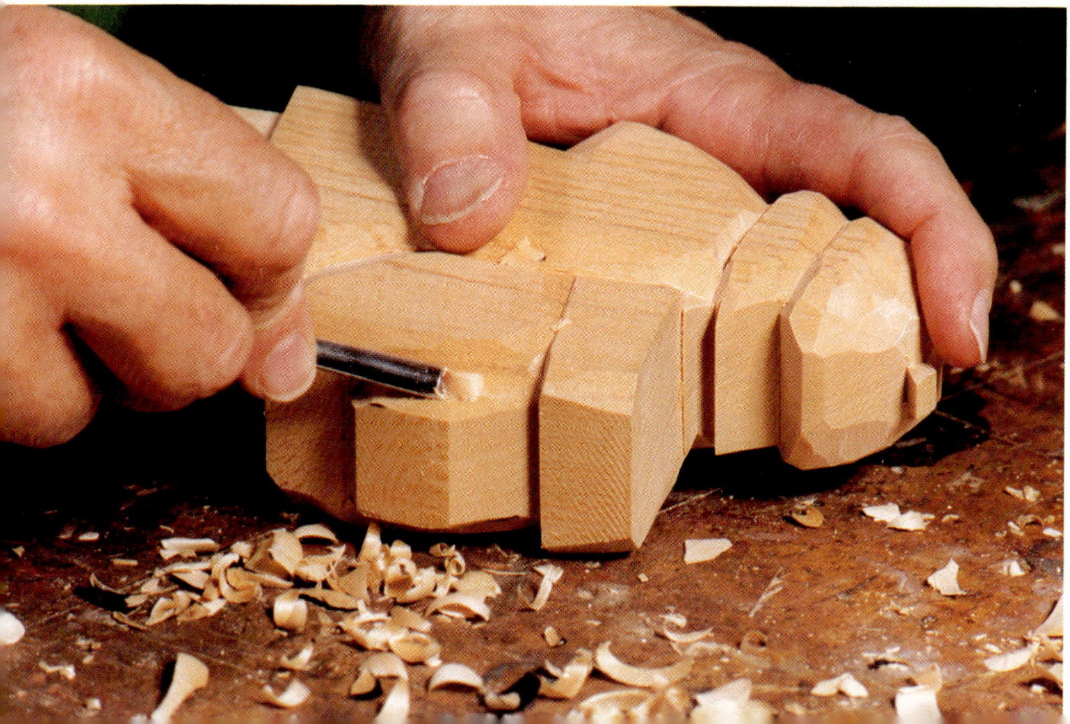

I've cleaned off the darkened area.

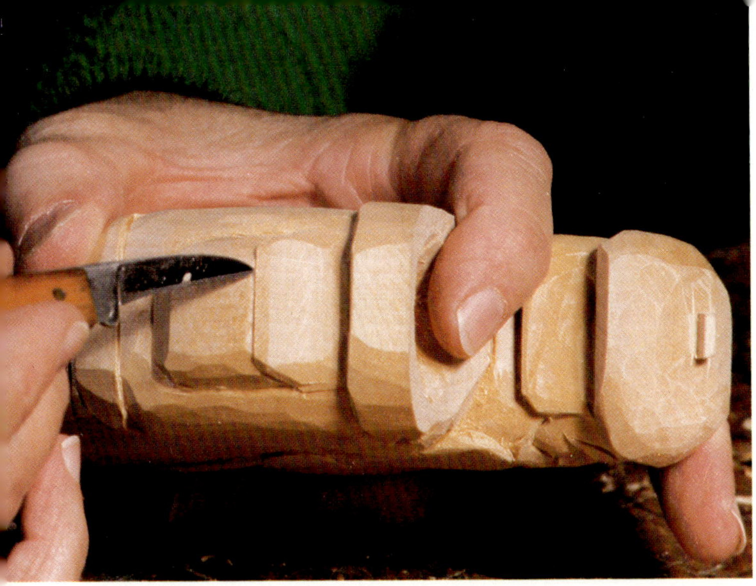

Cut a little line to show the flap of the pouch.

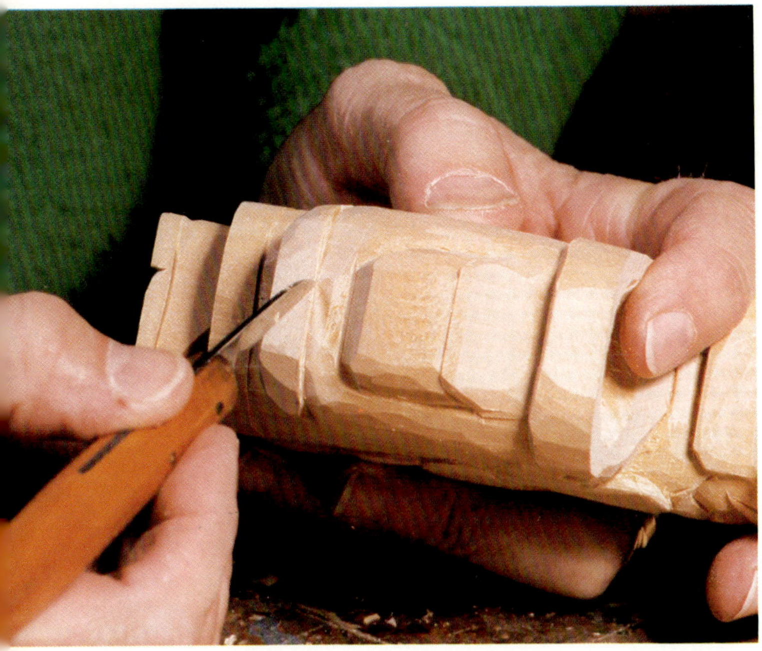

Add additional detail to the bottom of the golf bag.

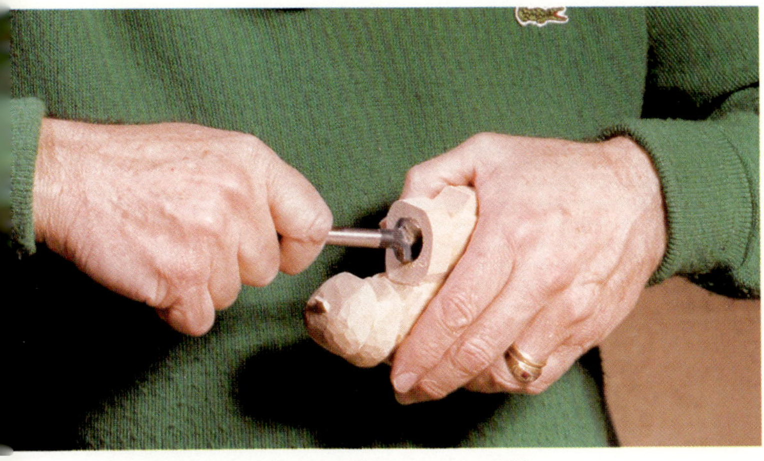

I couldn't generate enough r.p.m.'s to drill a hole in the bag and found it worked better in my drill press.

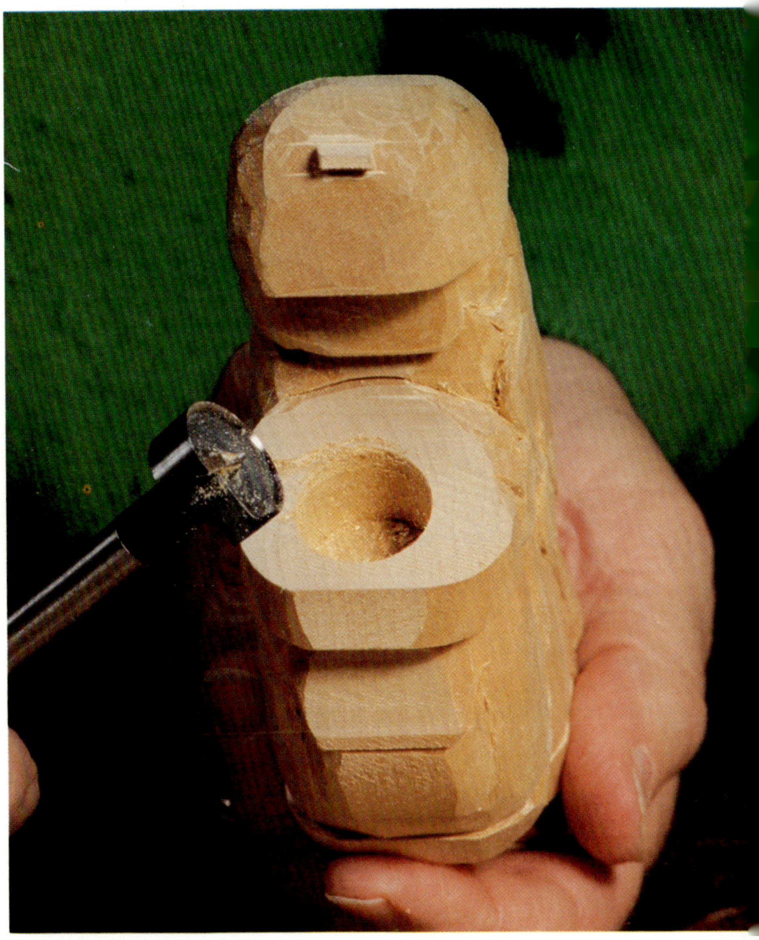

You could do this hole with a gouge and knife, but this Forstner bit works better.

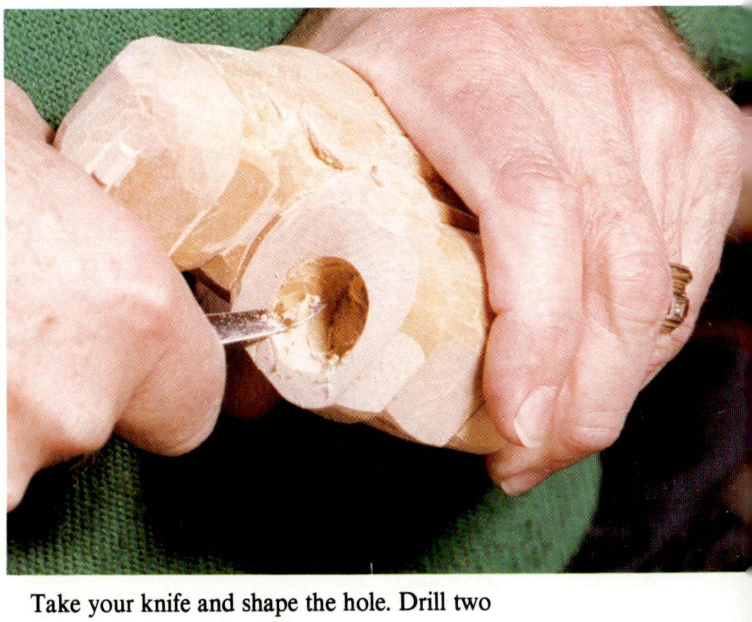

Take your knife and shape the hole. Drill two or more holes for the clubs.

Below are four views of the Golfing Santa.

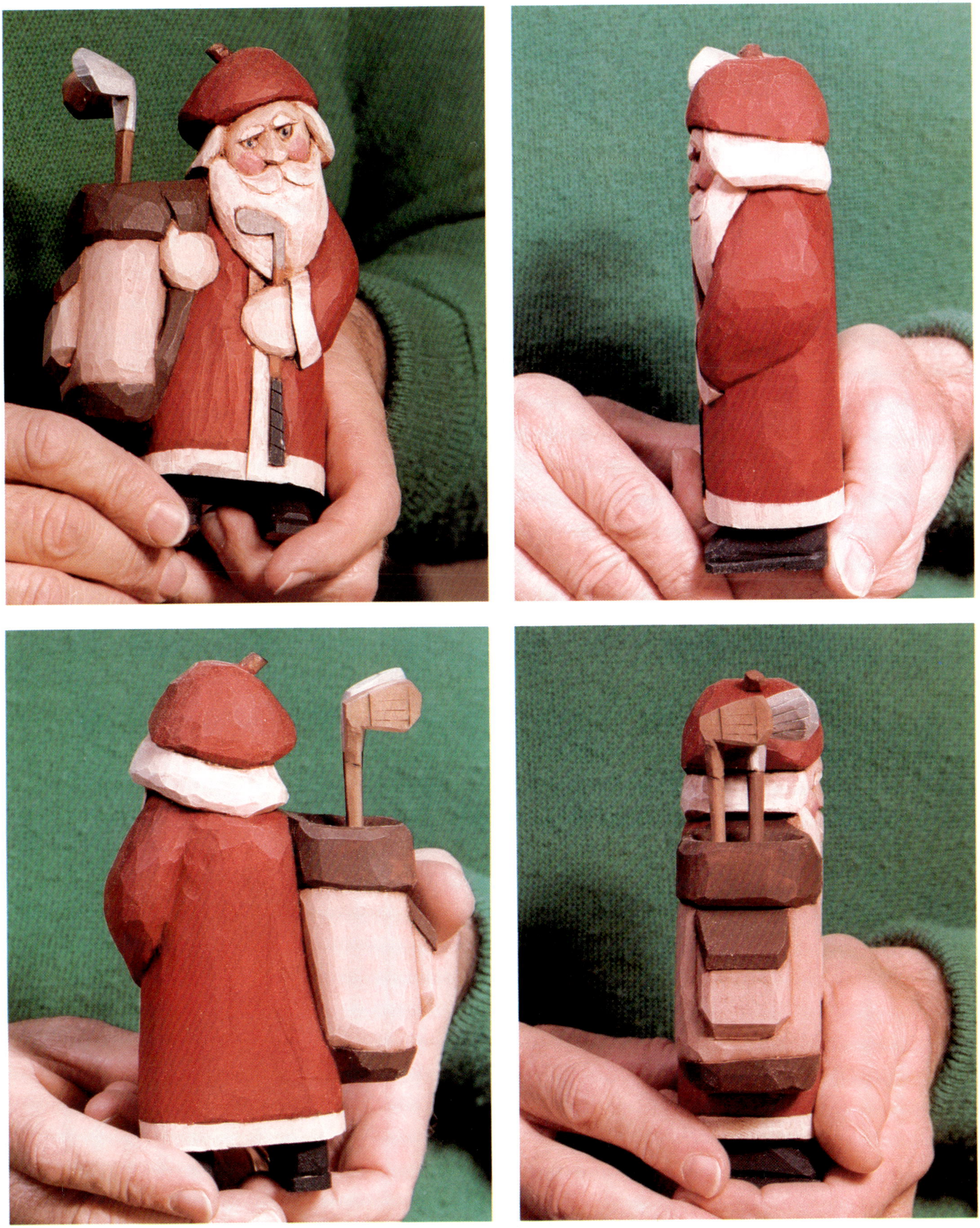

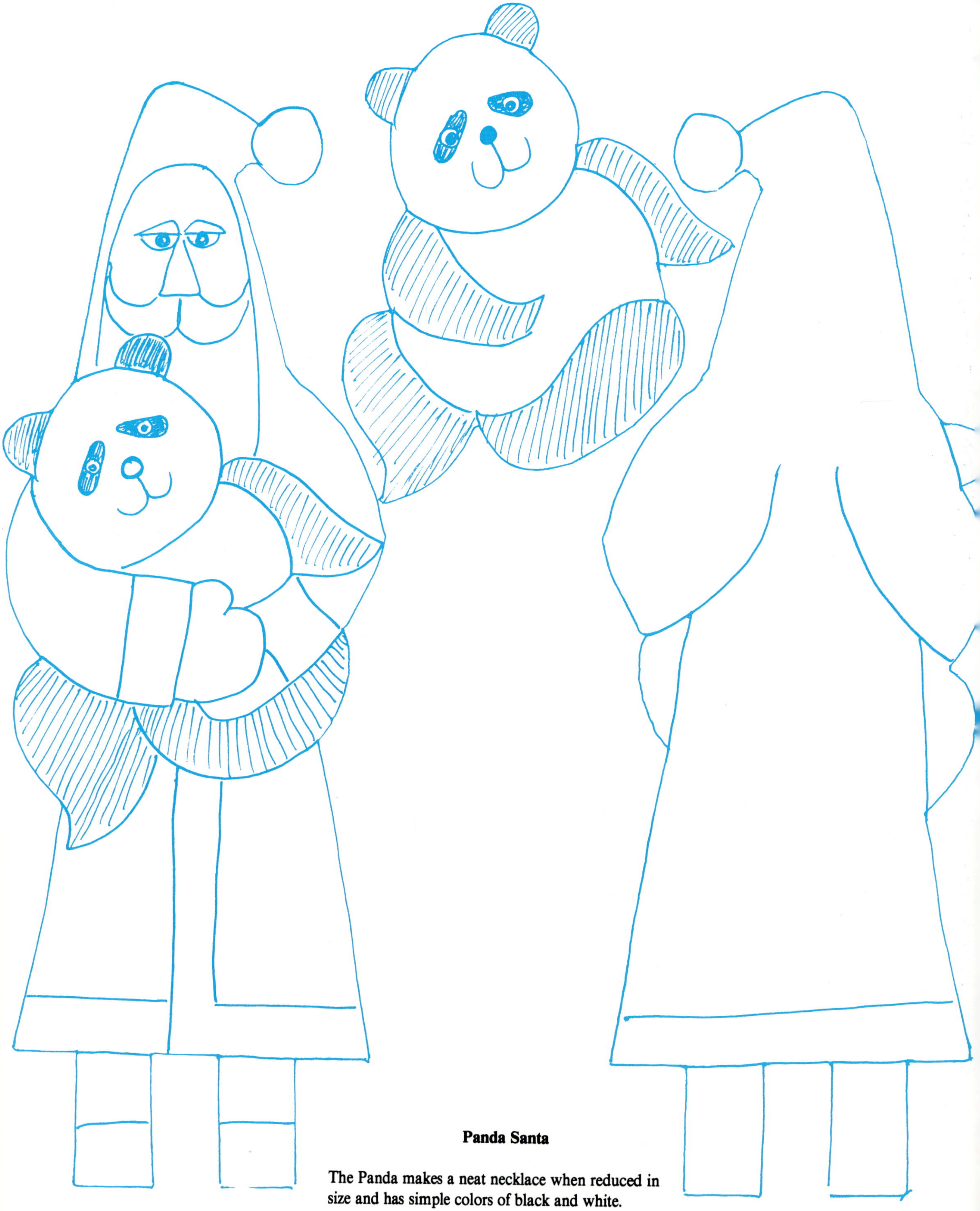

Panda Santa

The Panda makes a neat necklace when reduced in size and has simple colors of black and white.

Panda Santa

My first Panda Santa request came from Virginia Beach, Virginia. This Panda was borrowed from a friend in the antique business who tells me they are still very collectible.

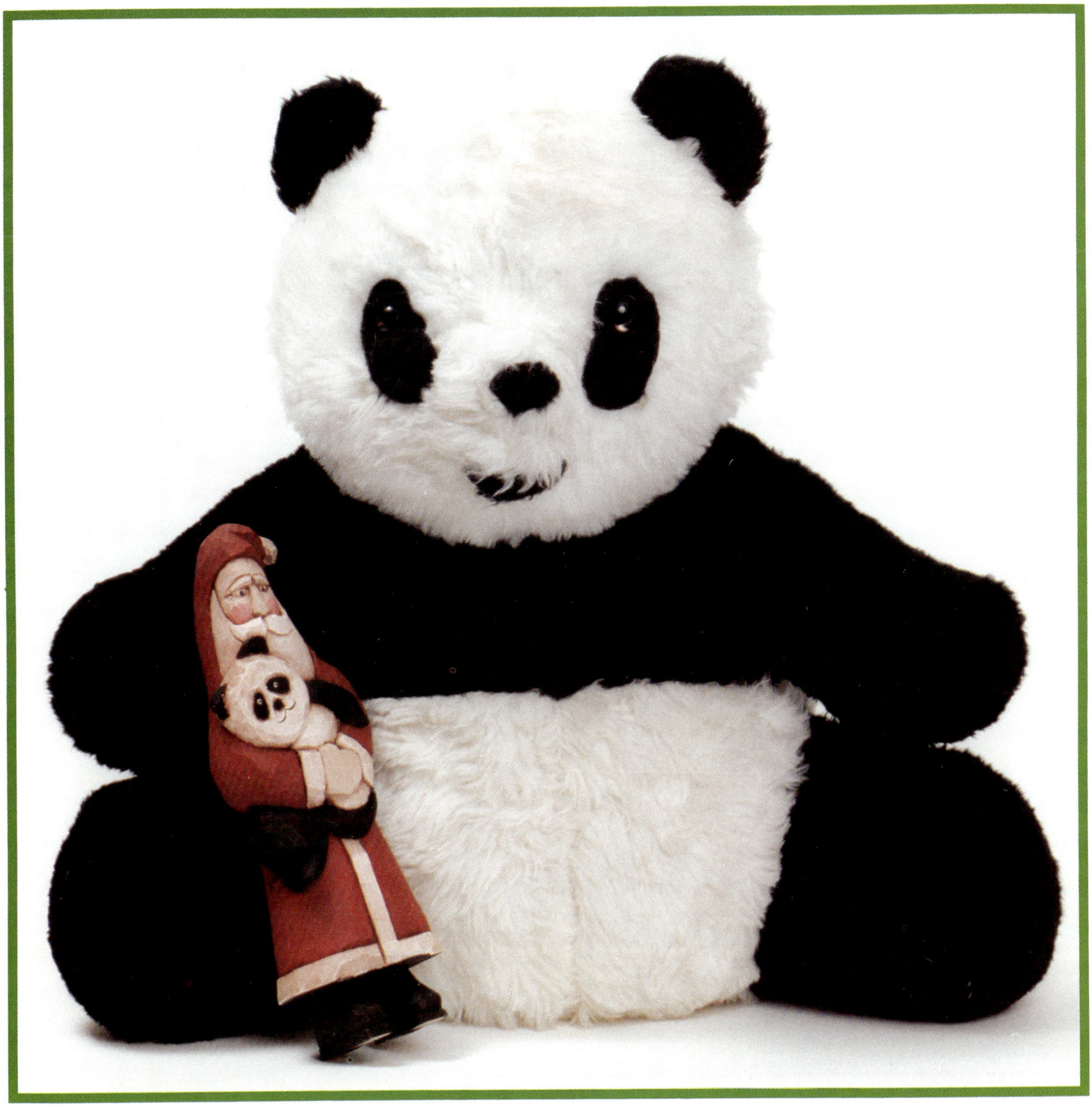

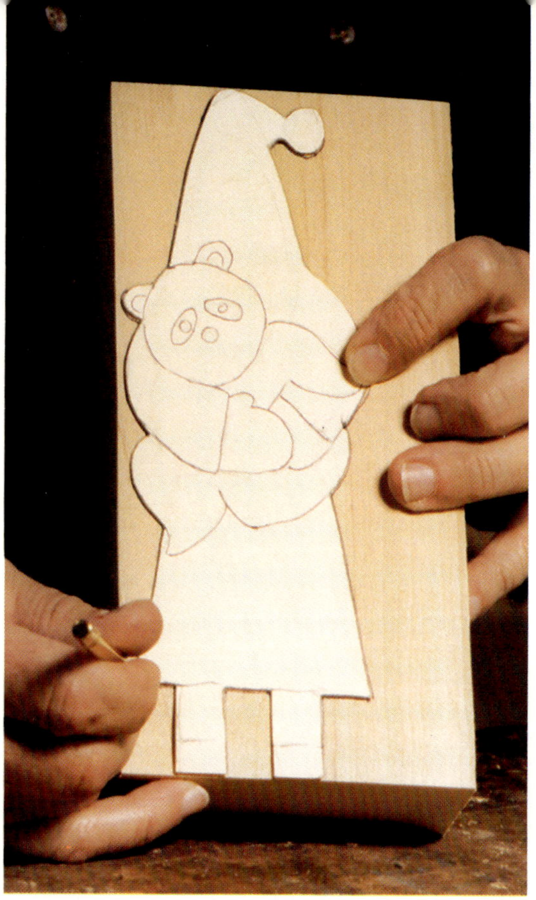

Trace the pattern on a block 8⅞" high, 3¼" wide, and 1¾" thick.

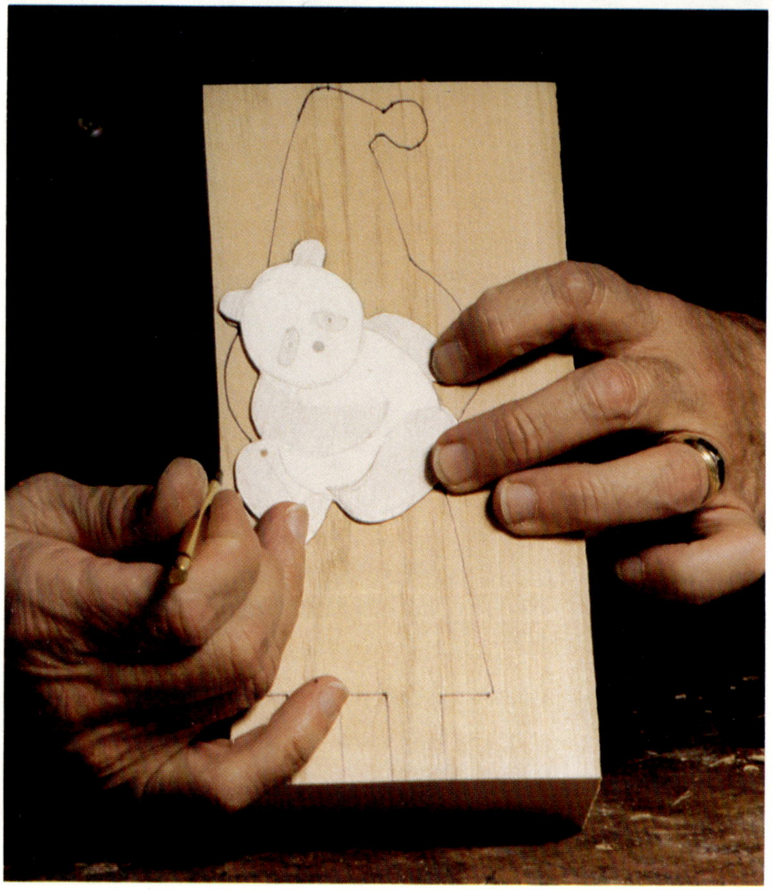

Choose where it fits best. Draw onto the block.

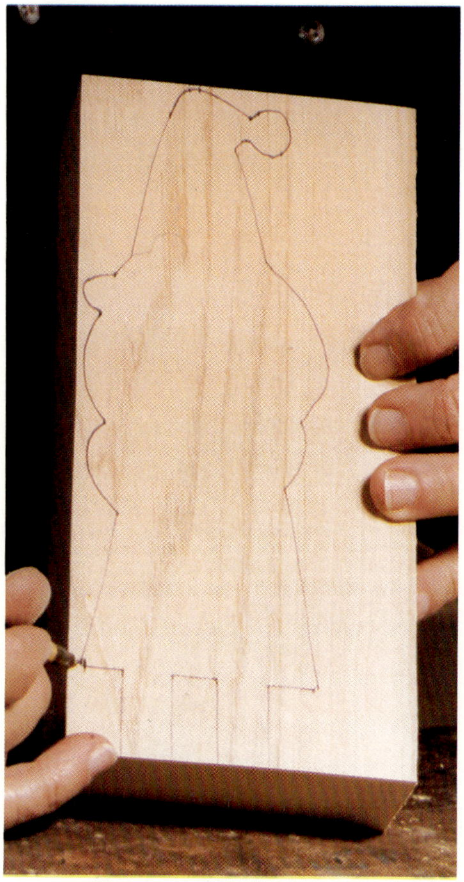

Cut the Panda pattern out.

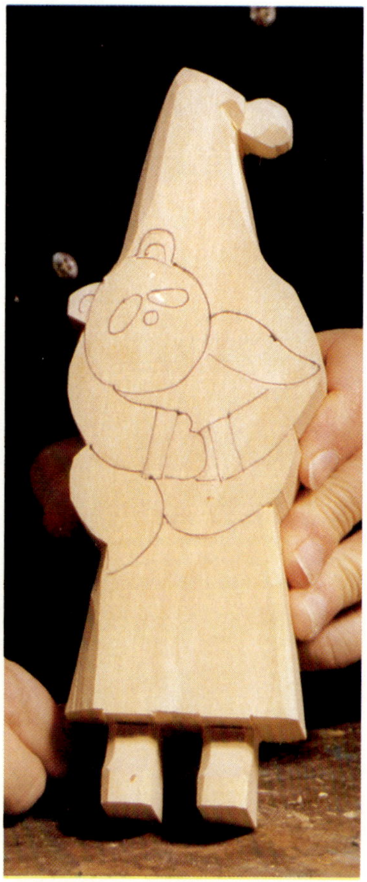

Saw, and you're ready to begin carving.

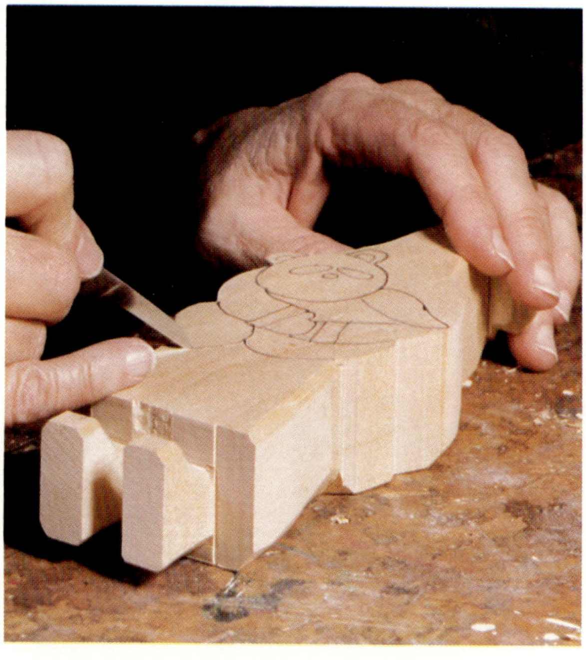

Incise the lines deeply. One of the members of my carving classes told me that what I called incising was scoring. I told him scoring was something you did in high school or college, sometimes on the athletic field.

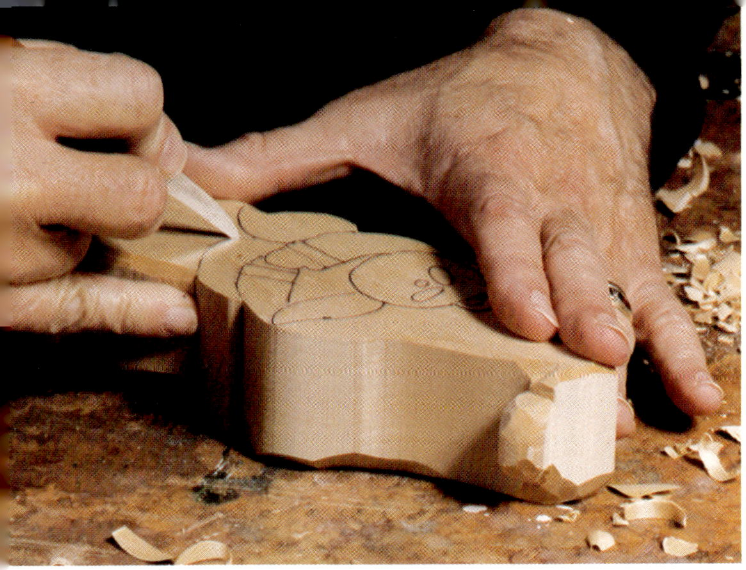

Incise each line.

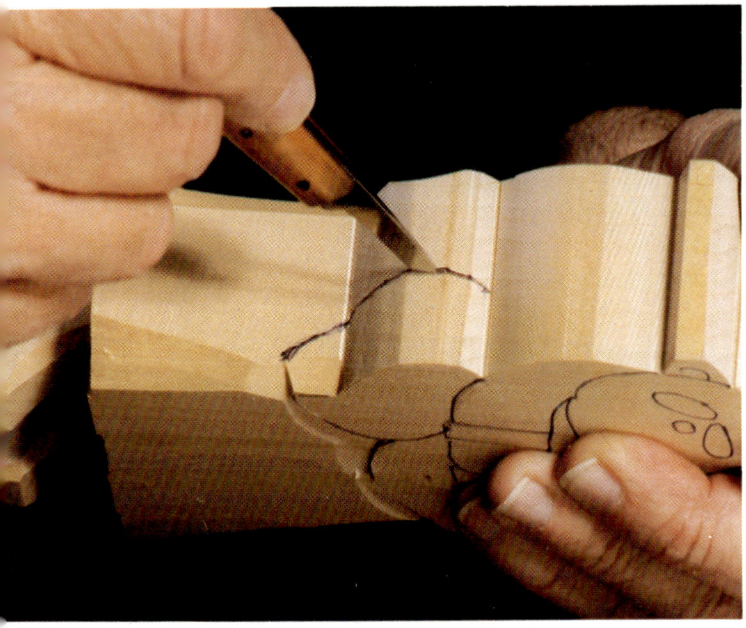

Draw a line where the Panda's leg should be.

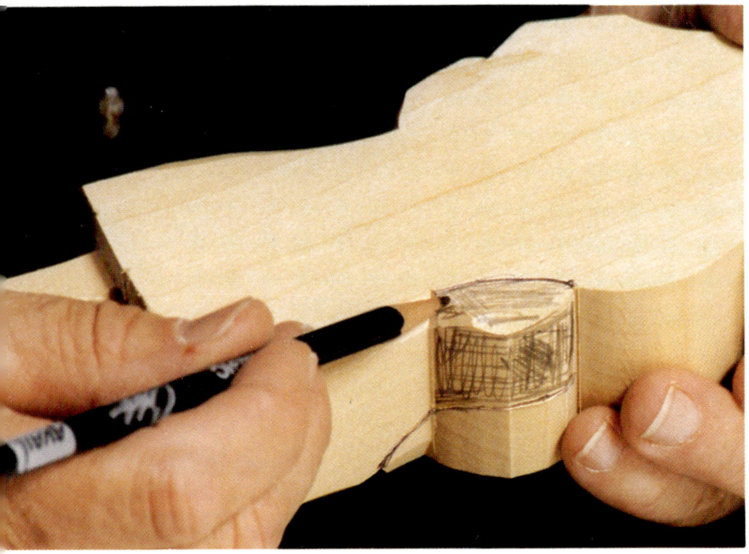

I've darkened the area to be removed.

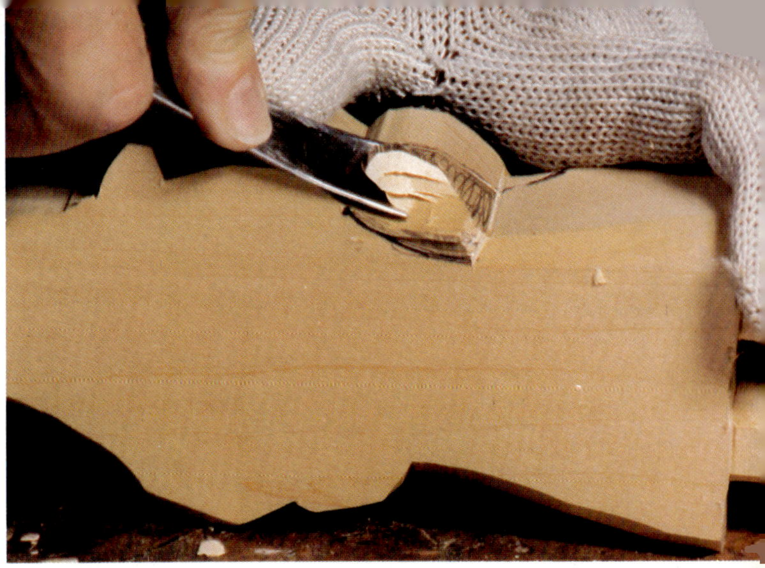

Use the gouge or a knife to take out the darkened area. I have put on the safety glove.

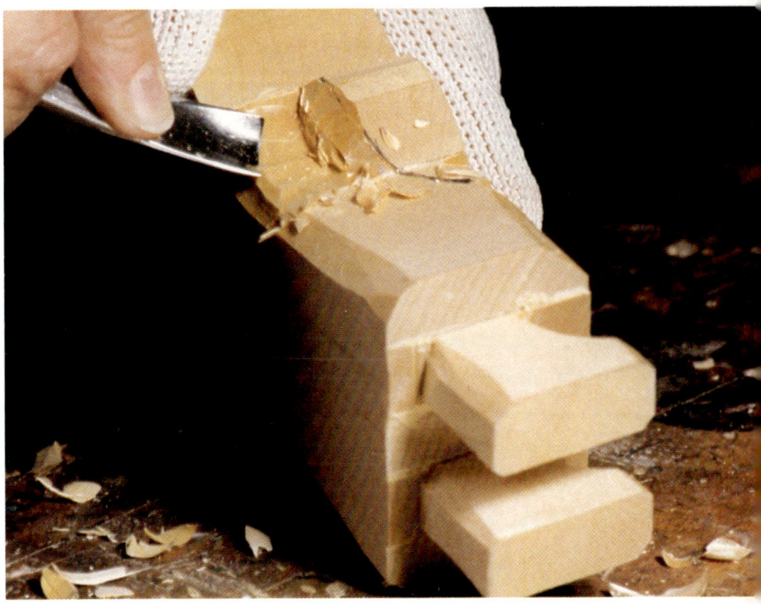

Leave enough of the Panda's leg to round.

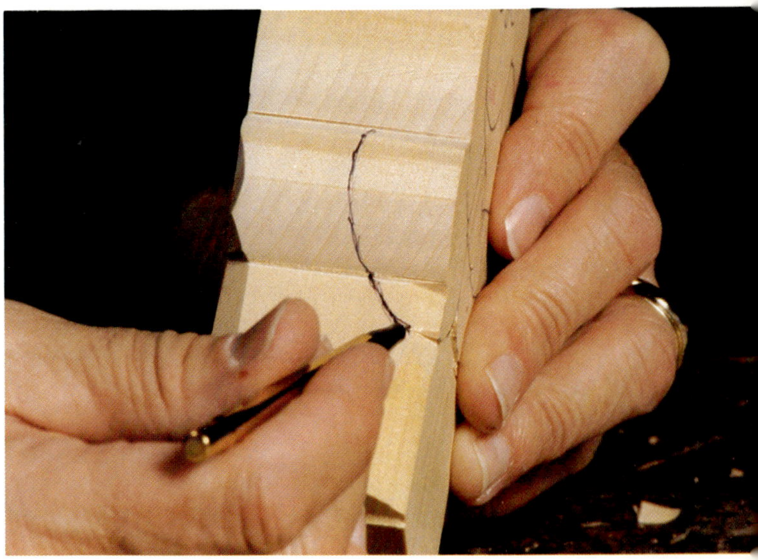

Draw a line outlining the Panda's head.

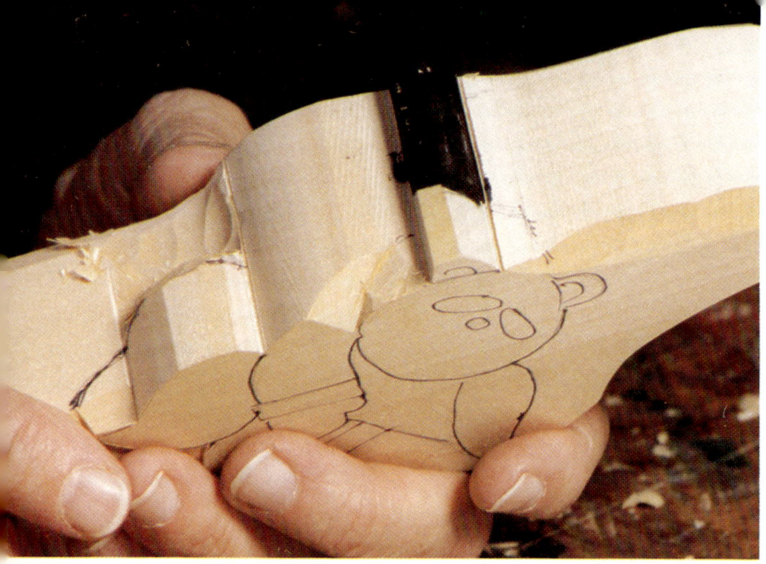

I've darkened the area to be removed.

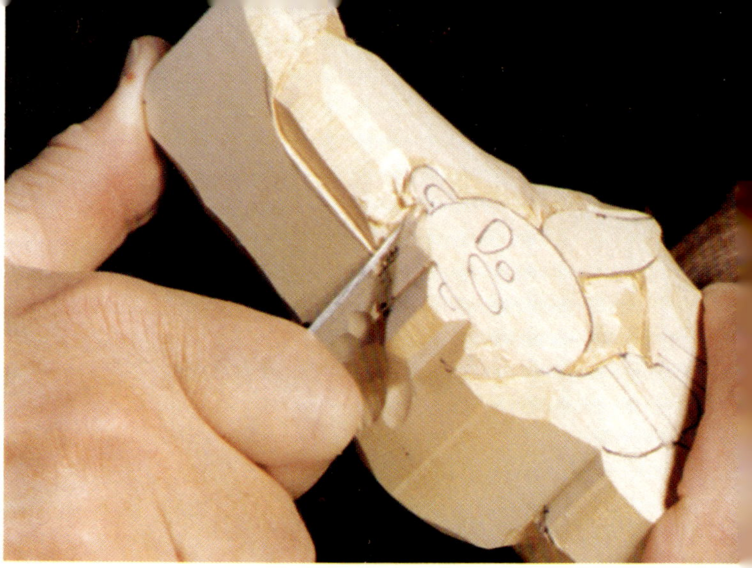

Round and blend the Panda's head into Santa's shoulder.

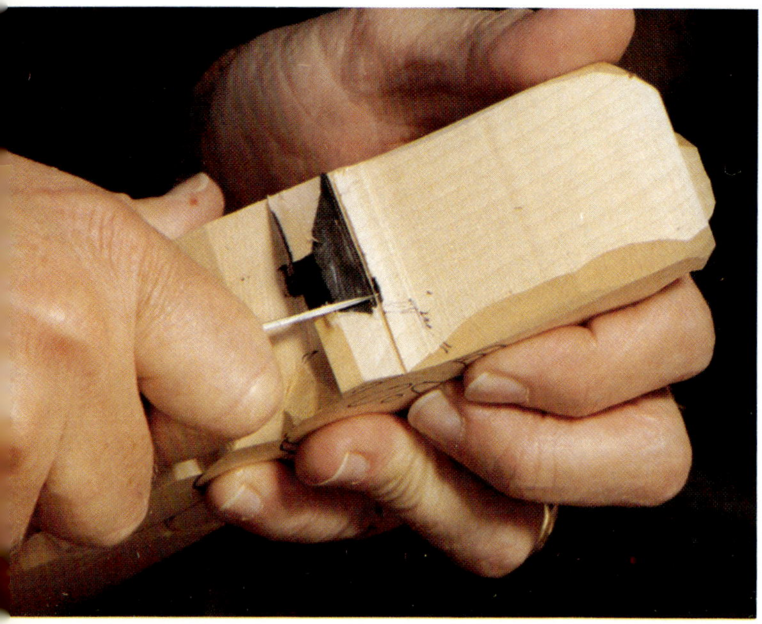

Make a stop cut.

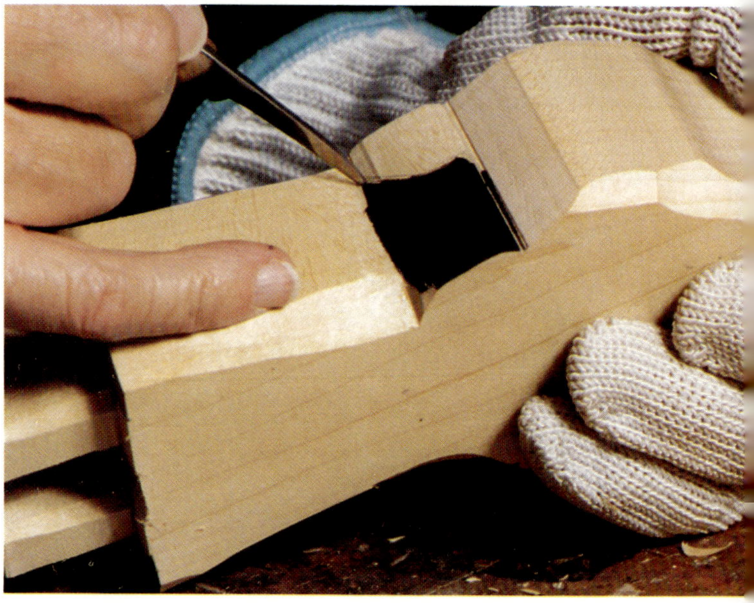

I have darkened the area on the Panda's left leg that should be removed.

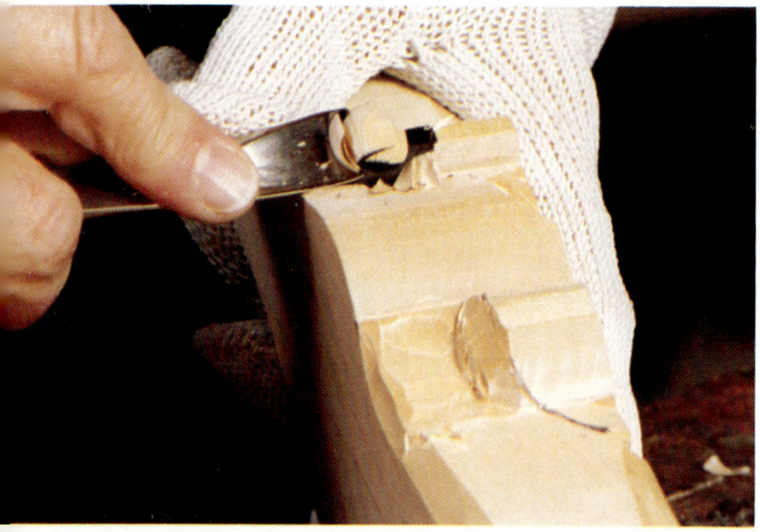

With a gouge or knife, remove the darkened area.

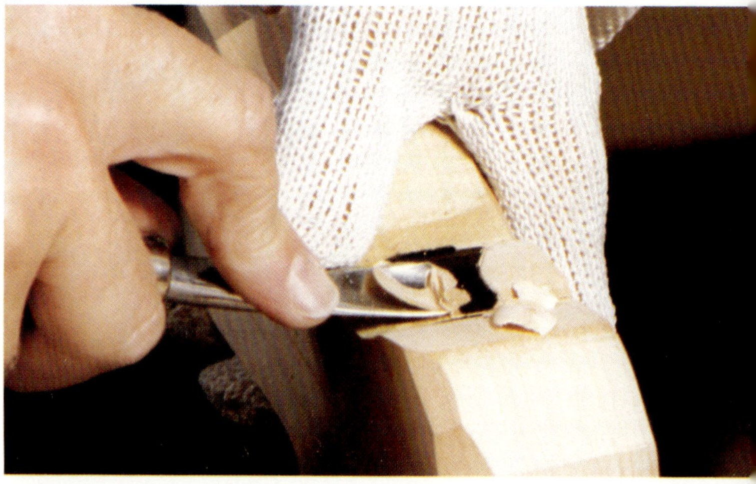

Remove the waste. Again, be sure to leave enough of the Panda's leg so that it can have a nice round look.

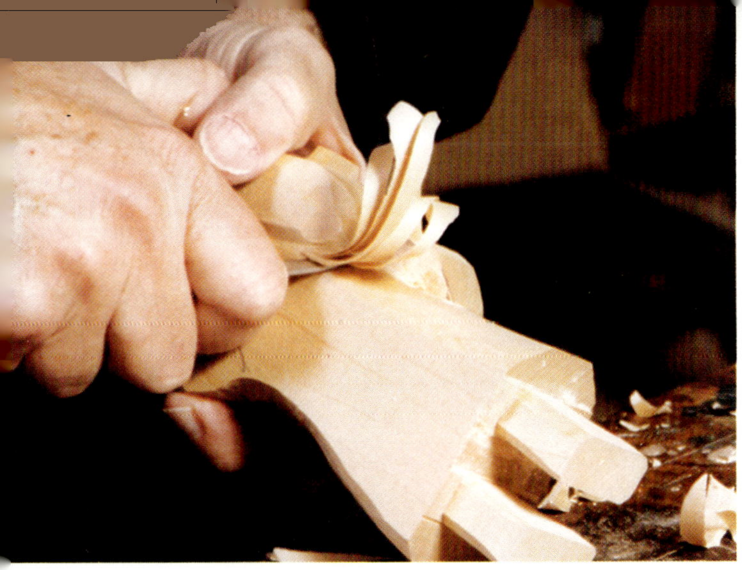

Continue to round as you go.

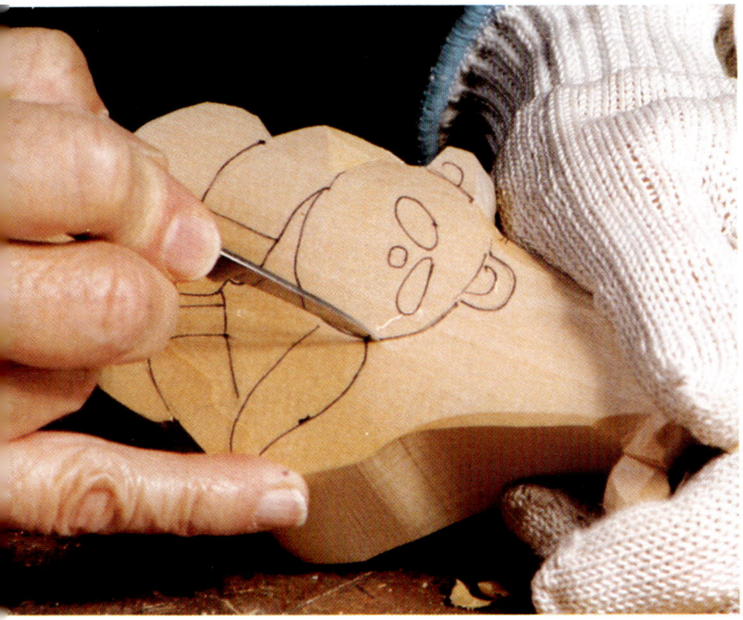

Incise any other area you may have missed. We will begin rounding the Panda's tummy.

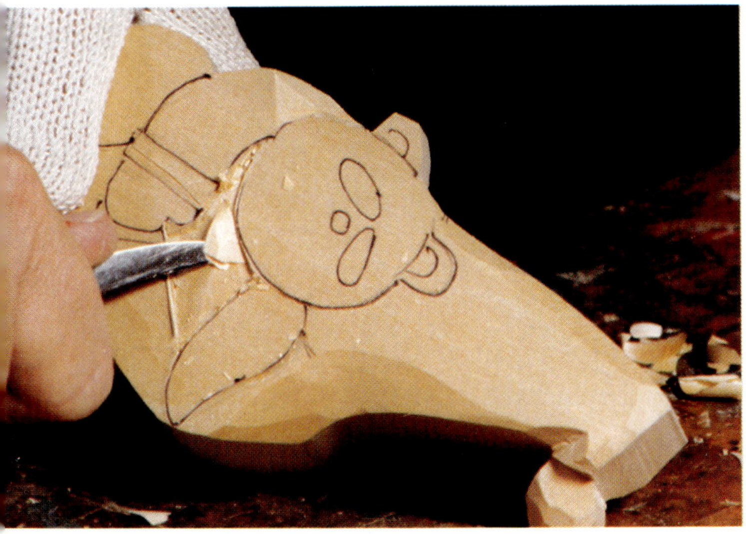

Blend the tummy into the chin.

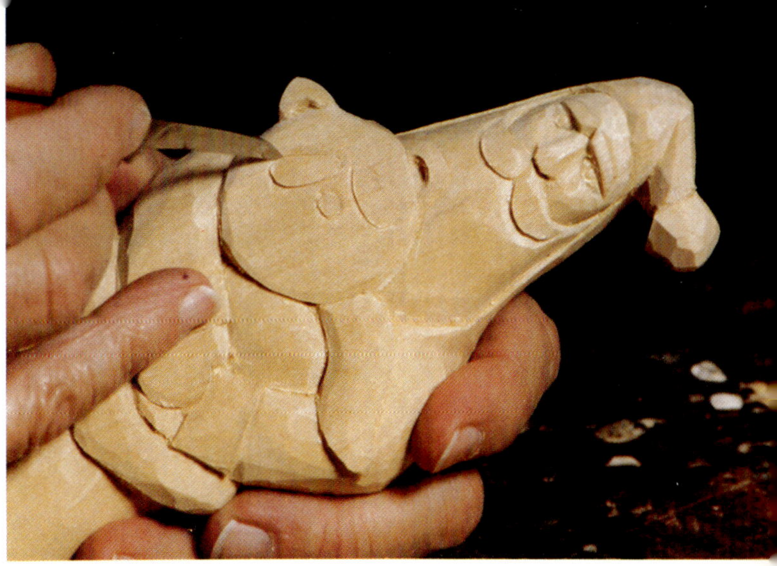

The Panda and Santa arms have been rounded. You may cut to make the eyes and nose stand out. You may simply paint these features in.

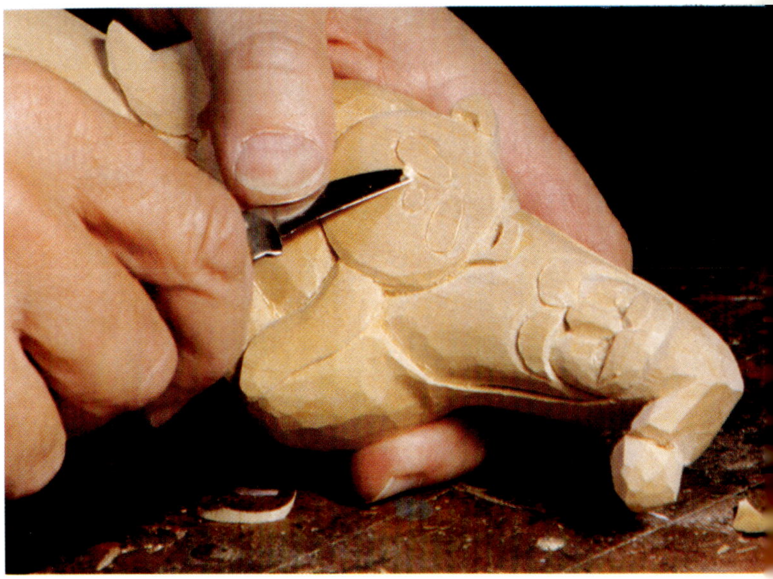

If you decide to cut the eyes and nose in, be sure to have a sharp knife.

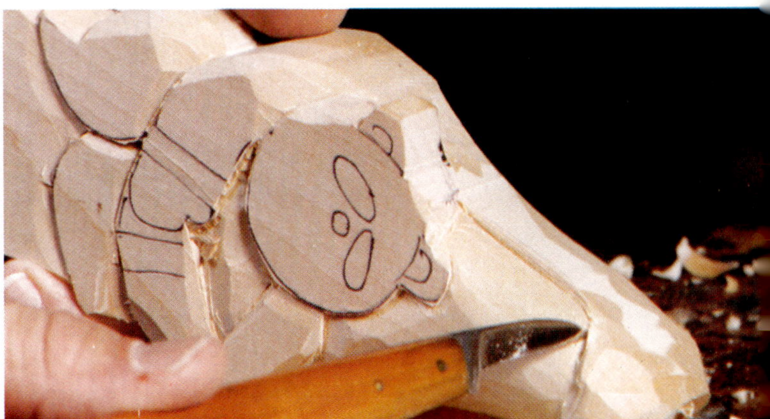

I don't want to be redundant, but remember the frying pan face. Begin giving the face the good egg shape.

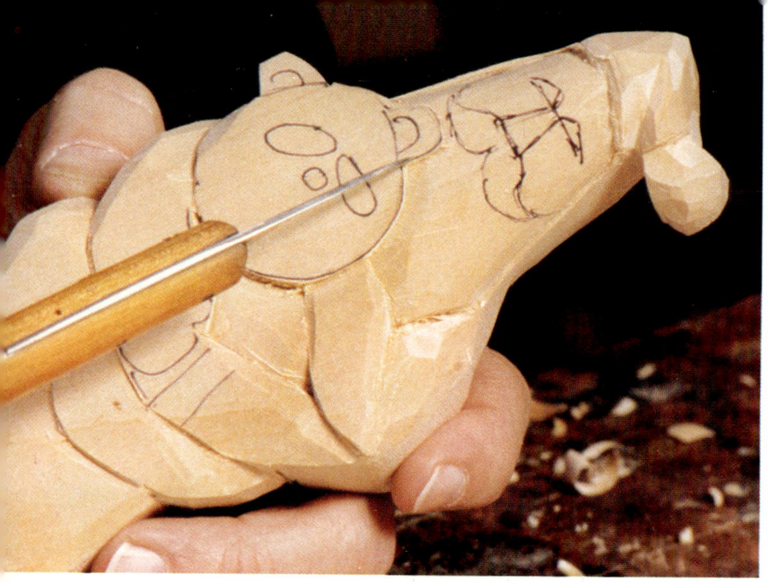

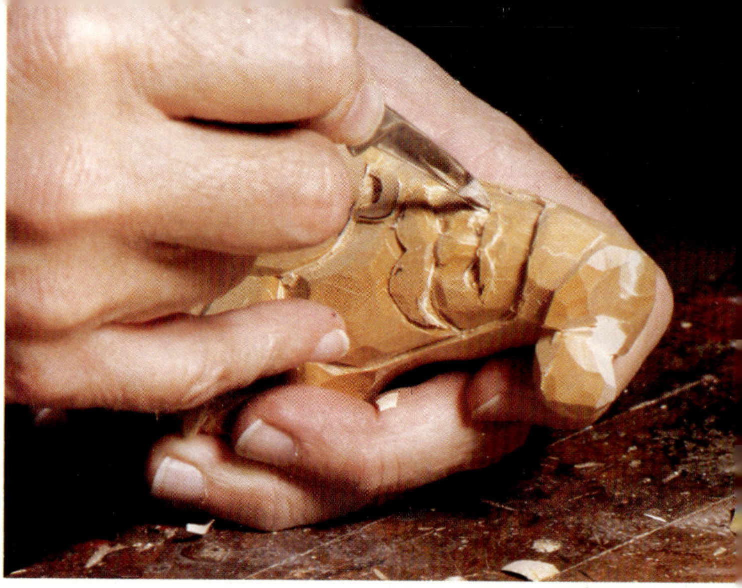

Blend the beard into the Panda's head. You don't want the beard and Panda head to look flat.

The face is just about ready.

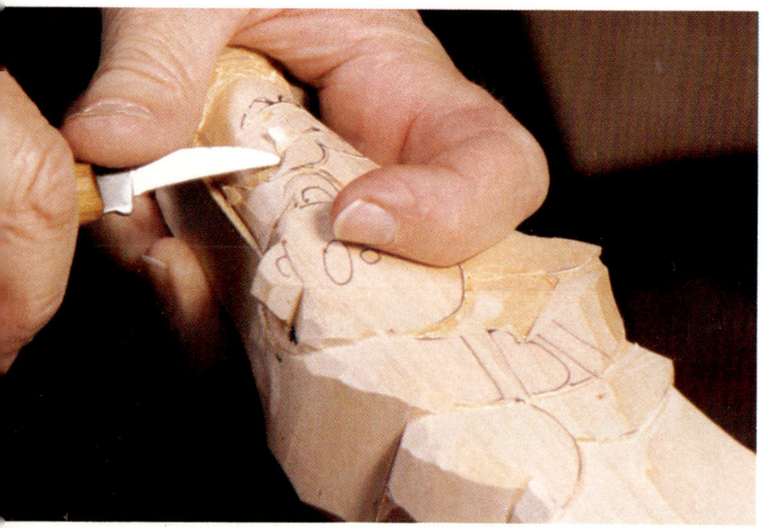

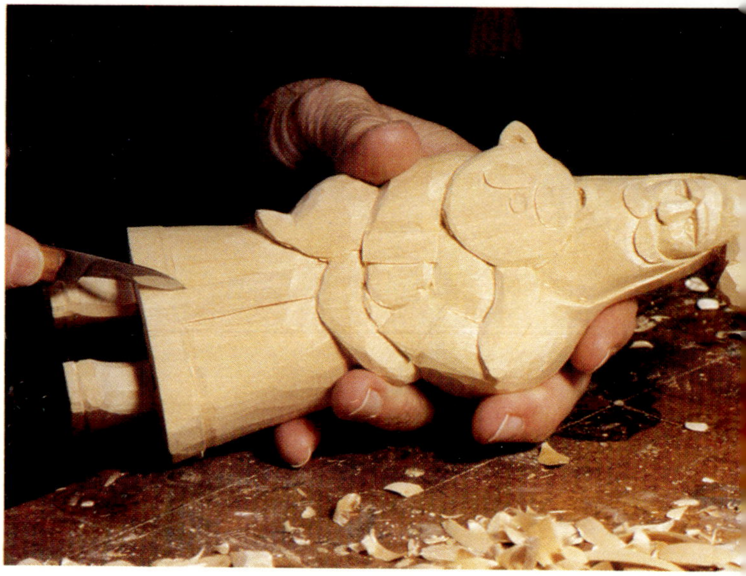

Round the cheek into the moustache.

Refer to the stocking Santa for face carving detail.

I'm adding the fur. Notice the roundness of the lower part of Santa.

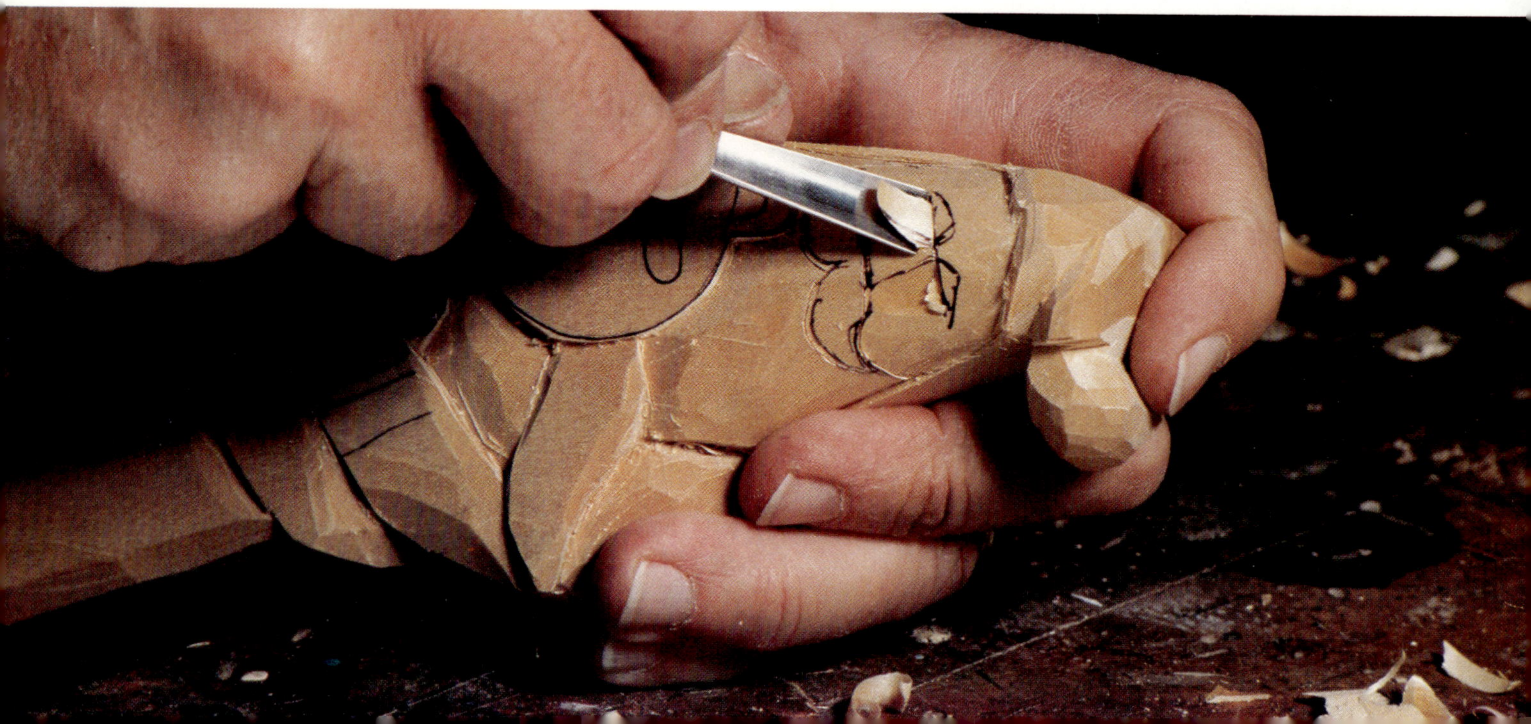

Four views of the Panda Santa.

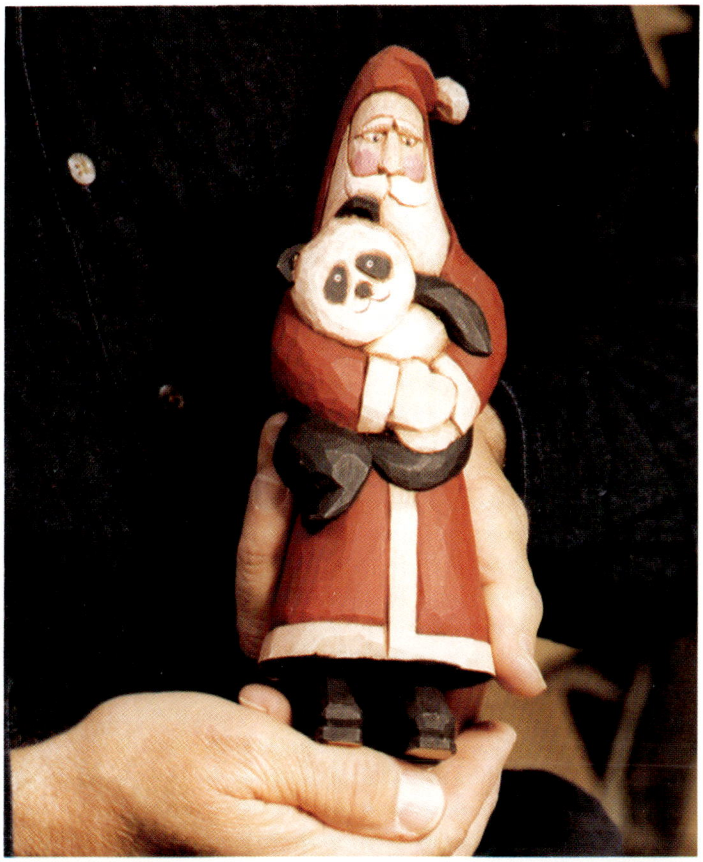

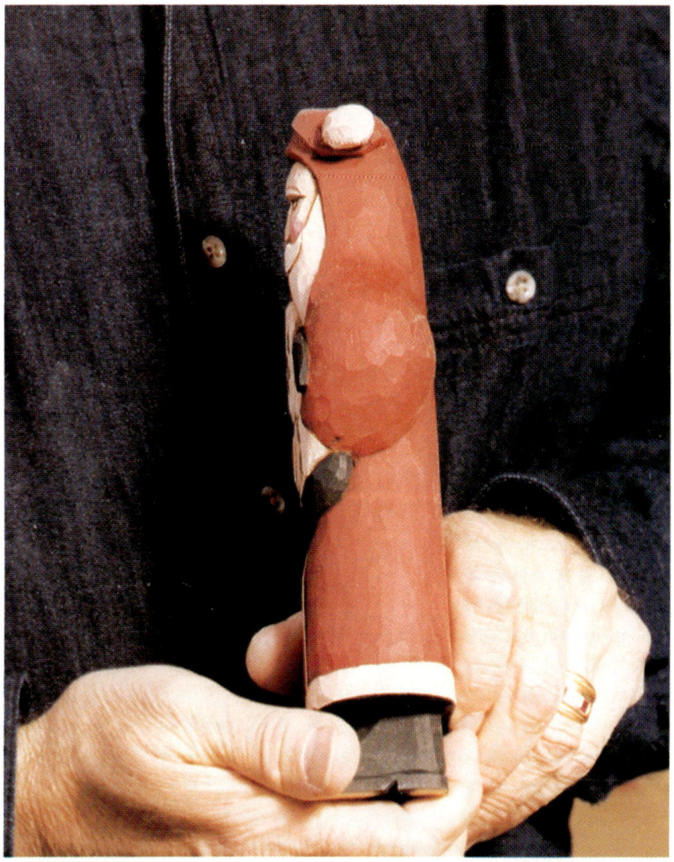

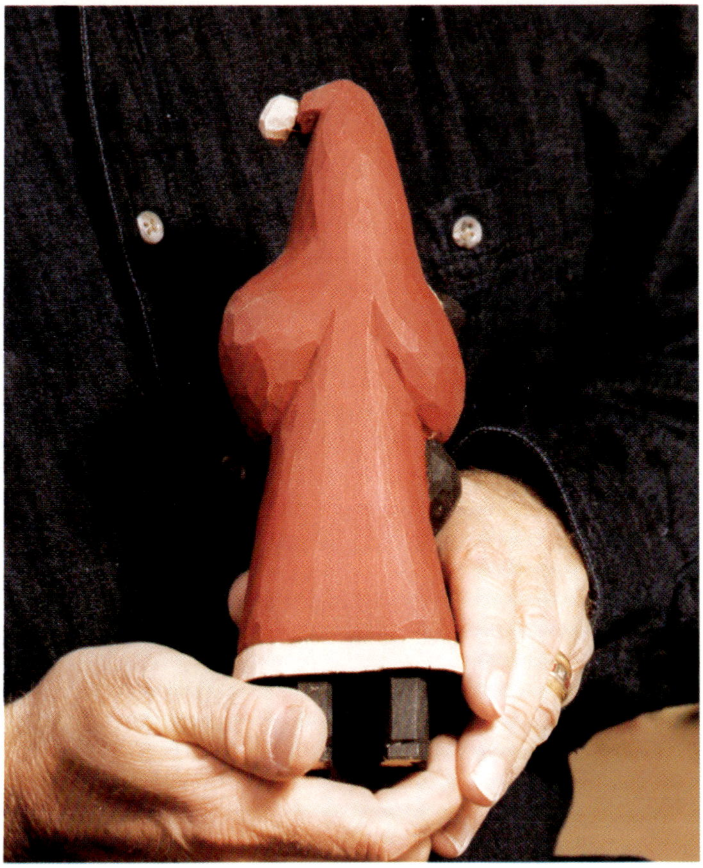

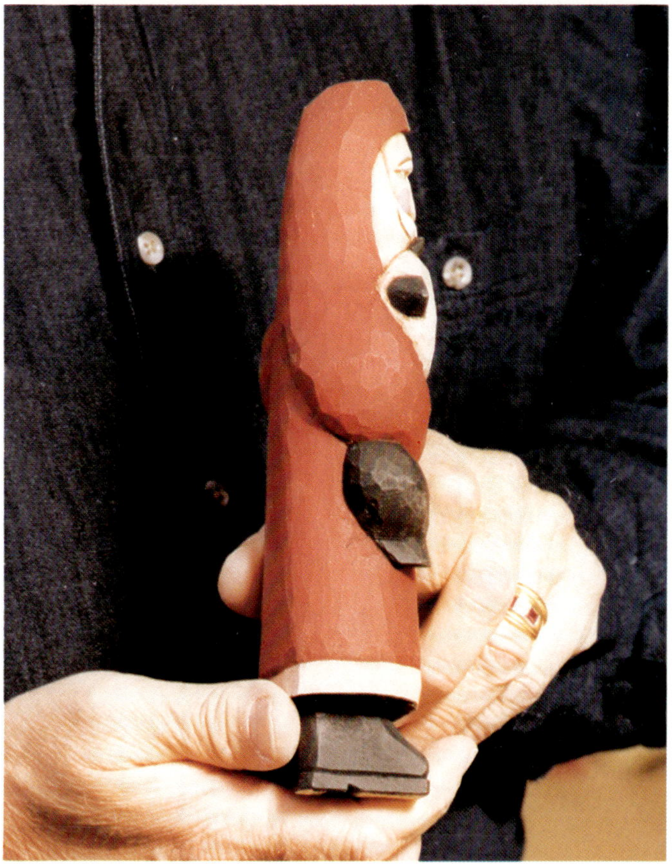

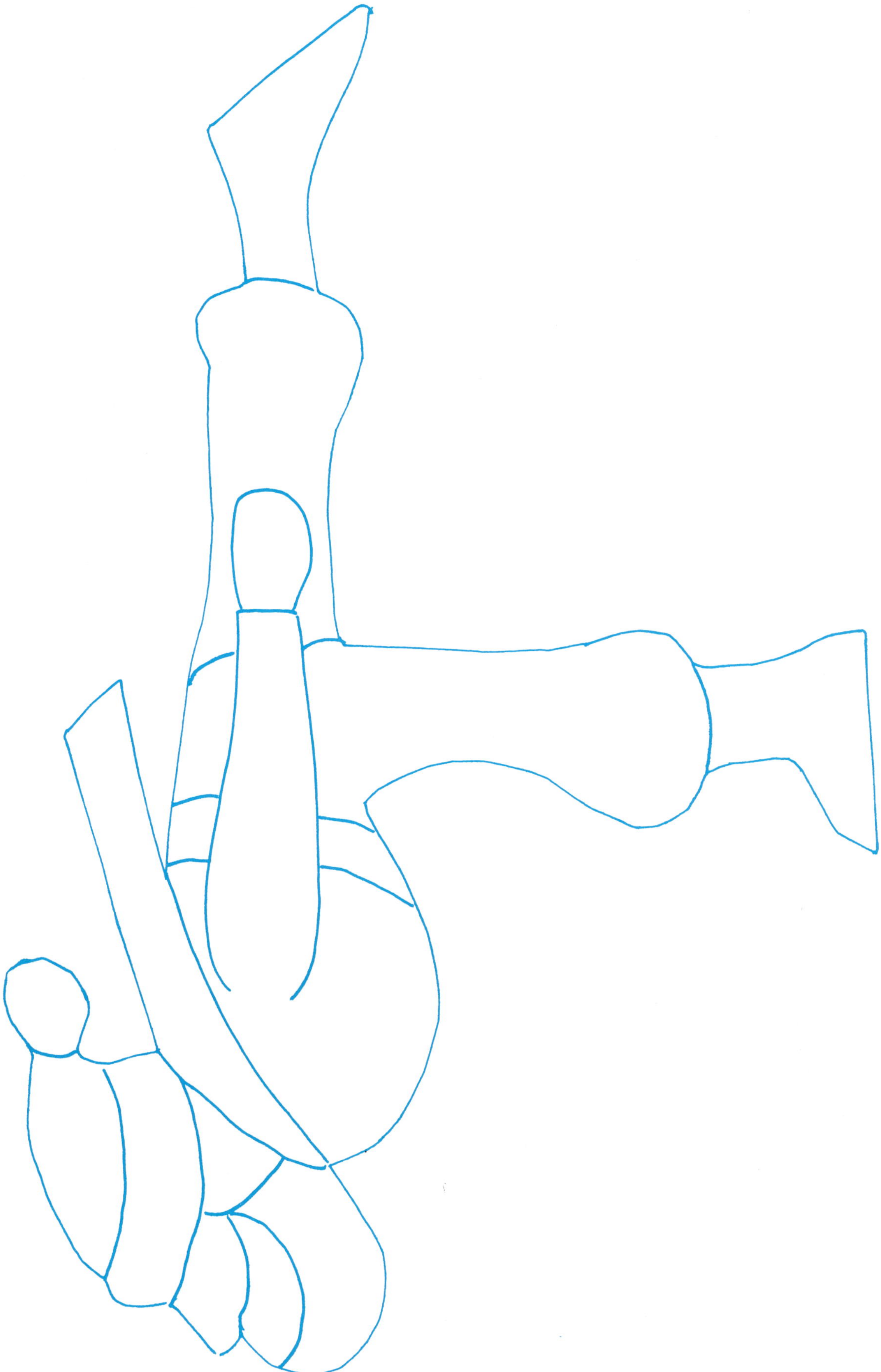

Santa Skier

Skiing Santa, Skating Uncle Sam, Turn Of The Century Skater

We do very little skiing this far south, but it can be done a few hours north of here. I want you to use your imagination in creating your own patterns. I was inspired to do the hot dog skier after seeing a skiing show at Six Flags Over Georgia in November. Keep your eyes open; inspiration can come at unusual times.

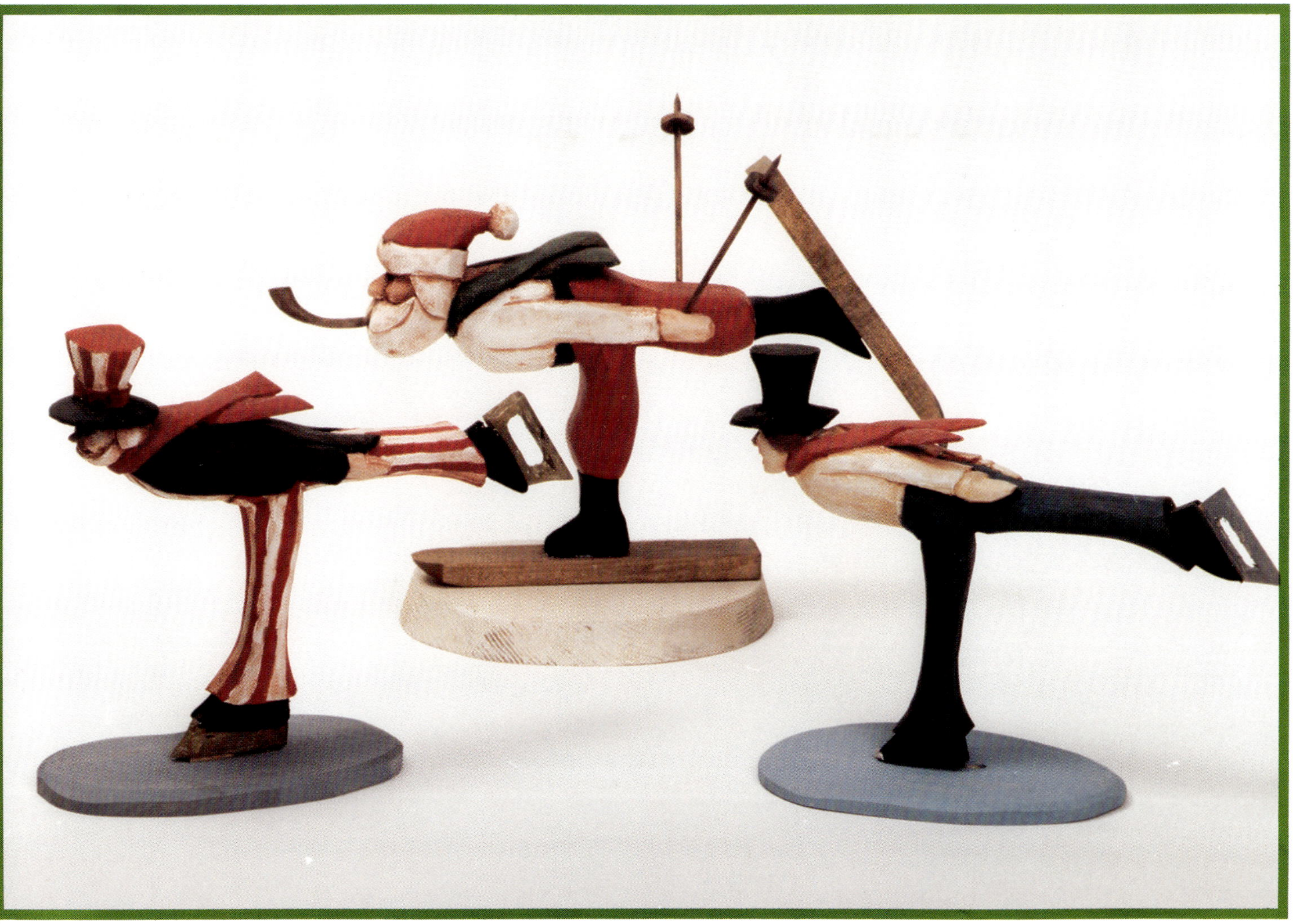

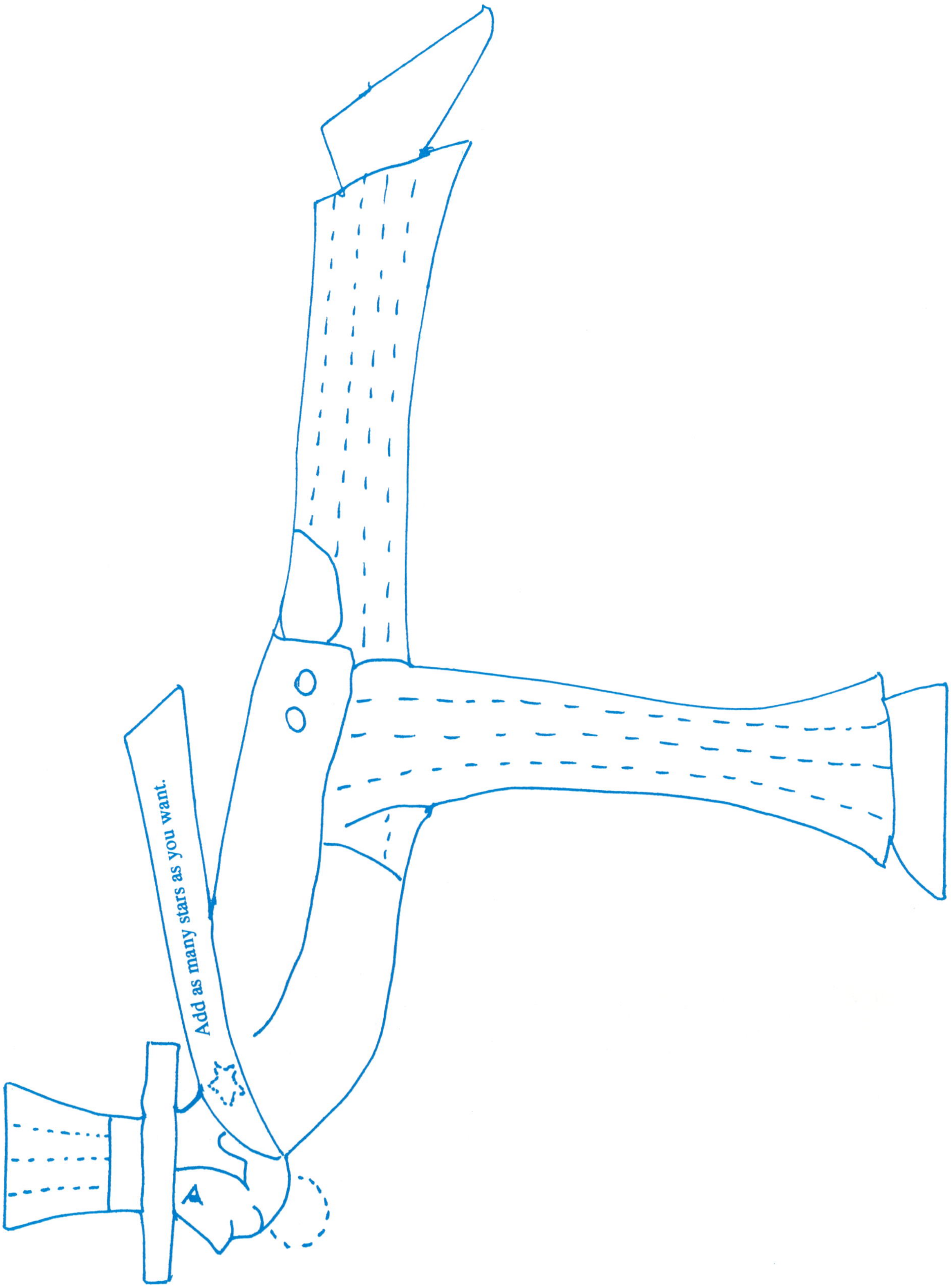

Early American Skater

or connect the dots and paint red, white, and blue for a patriotic Uncle Sam.

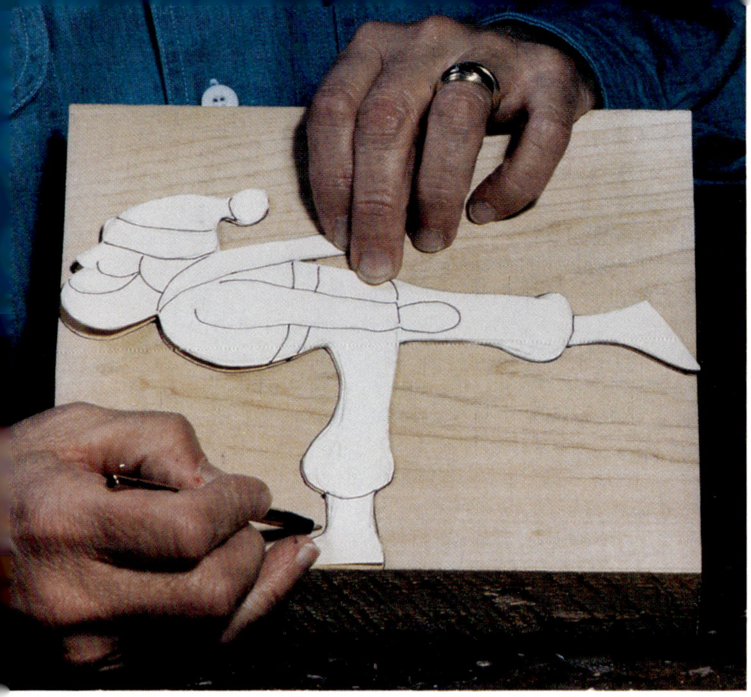

For the skiing Santa you will need a block 9¼" wide, 6½" high, and 1¾" thick.

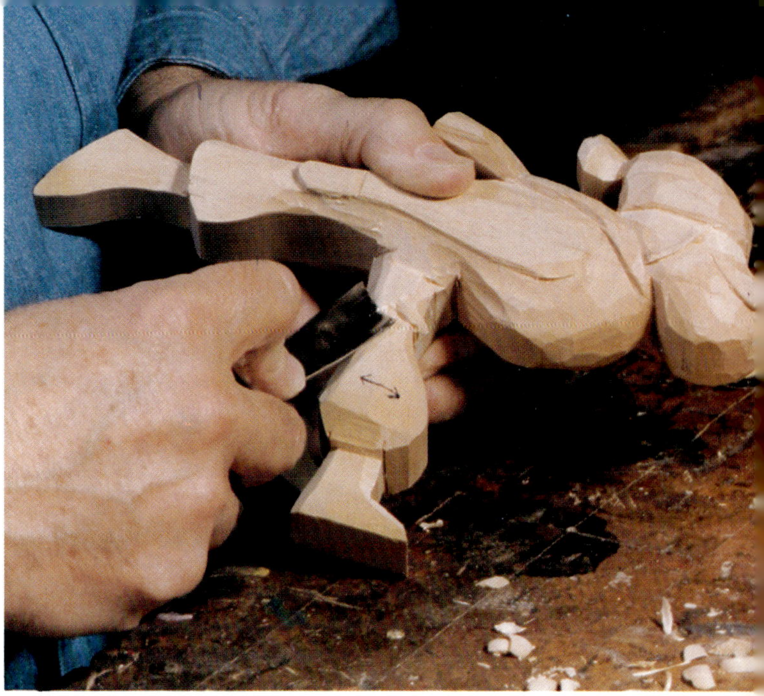

I've picked up the piece to show, by the arrow on the leg, which way the grain goes.

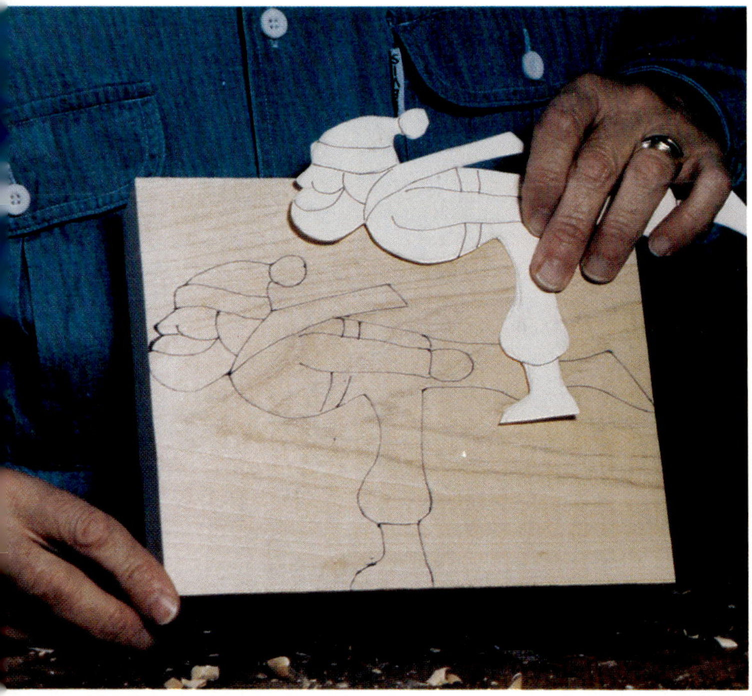

The pattern drawn on the block.

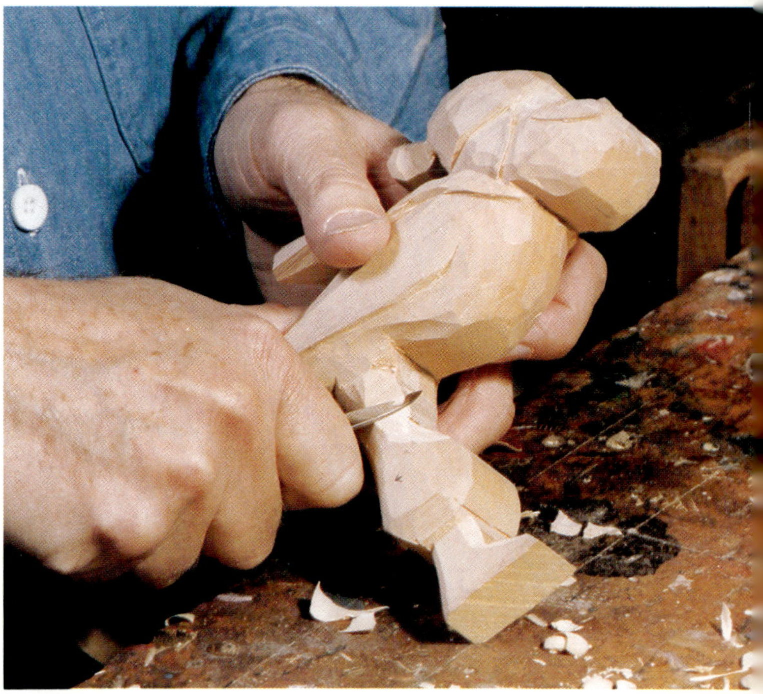

I'm now using my knife to start shaping the leg.

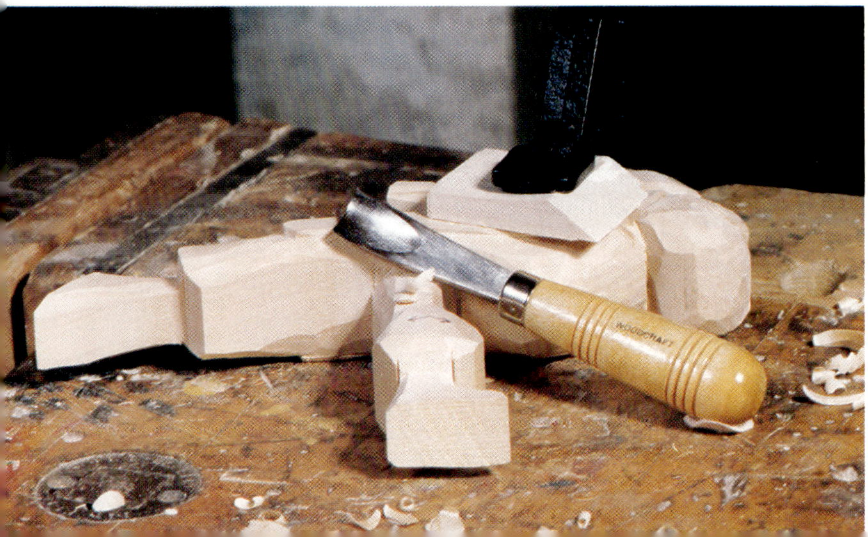

I've clamped the piece to my work bench. Use a scrap to keep from marring your wood. The right leg is carved cross-grain, and I found a good, sharp gouge helped move a great deal of wood.

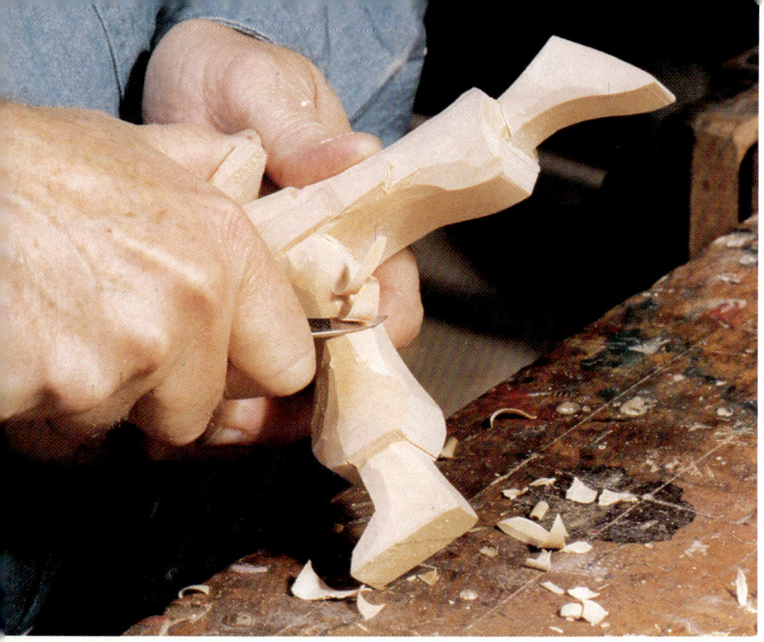

The leg is taking shape. Notice how the pants leg blends into the boot.

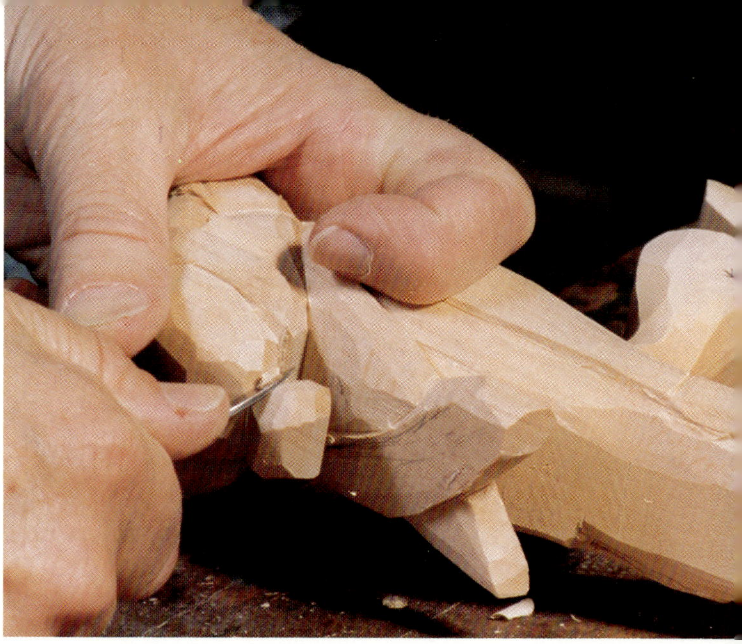

Start shaping the ball on the cap.

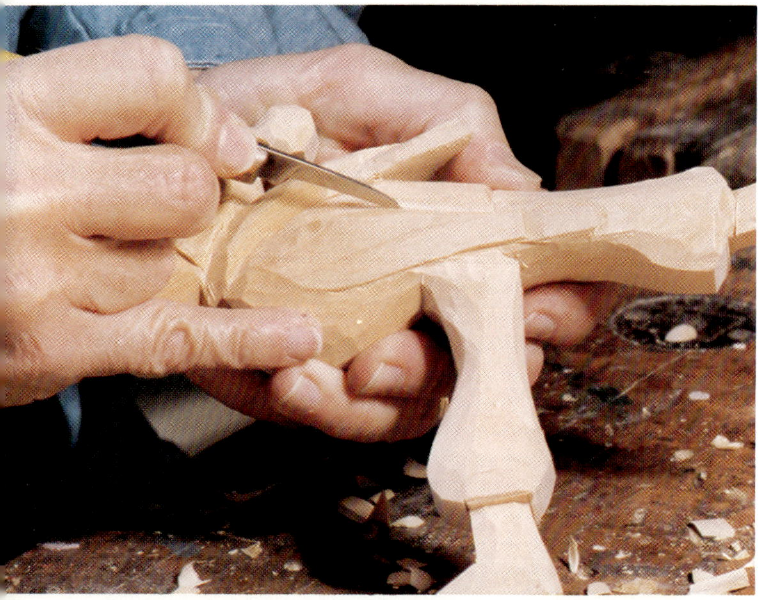

Incise around the arm and hand.

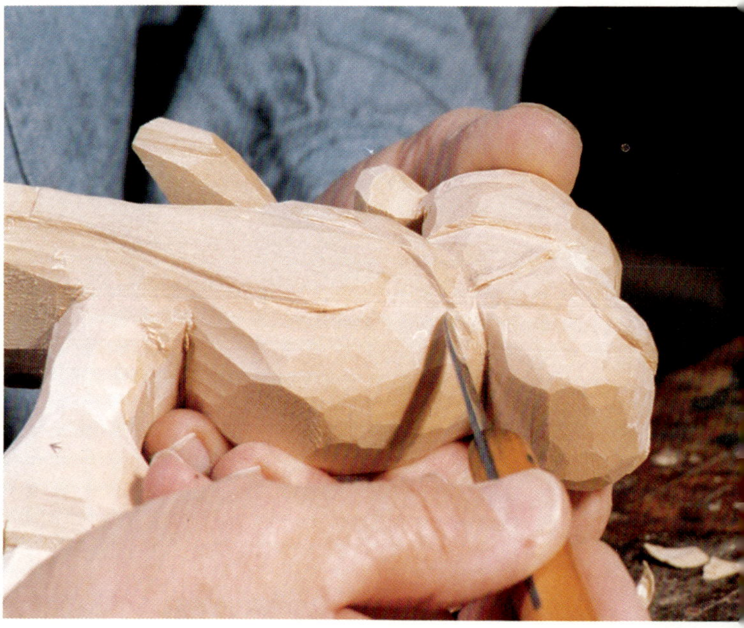

Trim around the scarf as it comes under the chin.

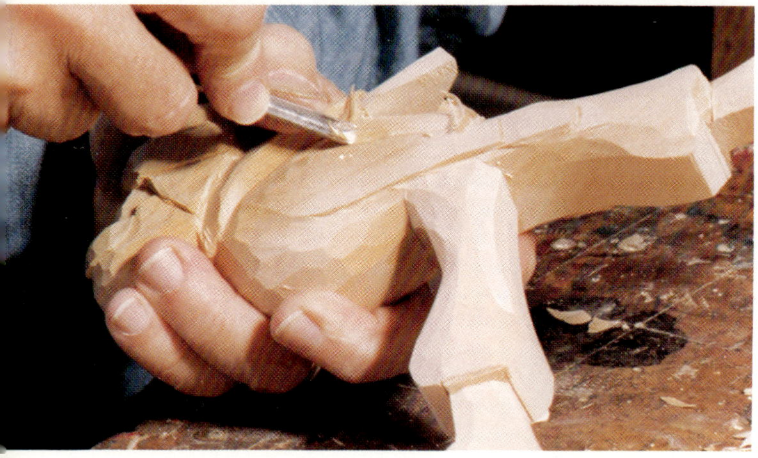

With a gouge or knife remove the waste around the arm and hand.

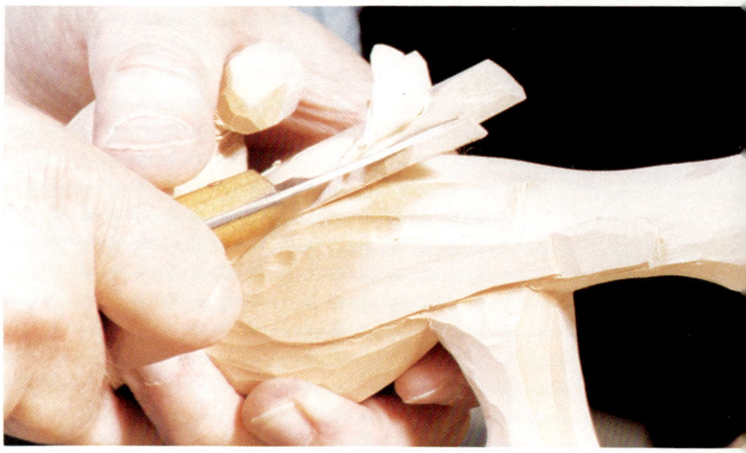

Trim the scarf.

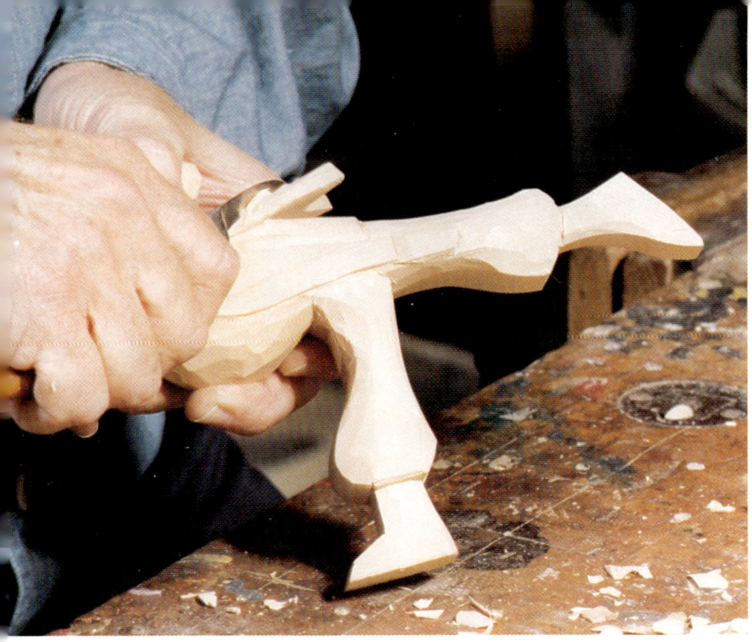

Support the scarf as you carve it or it may break off.

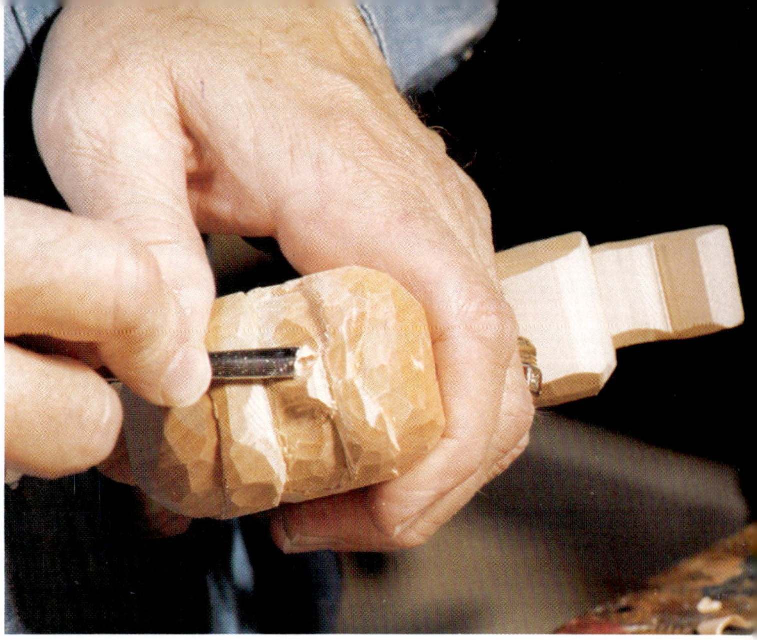

Trim the left side of the nose.

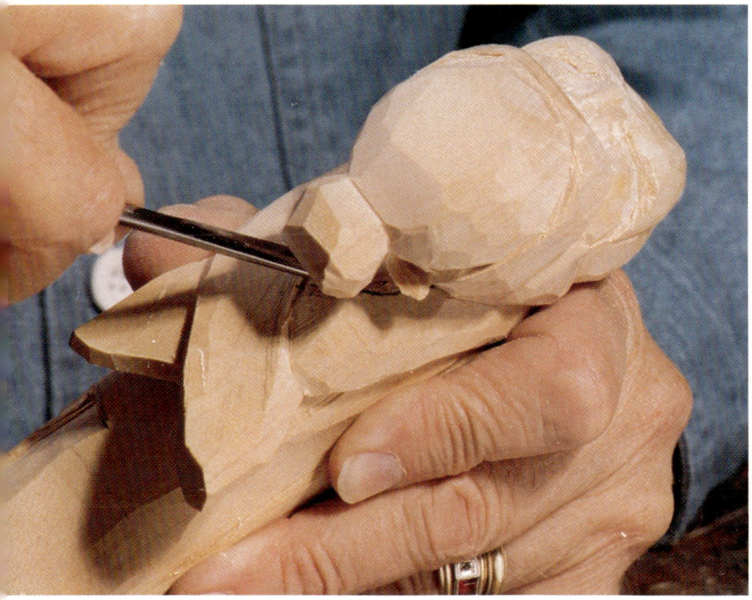

It is easier to get into this area between the back and the back of the neck with a gouge.

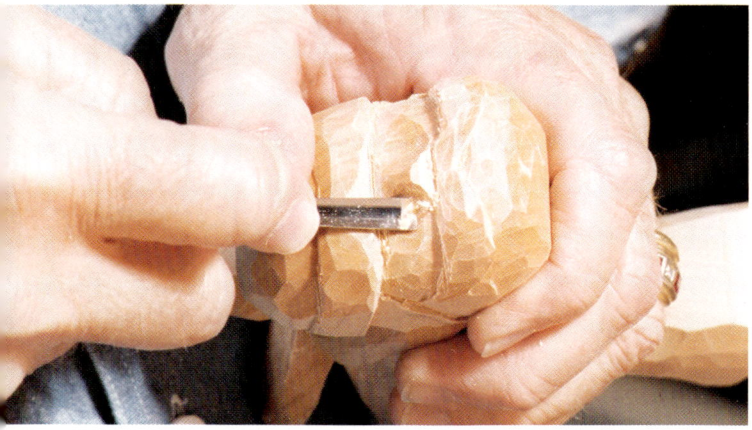

I've rounded the beard and cap and have begun to trim around the right side of the nose.

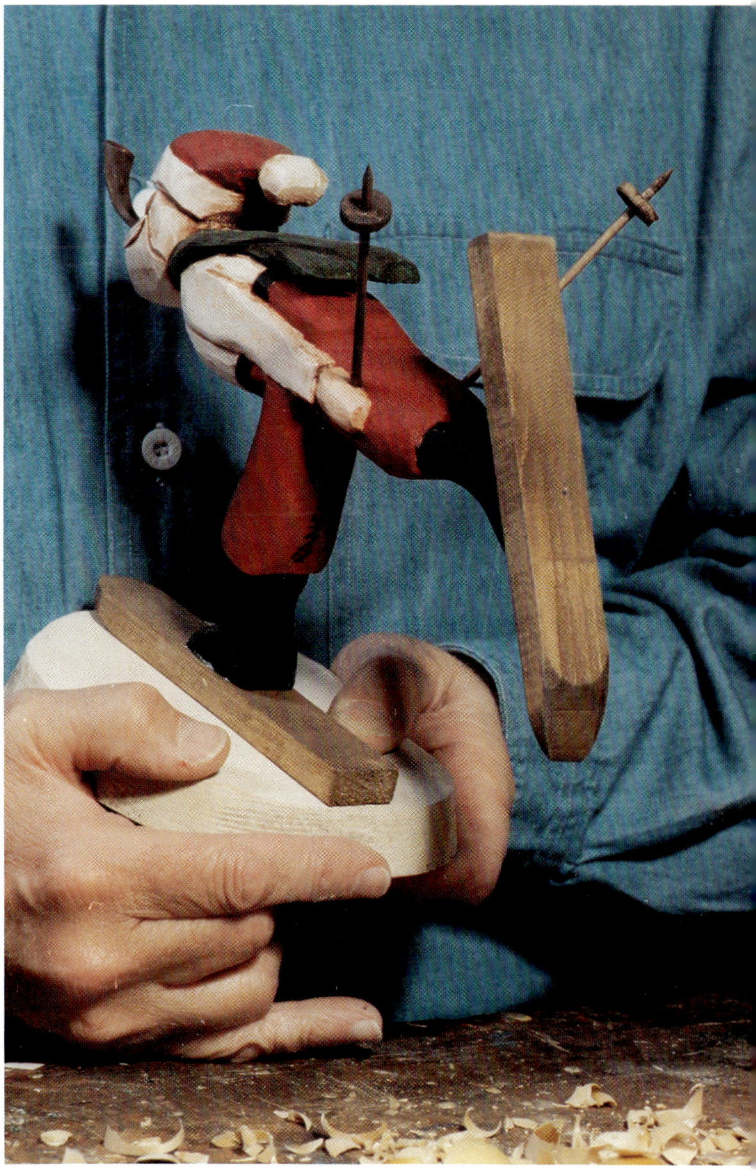

You will need to mount the skier.

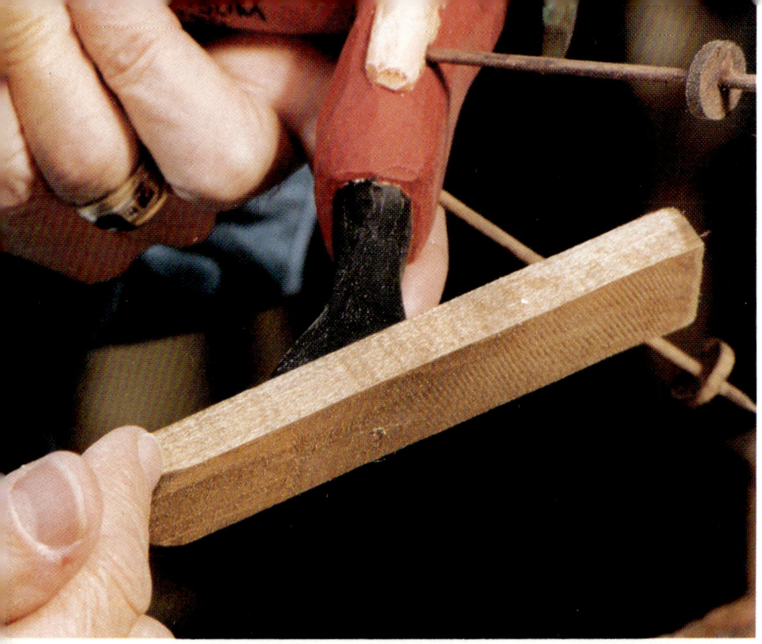

I will cut the skis thinner next time.

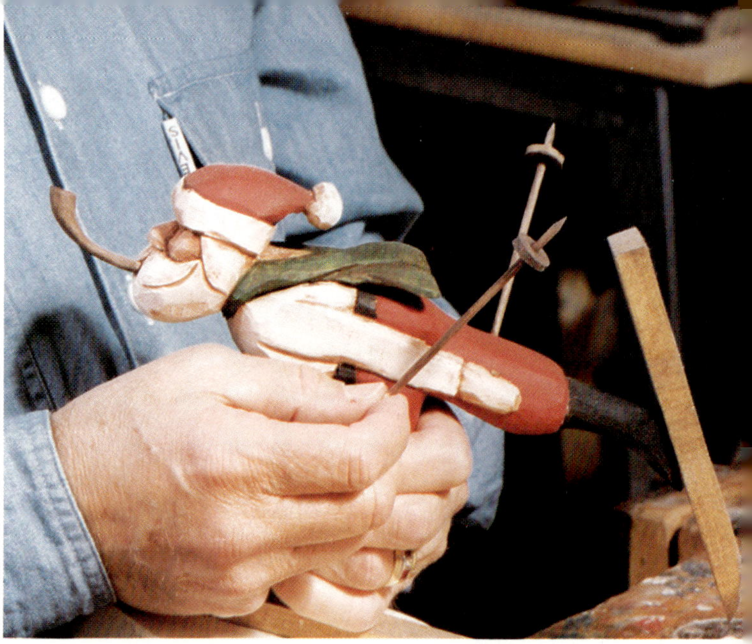

I used dowels to make the ski poles.

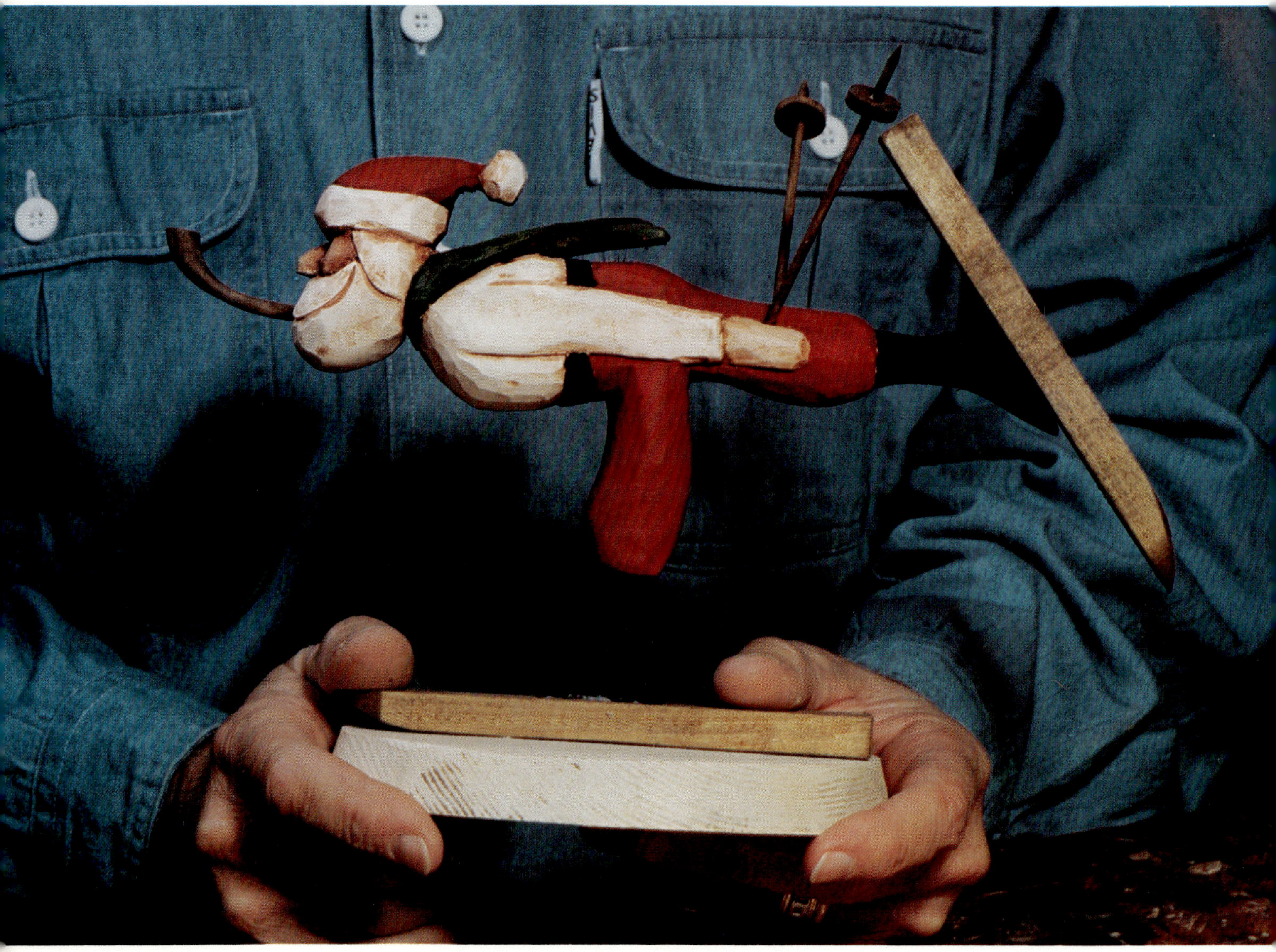

You will notice I've put a little pipe in the skier's mouth.

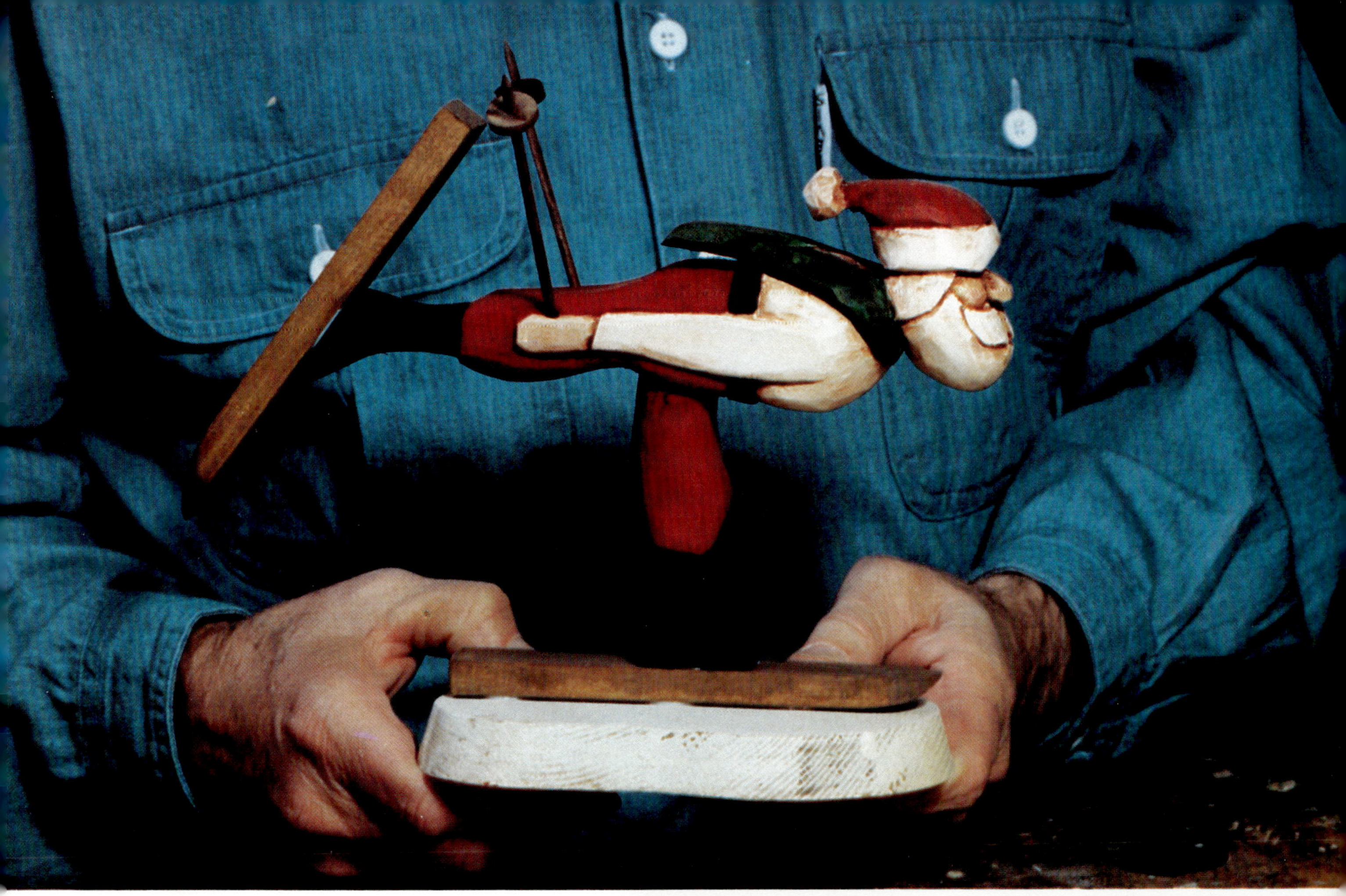

The only difference in the right and the left sides is the way the legs go into the body.

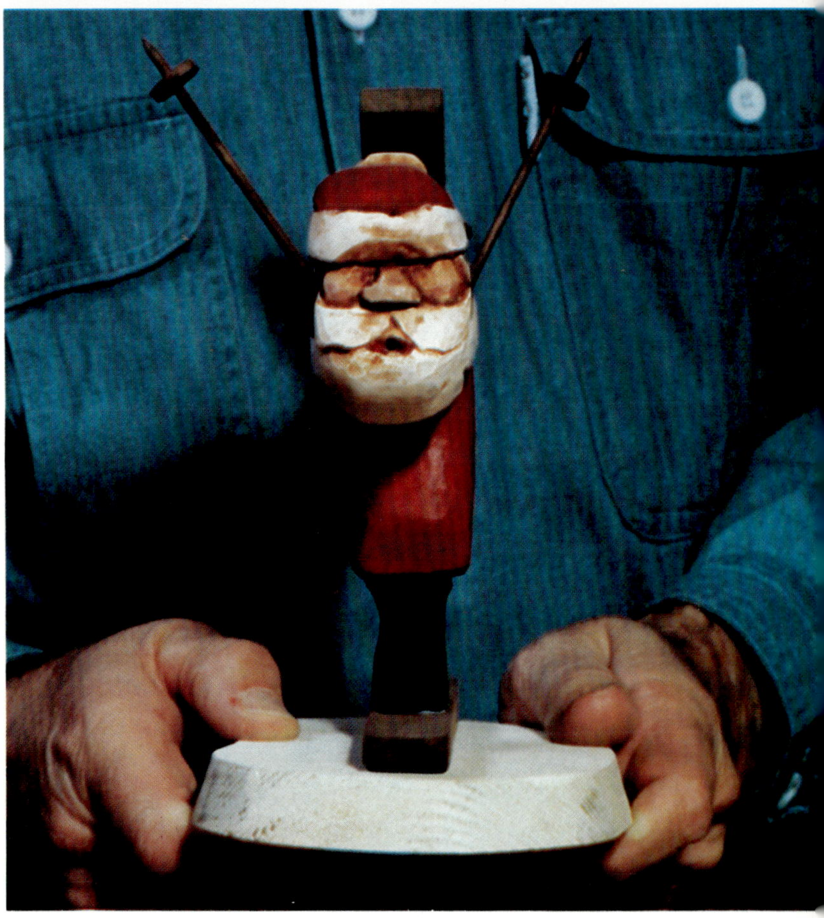

This Santa is to be viewed from either side and not head on.

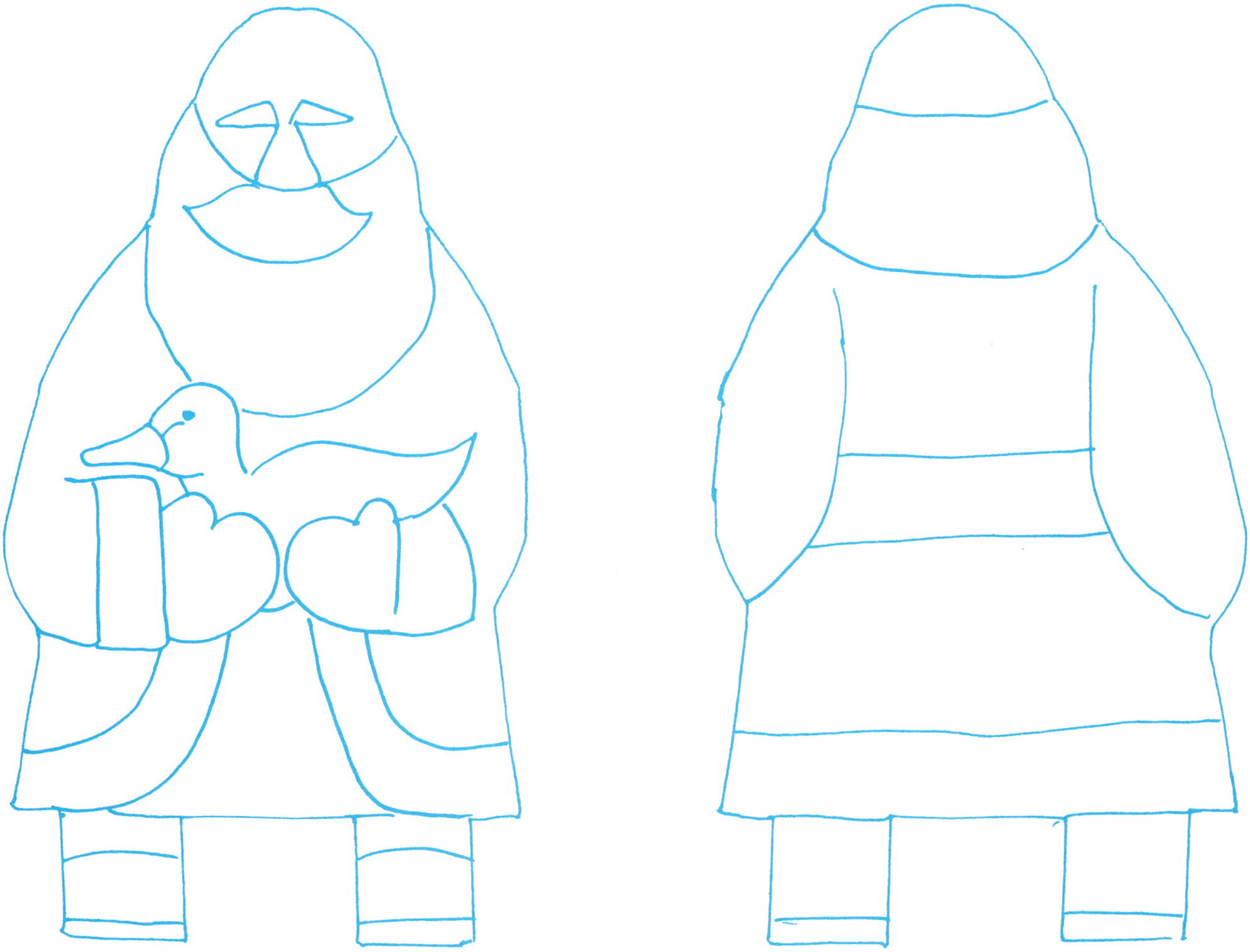

Santa with Decoy

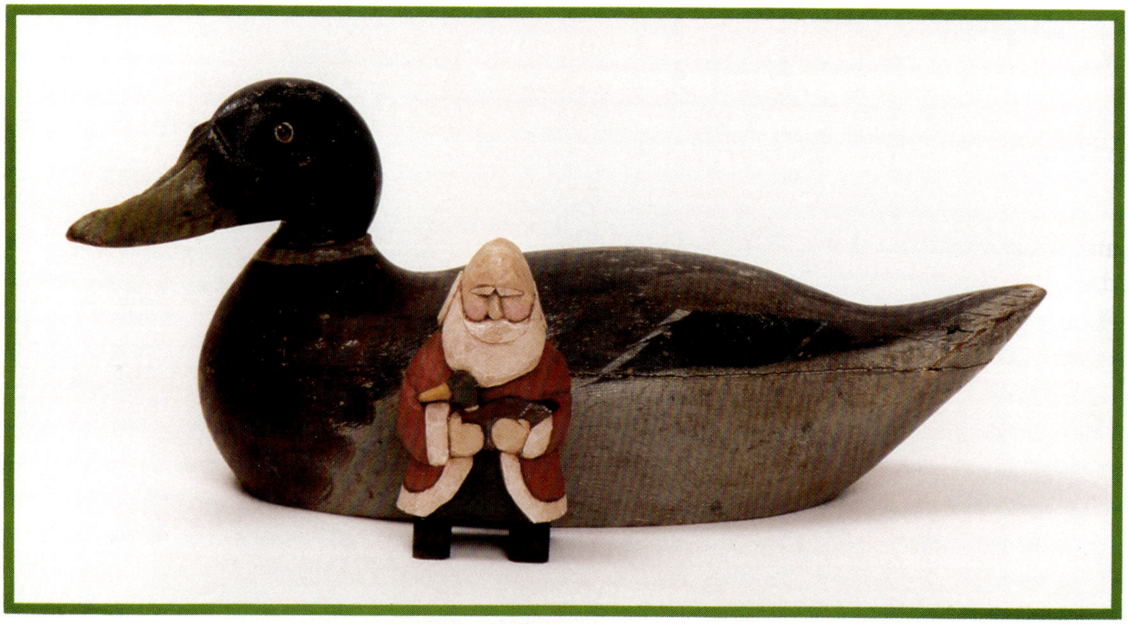

I am not a hunter, but I enjoy collecting old decoys. This Mason is one of my favorites. I've tried to duplicate him on the Santa, but by changing the color you can make him into any duck you wish.

Santa with Decoy

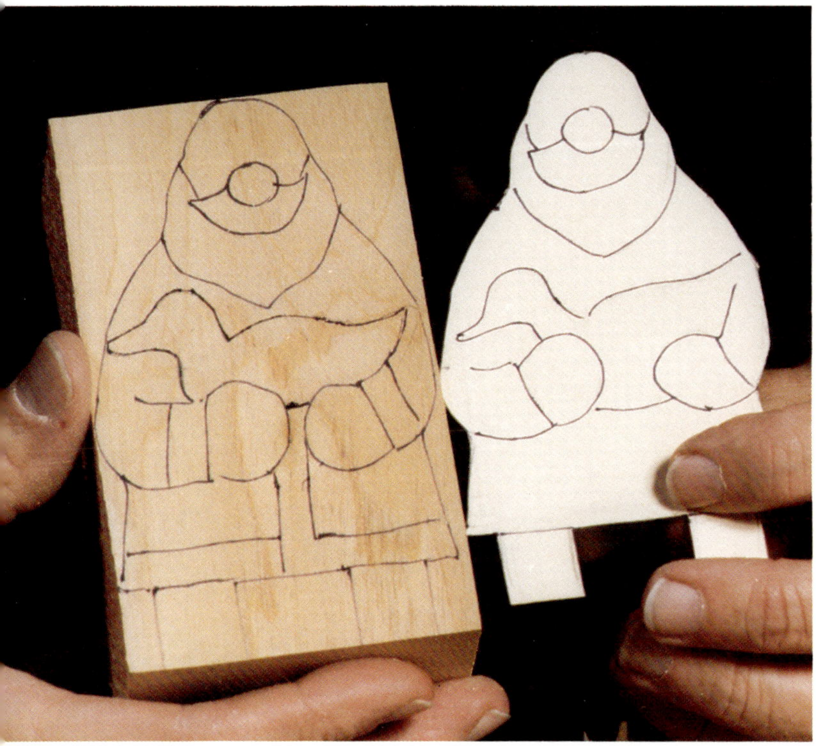

Trace the pattern on a 3" wide, 5" high, and 1¾" thick block.

Cut out and begin rounding and shaping body and bald head.

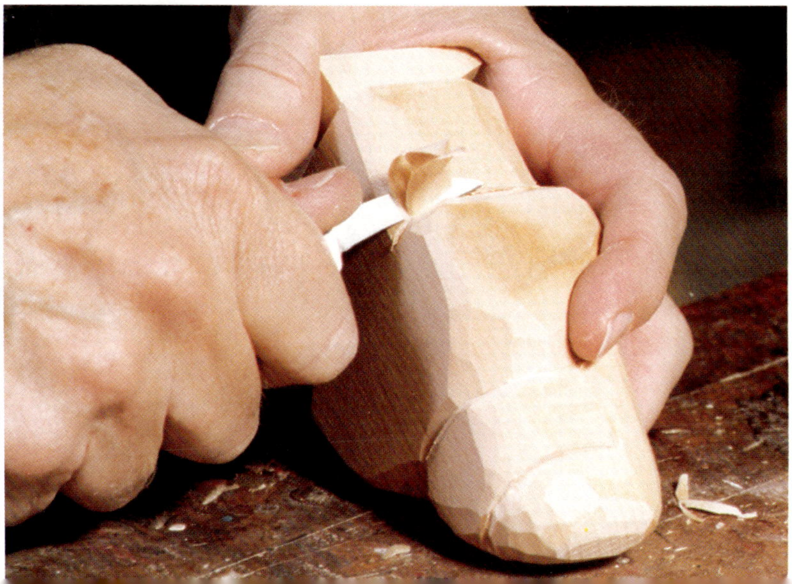

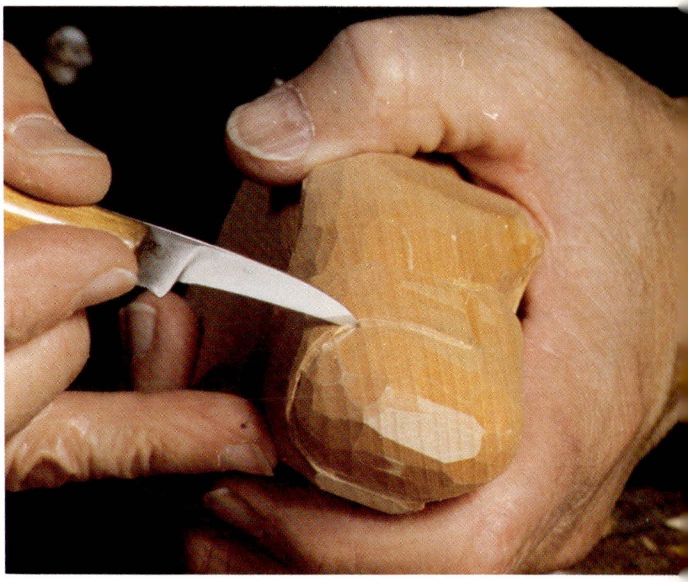

After rounding the head, incise the hair line.

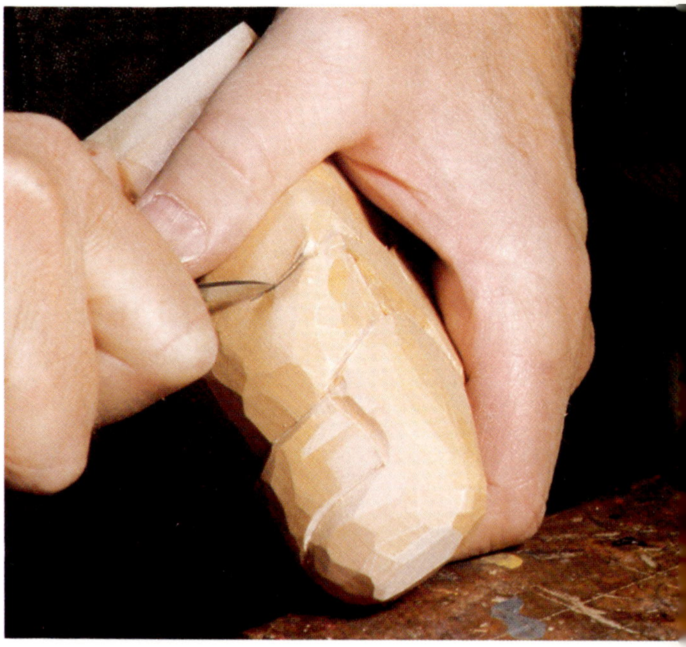

Define the hair around the bald head. Cut the left arm and shape.

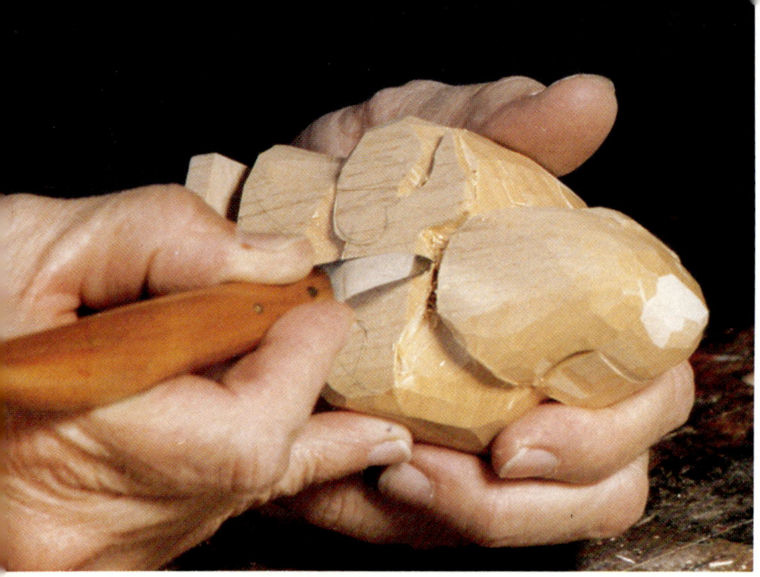

Cut out where the beard meets the body.

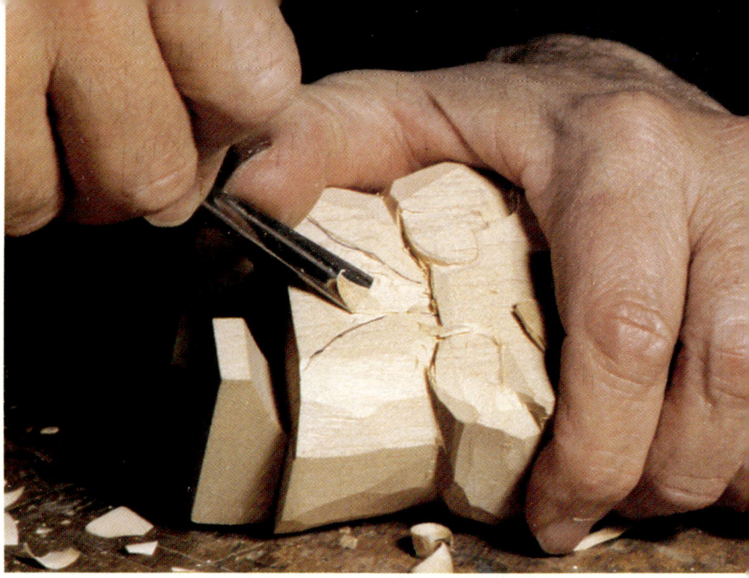

Trim away the area where the robe flares.

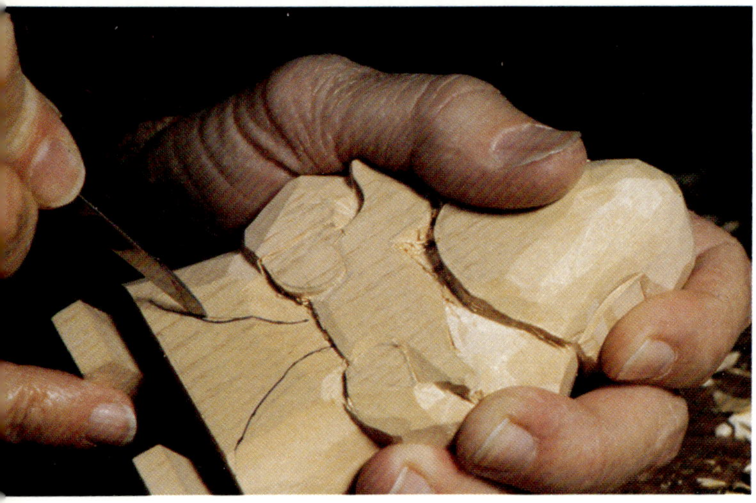

Rough in the arms and the duck. Incise where the robe flares.

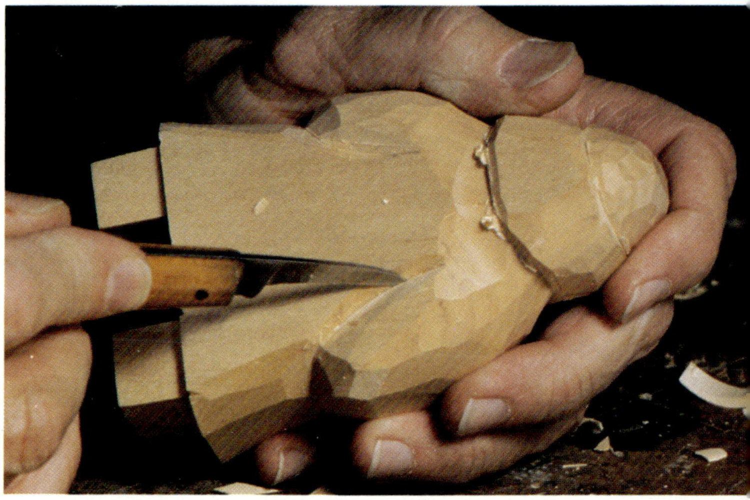

Do the back arm with a knife or gouge.

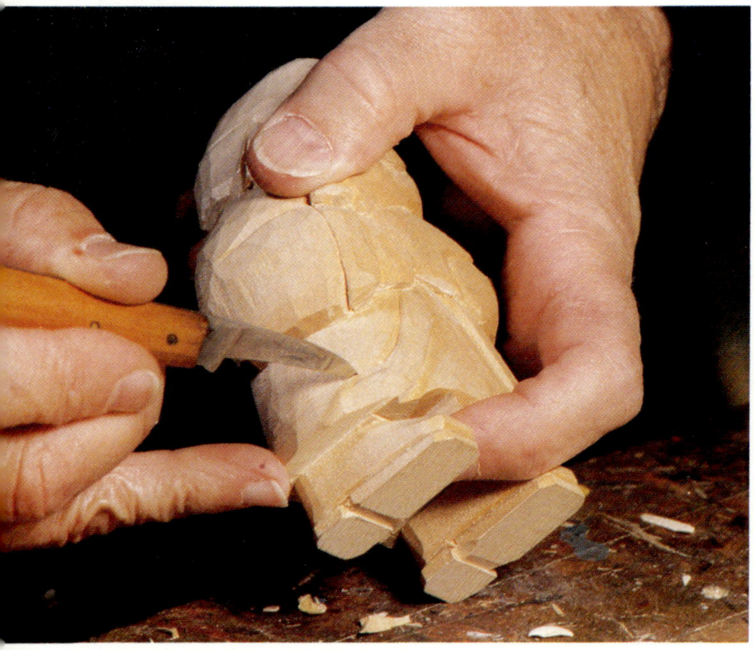

Incise the fur line on all sides of the Santa.

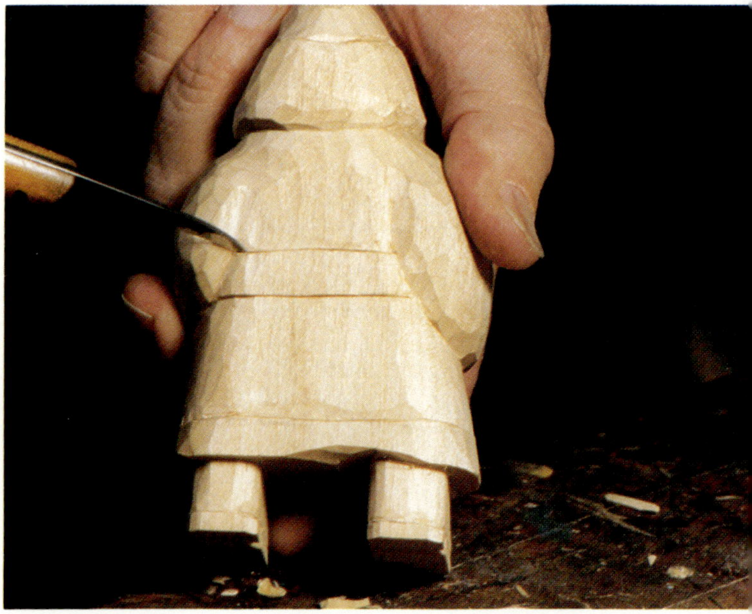

After shaping the back side of the arms, incise for a belt. Don't cut too deeply or you will have to paint the top and bottom sides of the belt.

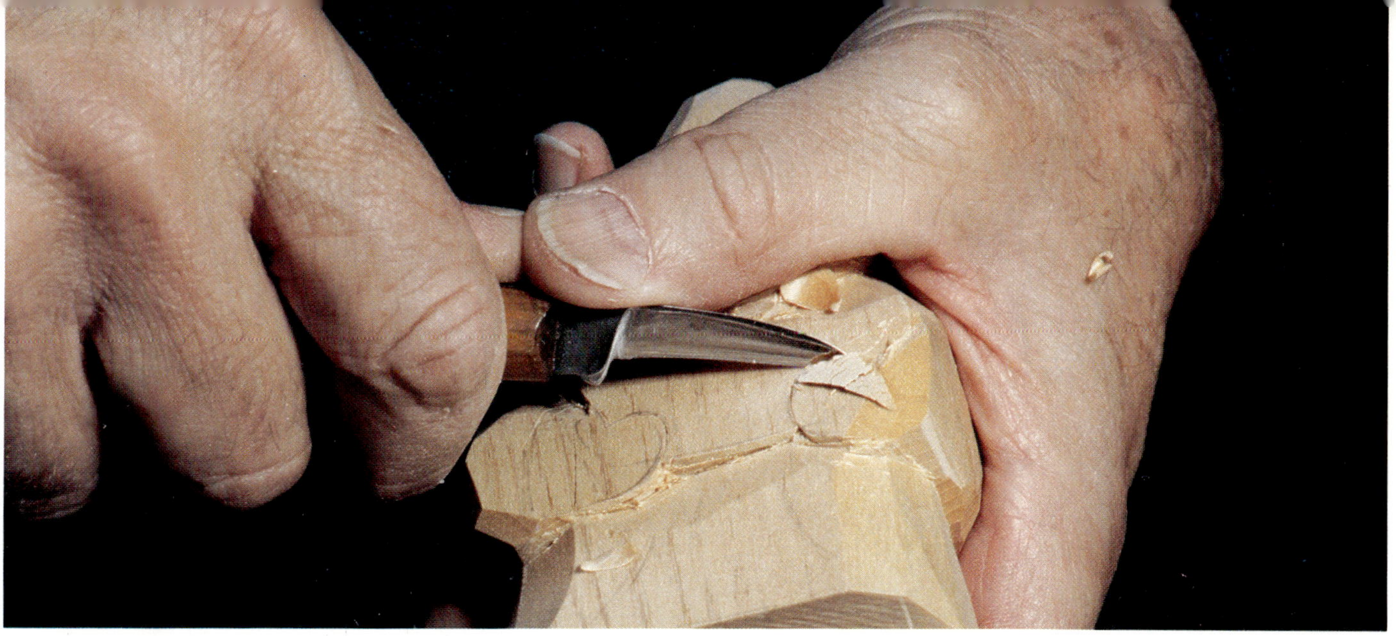

Continue to shape the duck.

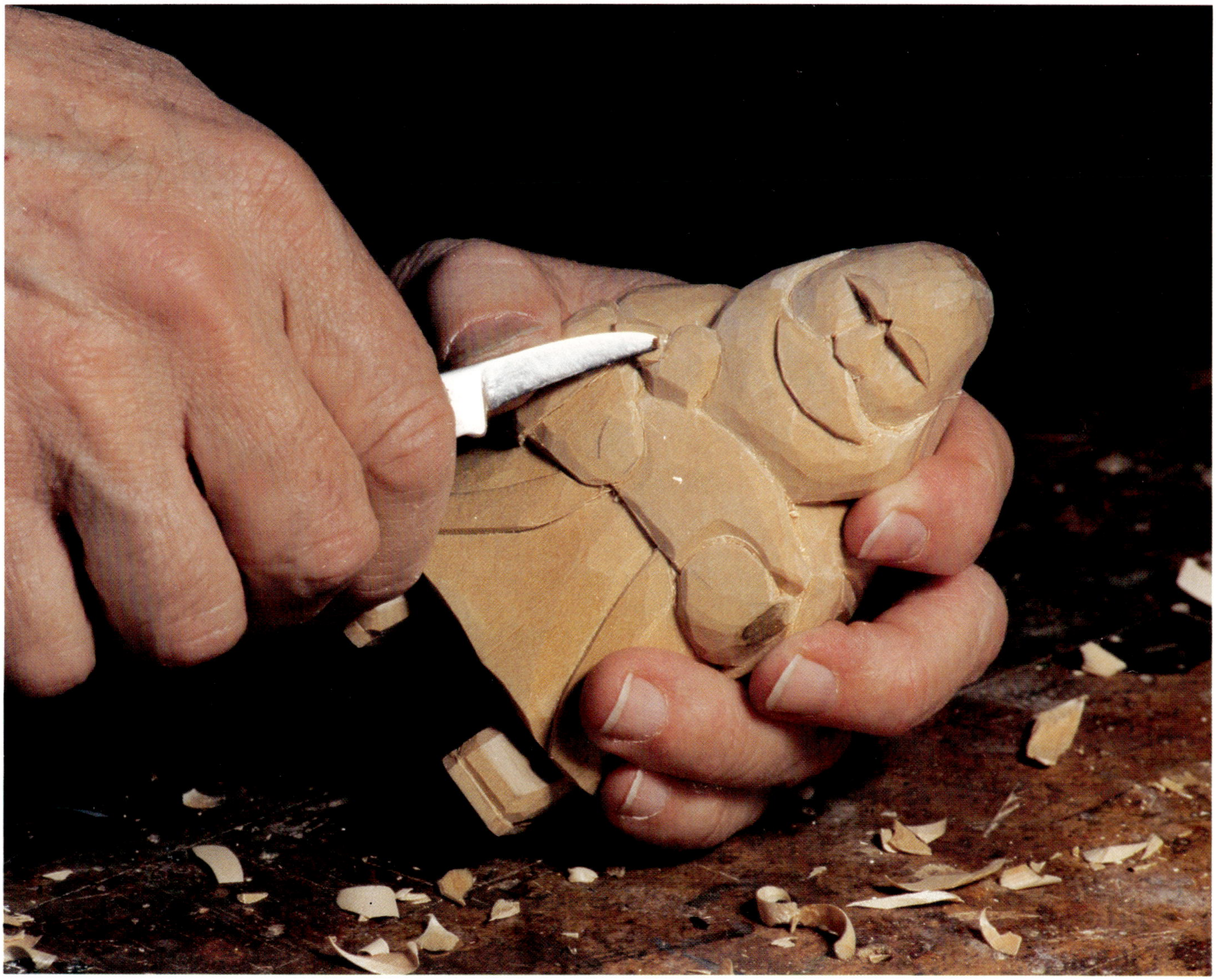

Put as much detail as you want into the decoy.

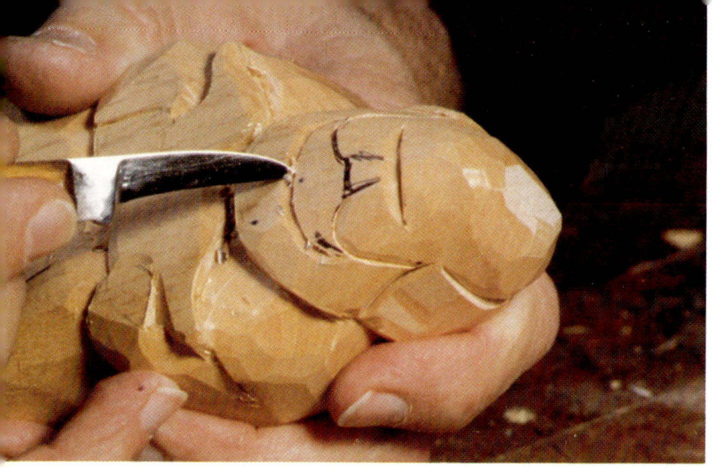

Cut this moustache in the shape of a smile. This should be a happy, fat face.

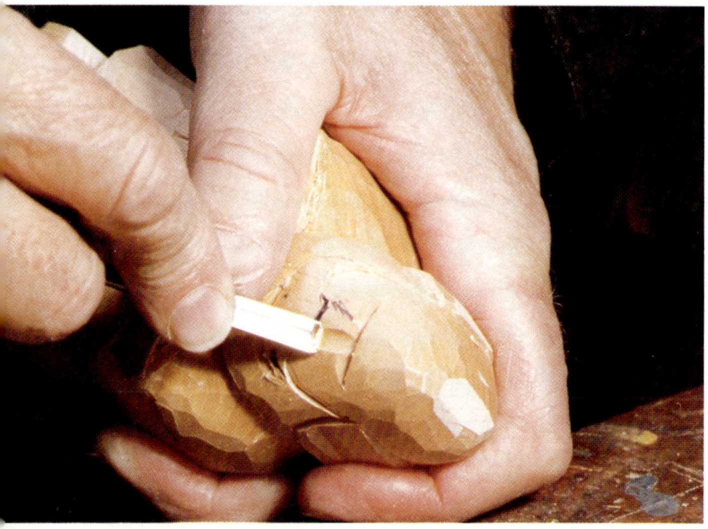

Trim around each side of the nose. I did not cut any eyes into this Santa. The shadow from the brow makes it look like his eyes have disappeared.

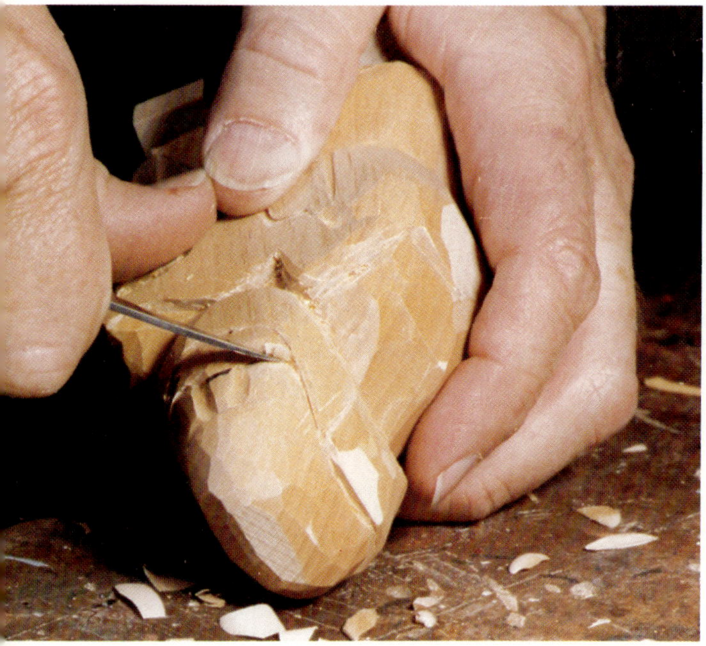

Round the cheek into the moustache.

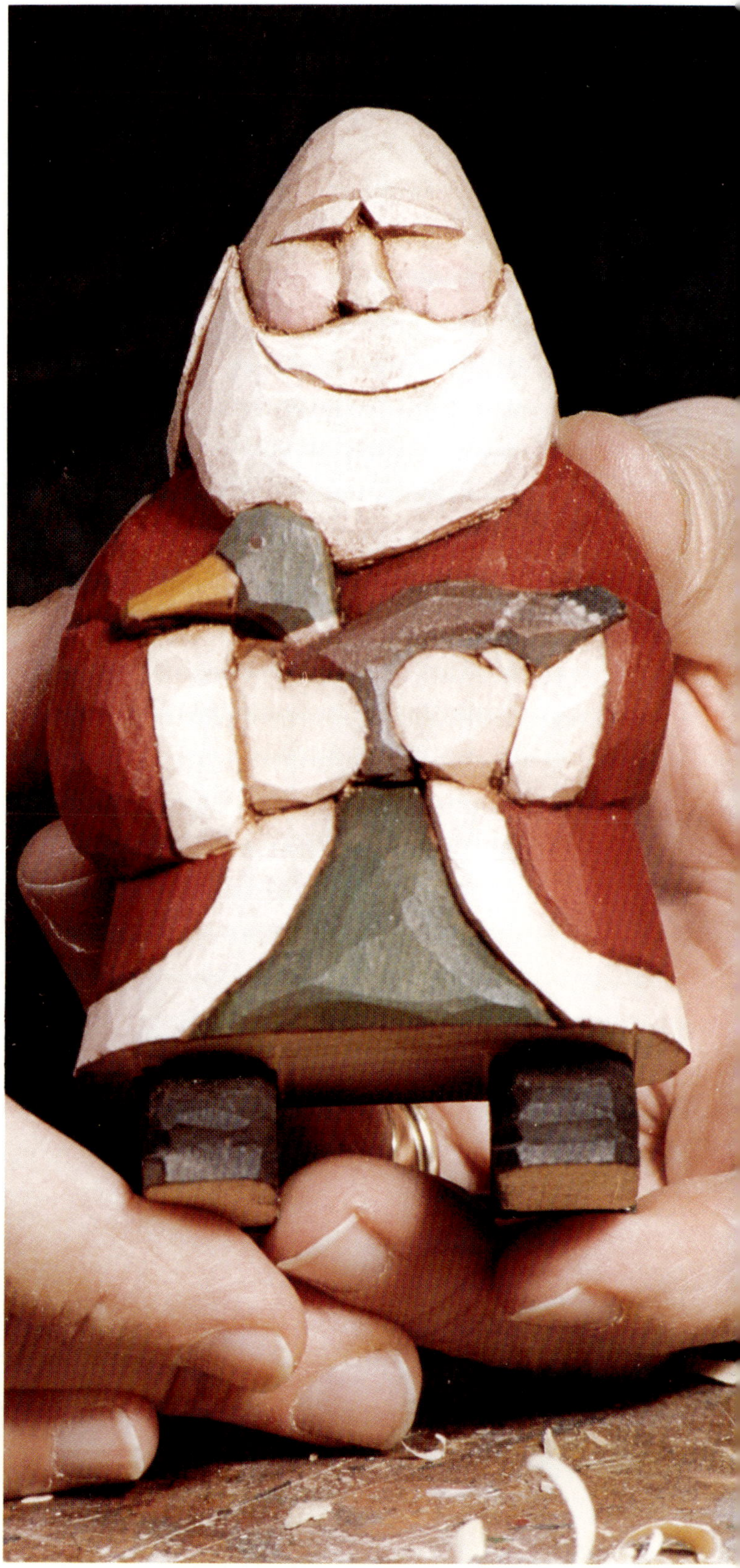

Views of the Decoy Santa.

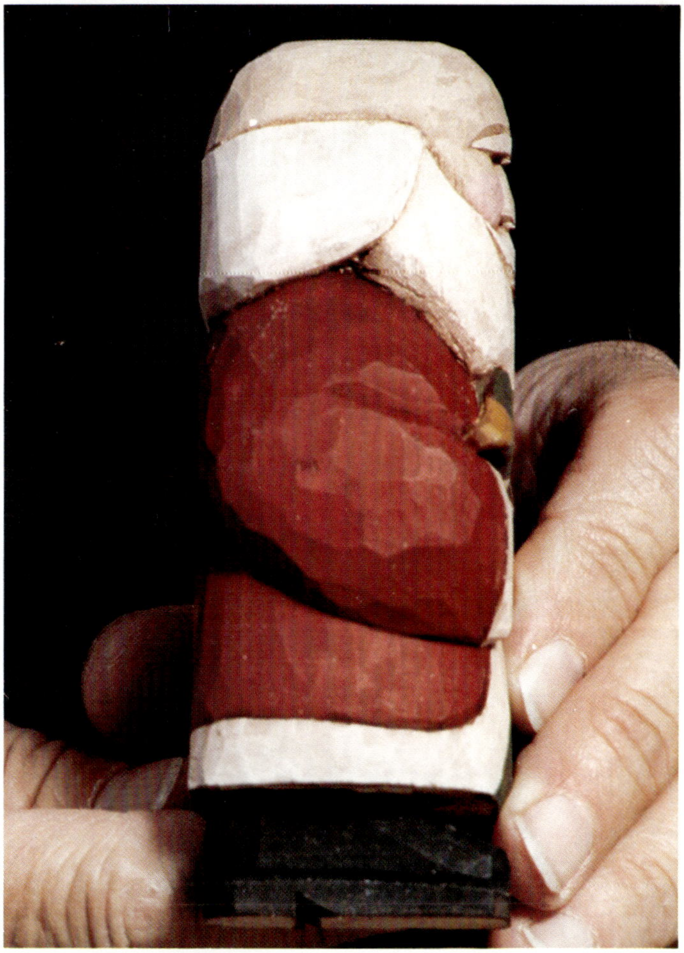
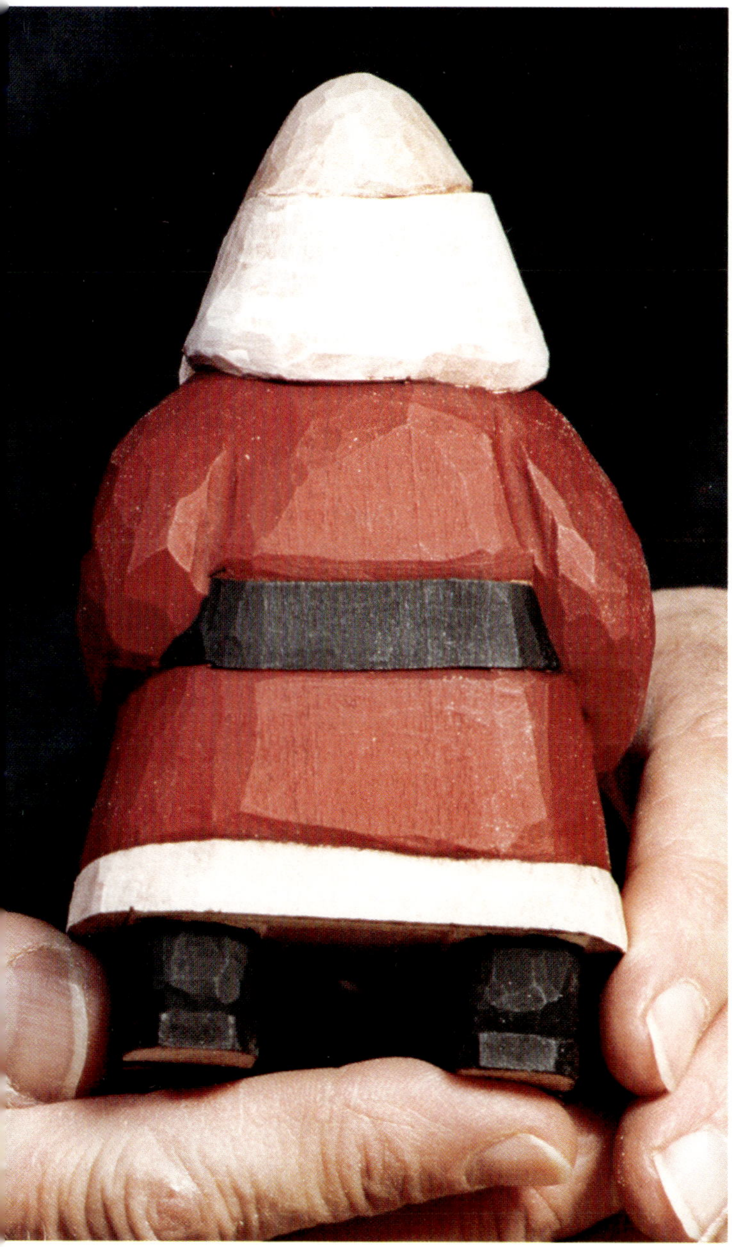
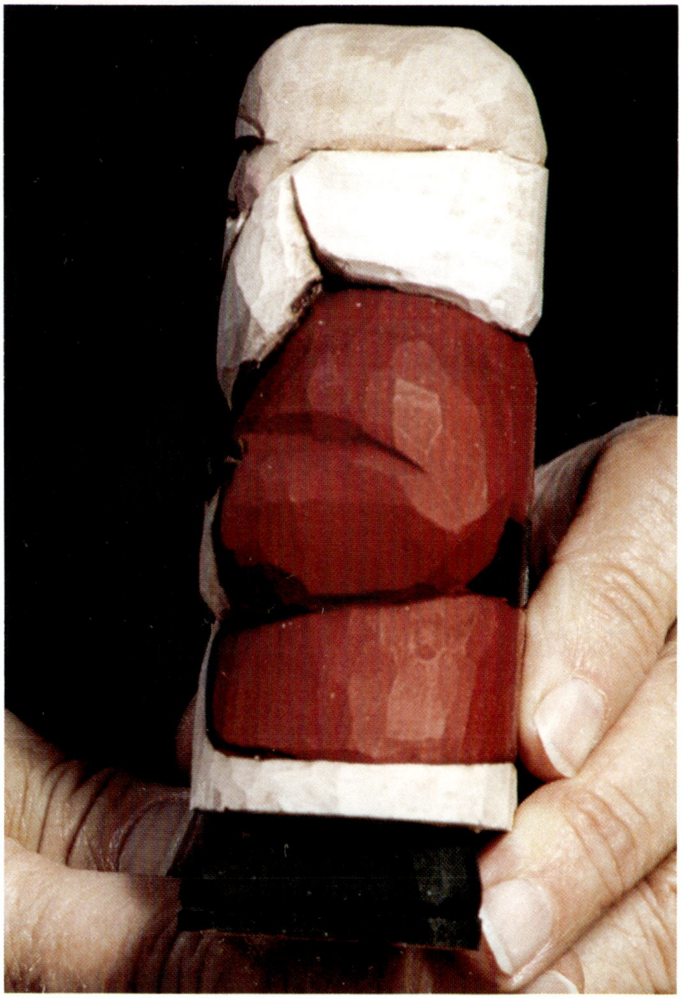

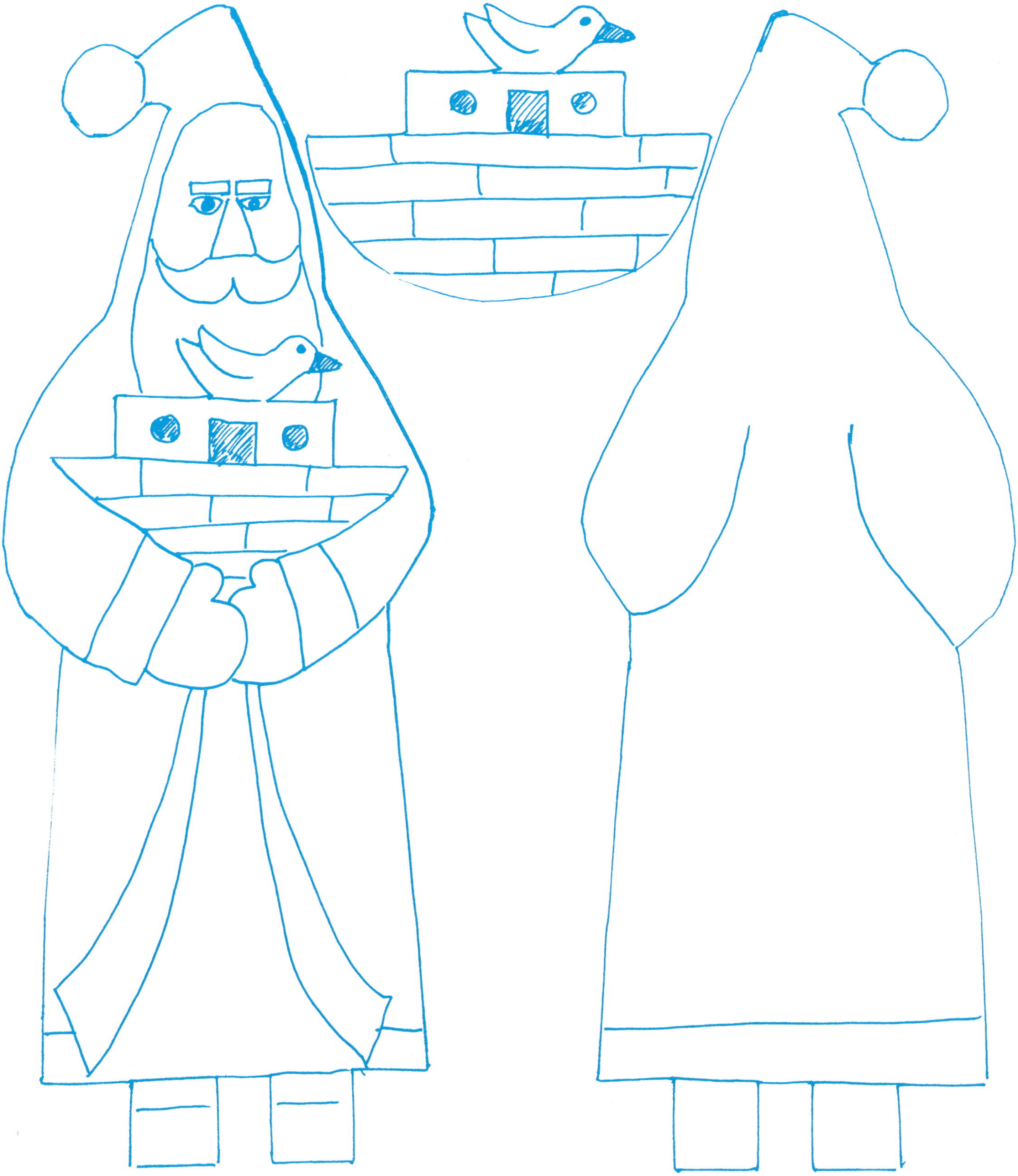

Santa with Ark

Burn the lines into the ark with a woodburner.

Santa With Ark

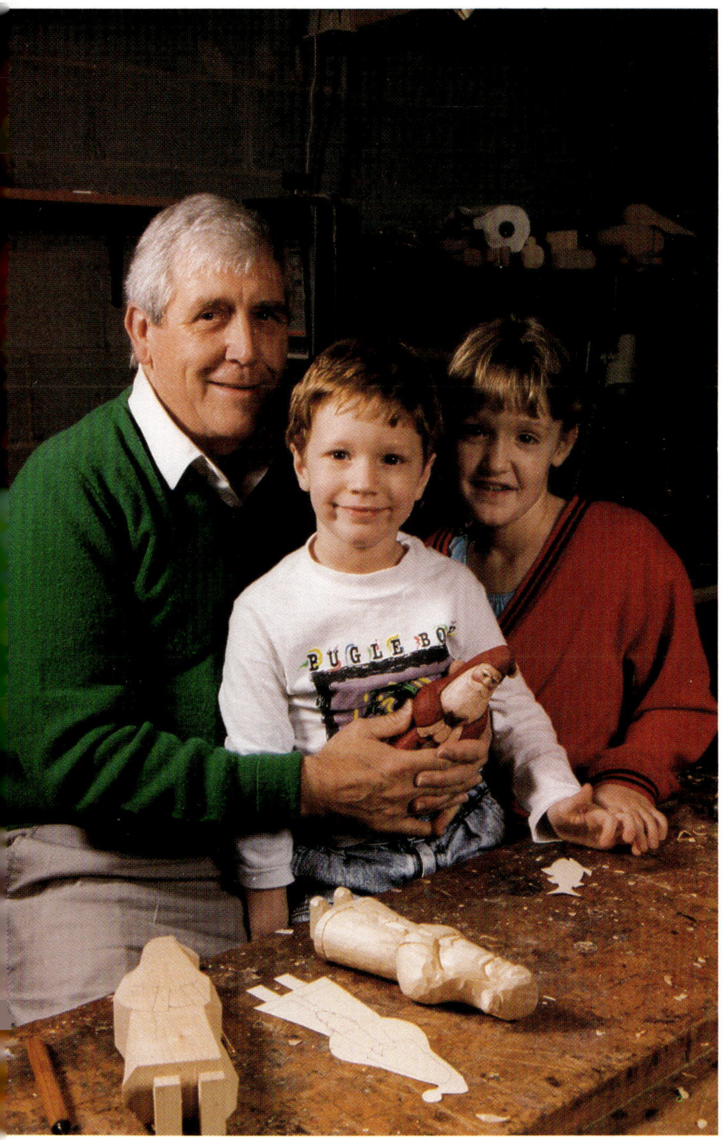

Taking a break with two of my favorite students, Tyler and Meredith. Ronnie, my other grandchild, was not available for the photo.

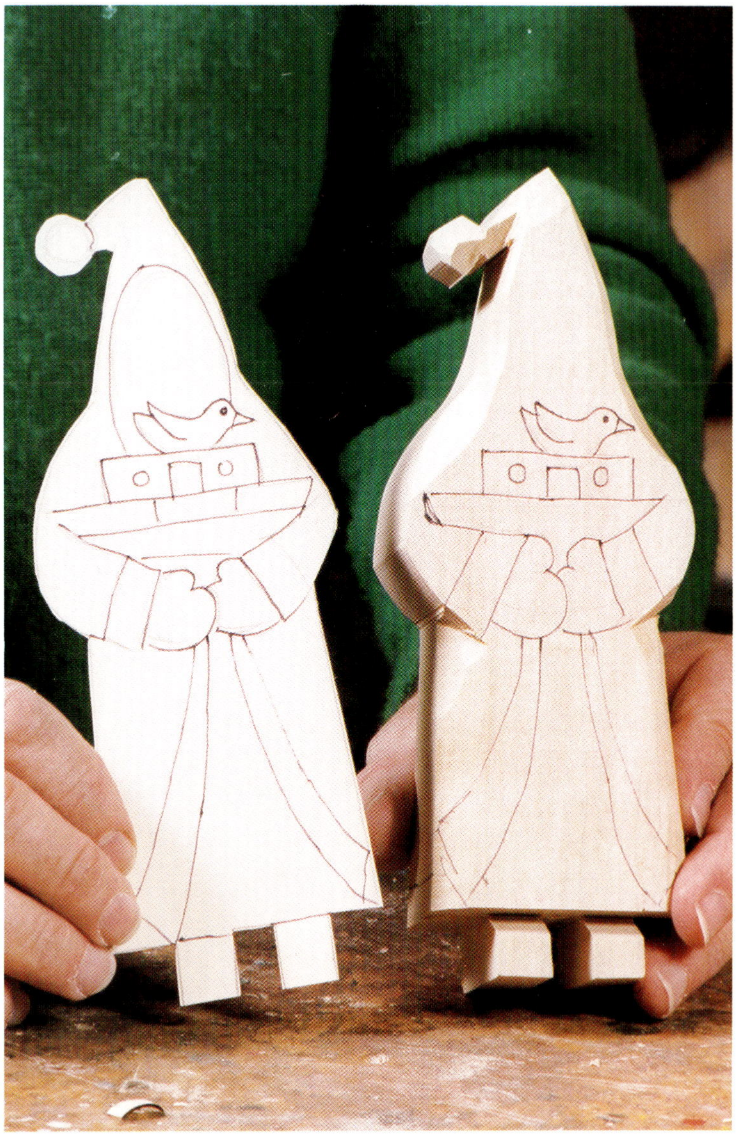

I've found the Noah's Ark Santa to be very popular.

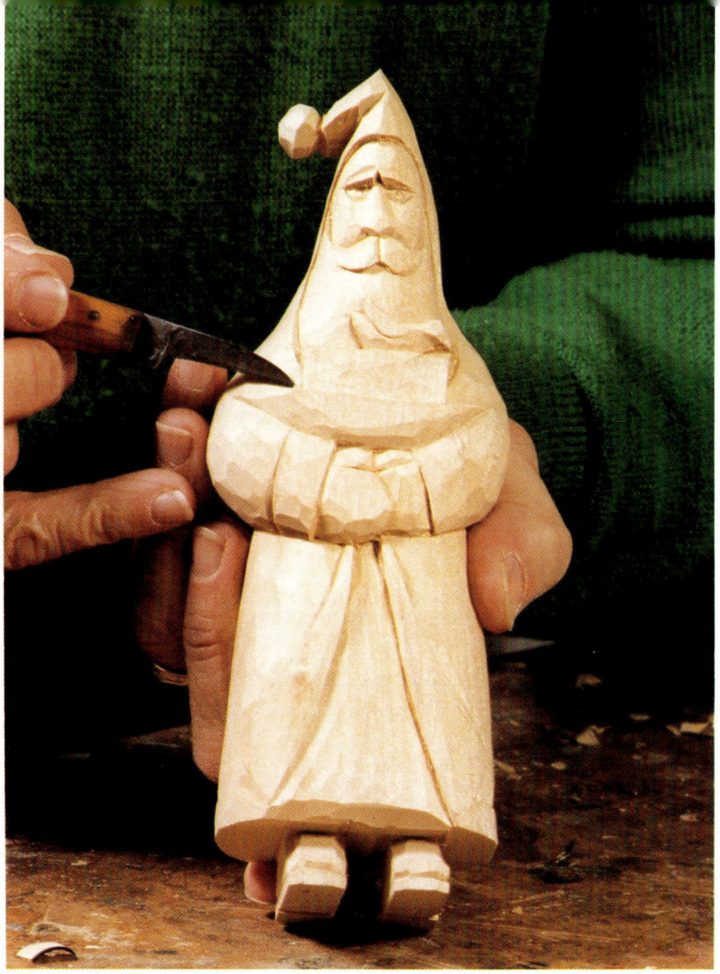

Other than the ark, bird and open robe, this Santa is similar to the other tall Santas shown earlier.
By now you've gotten so good you will want to be sure the back is as good as the front of your Santa.

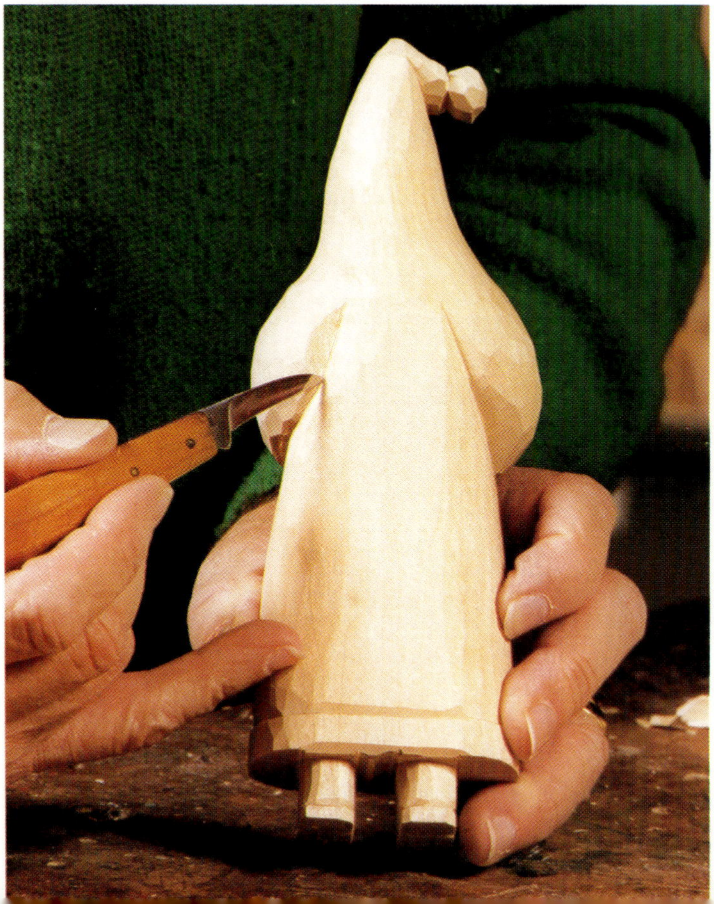

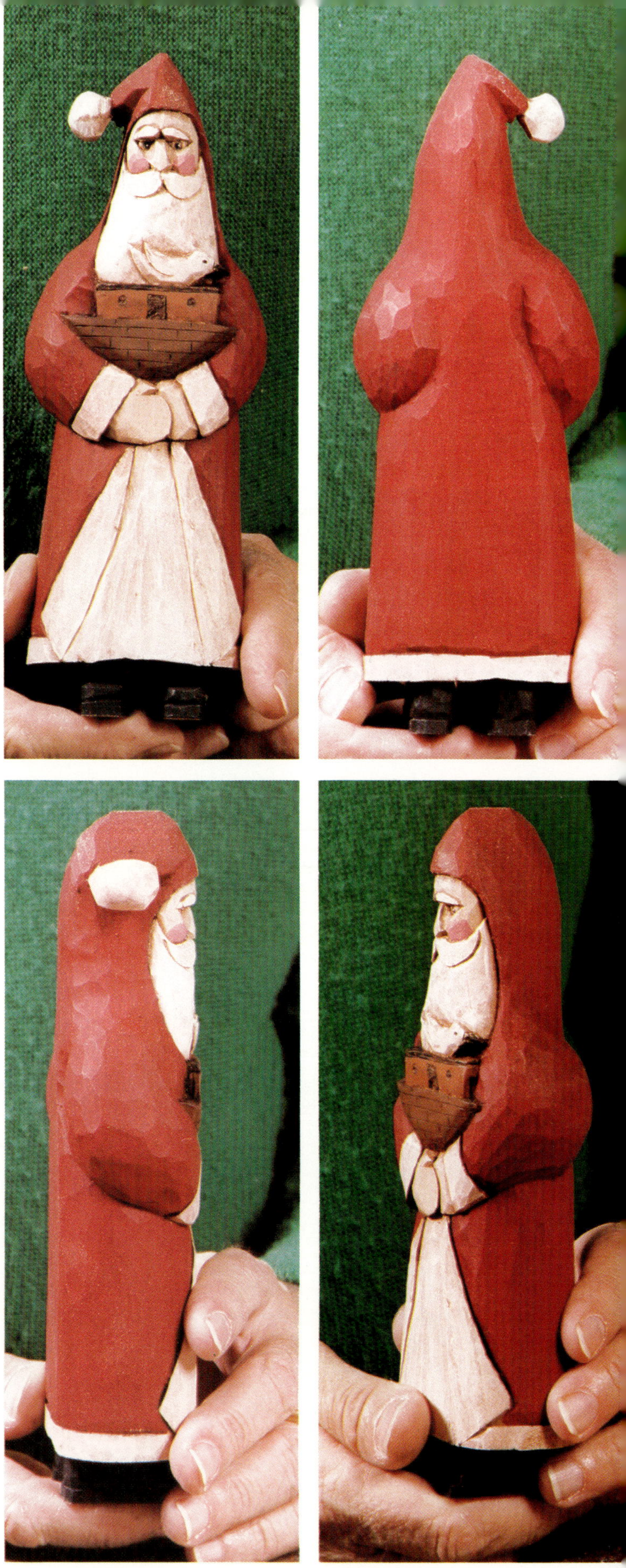

Views of the Ark Santa

Fisher Santas

The next two Santas are fishers. Obviously, fishing is very good at the North Pole. Chances are you've probably never fished there and will not recognize the species of fish the Santas are holding. I don't fish nor do I eat them. My doctor has told me that eating fish is a good way to get my cholesterol down. If you know a type of fish that doesn't taste fishy, please let me know.

The old fishing creel is one of our collectibles that my wife purchased from one of my Santa carving friends, Lee Perkins, at an antique show in Nashville, Tennessee.

Being as these are the last two patterns and you've been practicing your techniques, I'm not going into a lot of detail. If you are a new carver, I would try some of the other patterns before attempting the Santa with the string of fish.

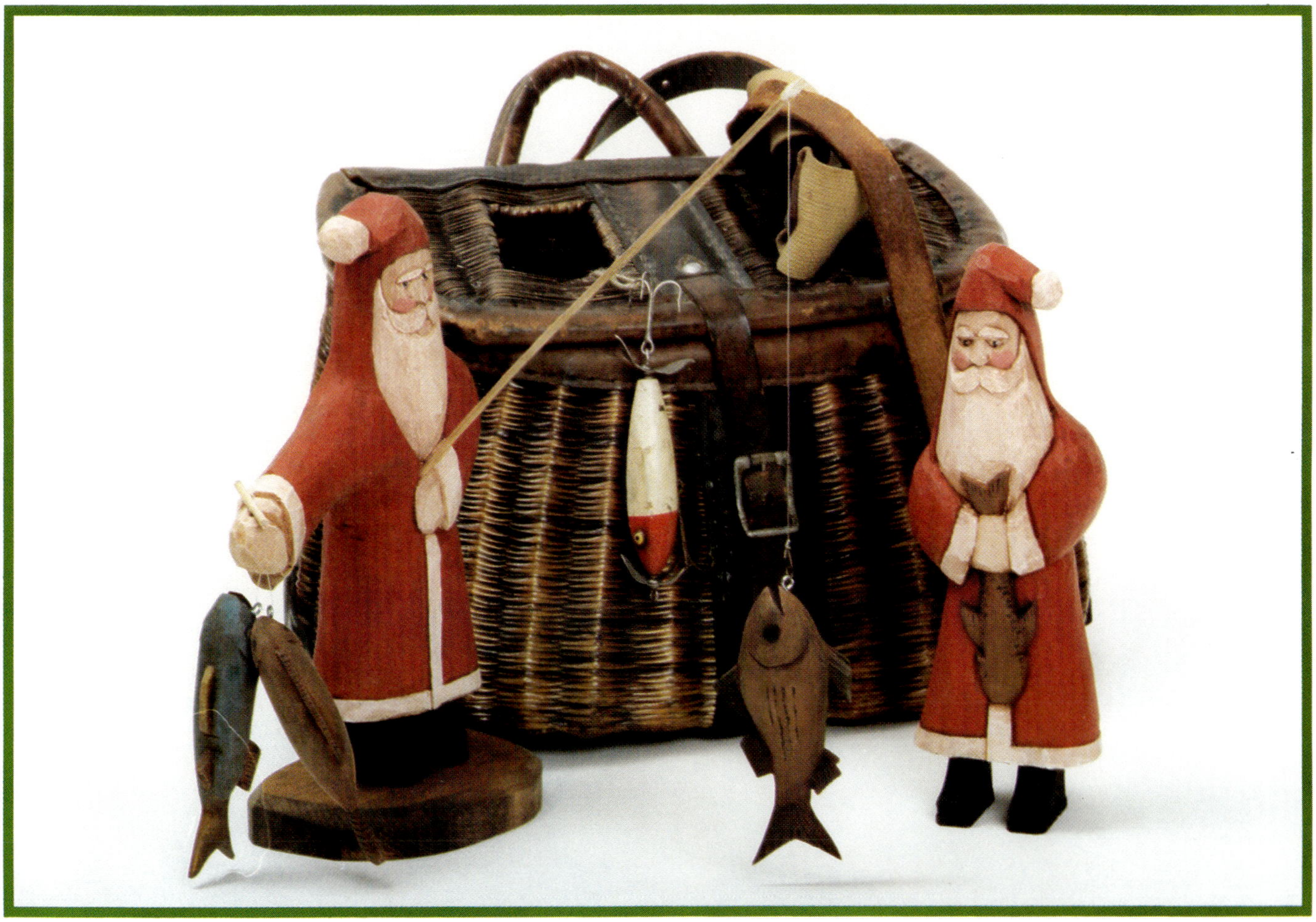

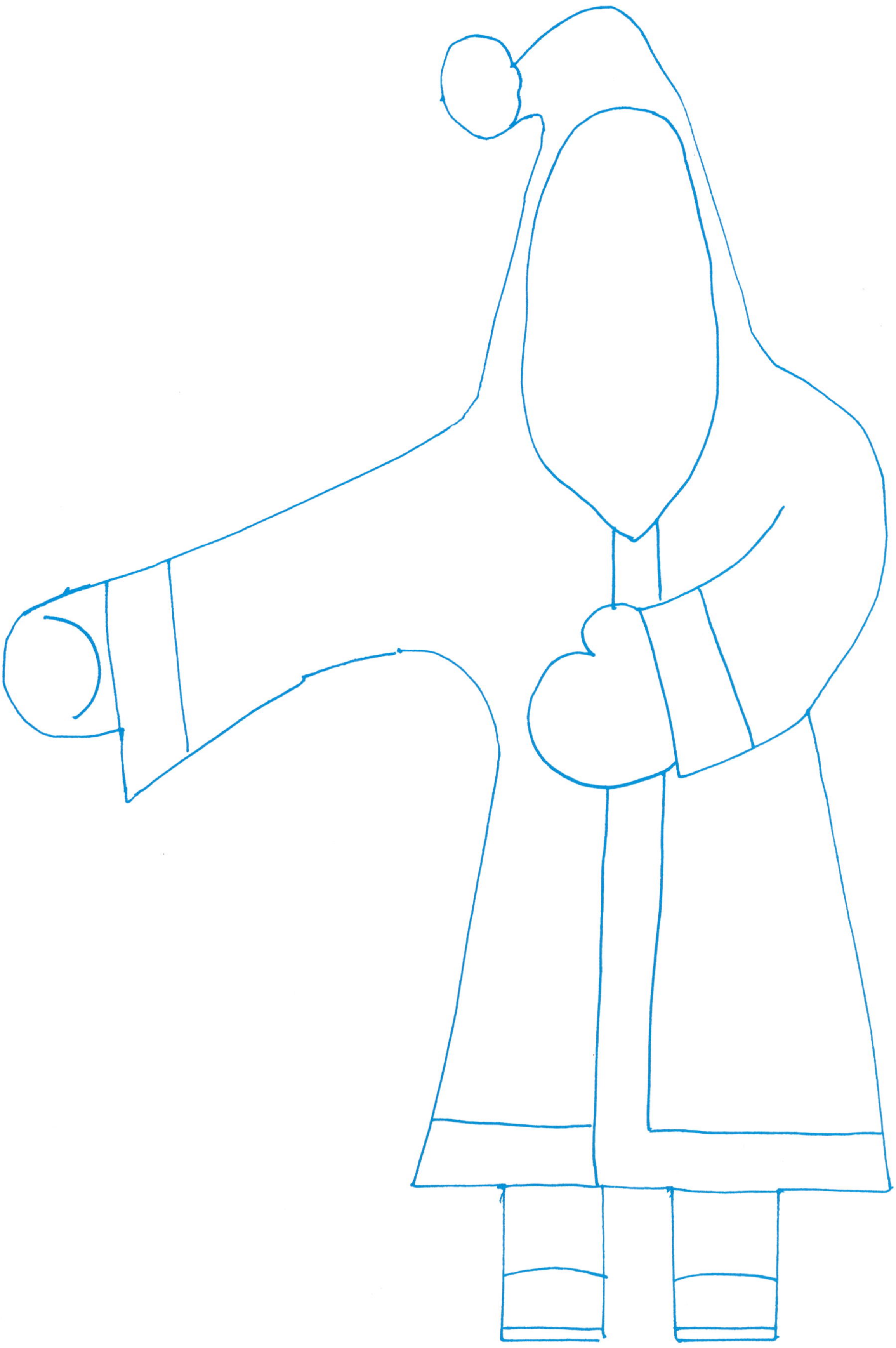

Santa with Catch

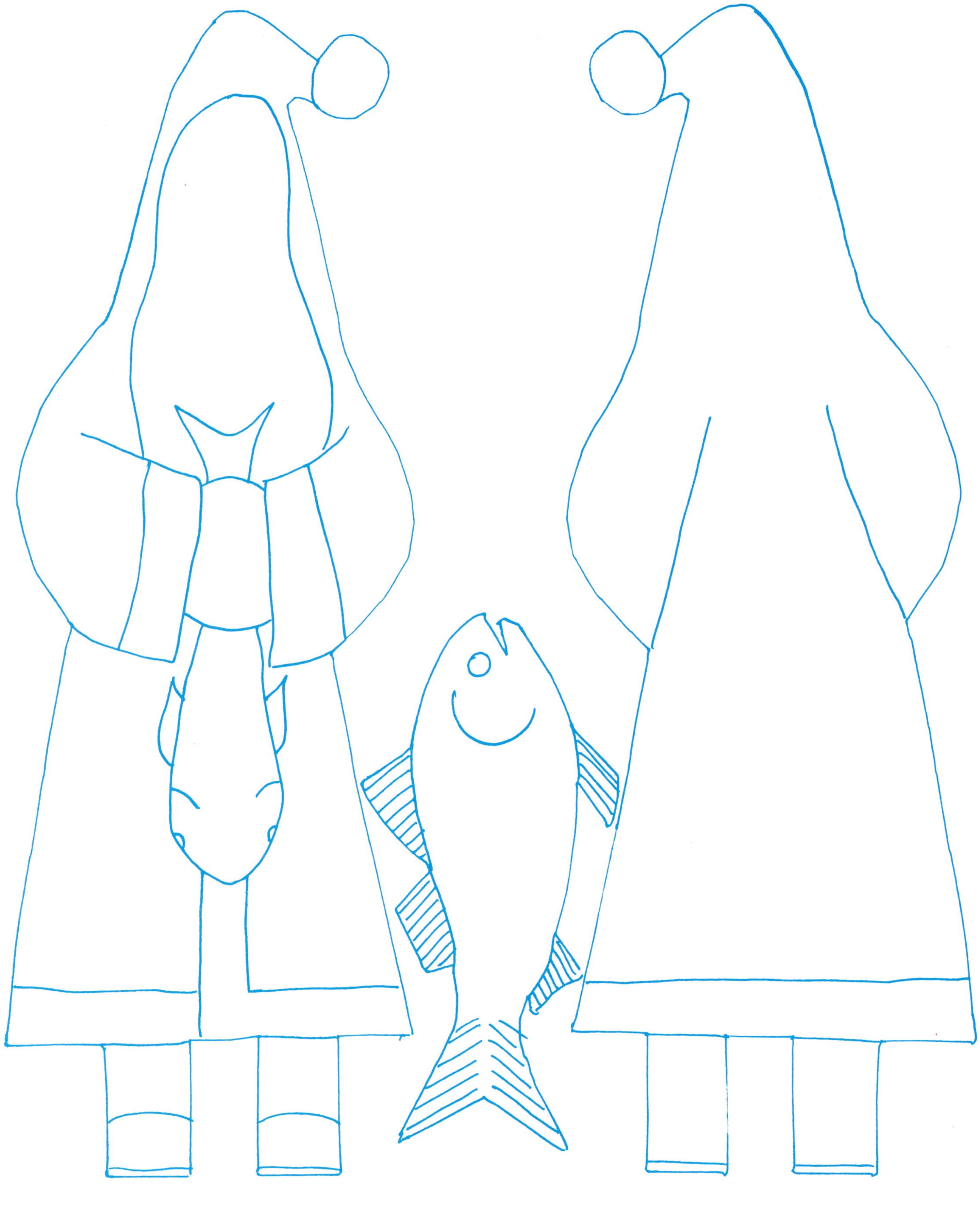

Fisherman Santa

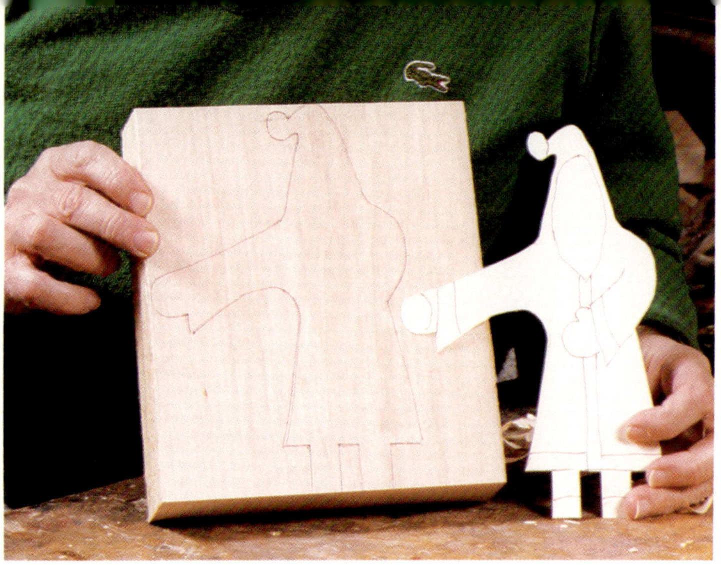

You will need a block 6¼" wide, 9" high, and 1¾" thick. Trace the pattern and cut.

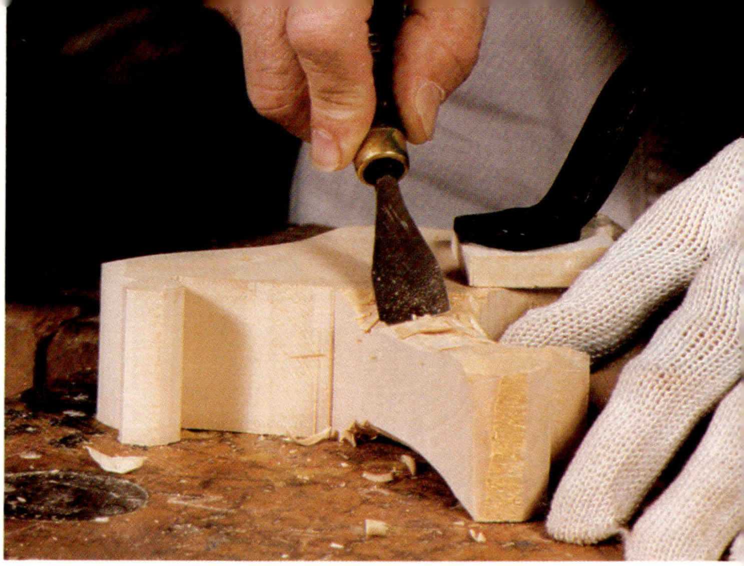

As you can see, I've clamped the piece and am using the glove for safety. The fish tail gouge will remove a great deal of the waste.

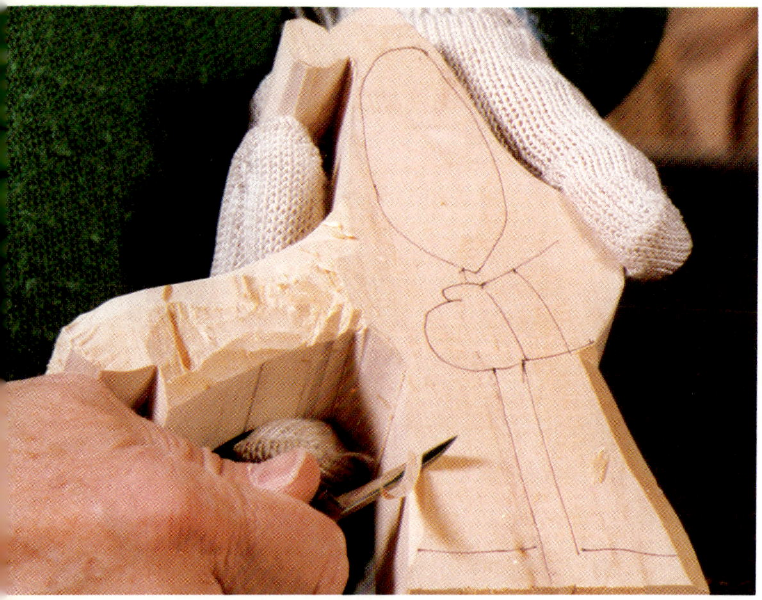

The main difference between this and the previous patterns is the arm and hand holding the fish and pole. Round and shape as before.

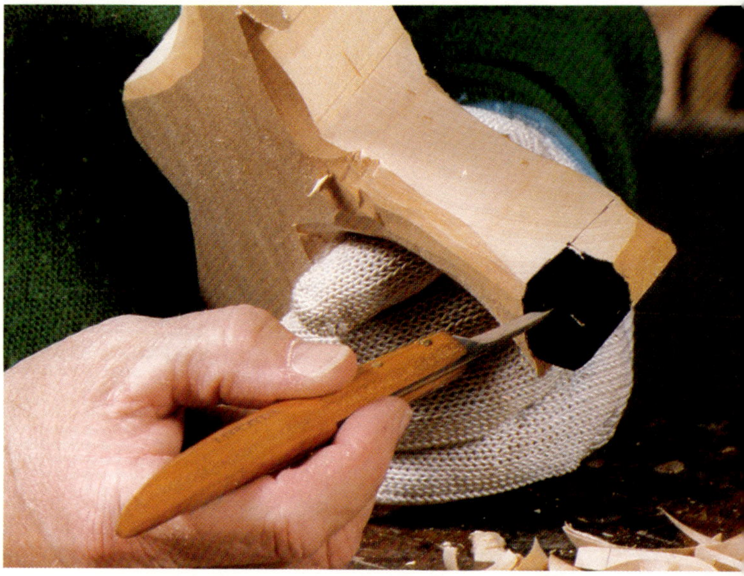

I've again blackened the area to remove.

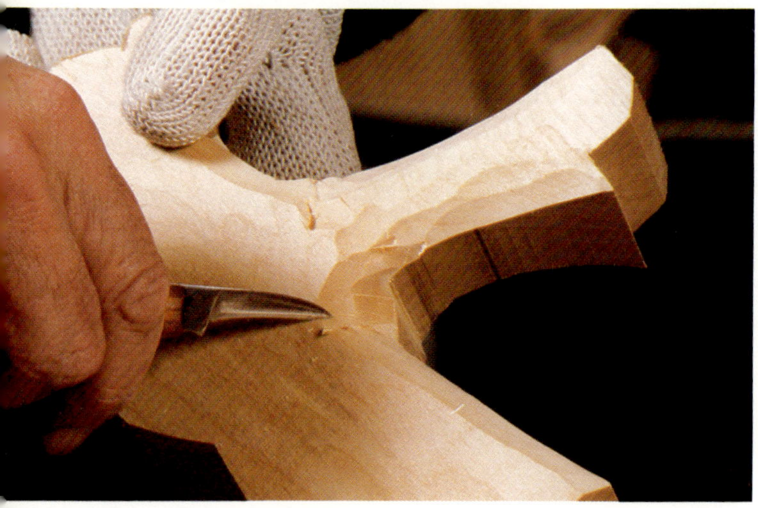

Shape the back side of the arm and robe.

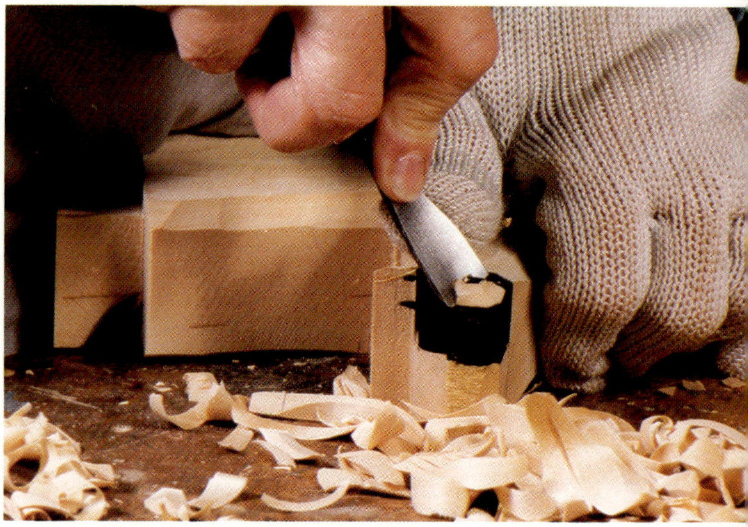

The smaller gouge is good here or use your knife.

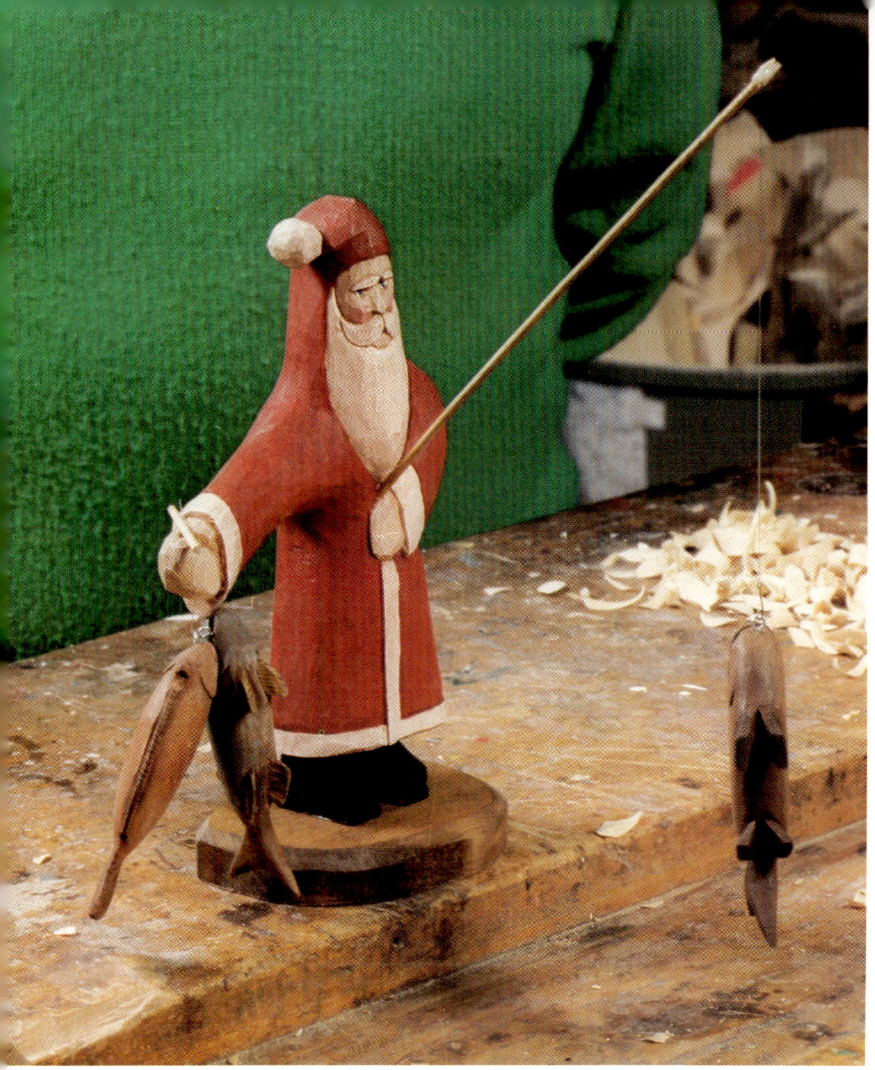

You will need to mount the fishing Santa on a base. I've drilled a hole through the right hand and another hole the size of the fishing pole over his left hand. Refer to the large color photo for better detail.

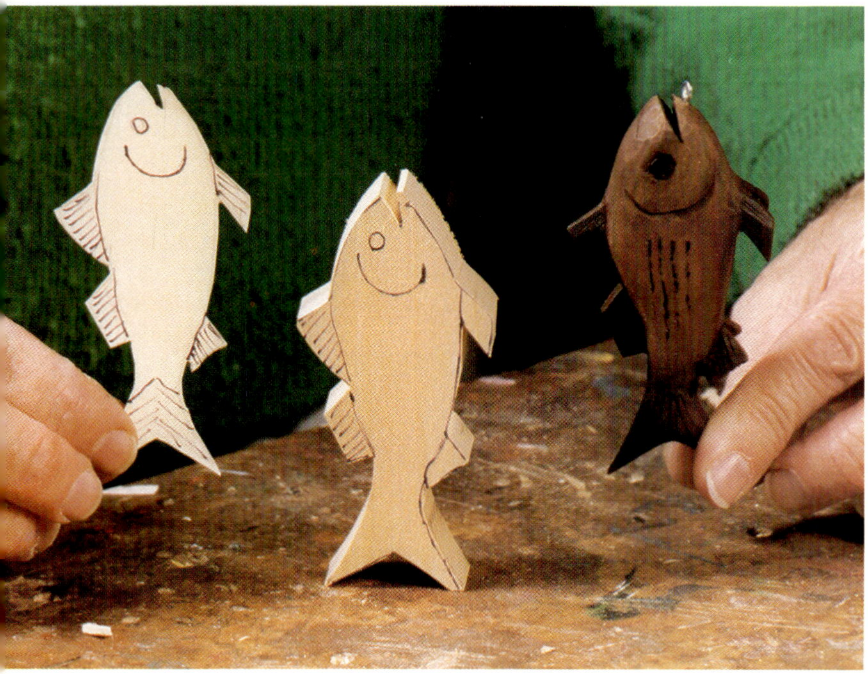

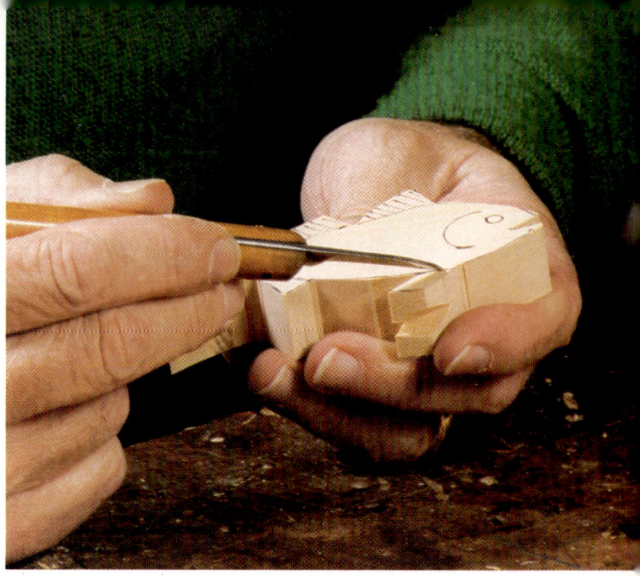

Make a notch between the fins on the bottom of the fish and shape.

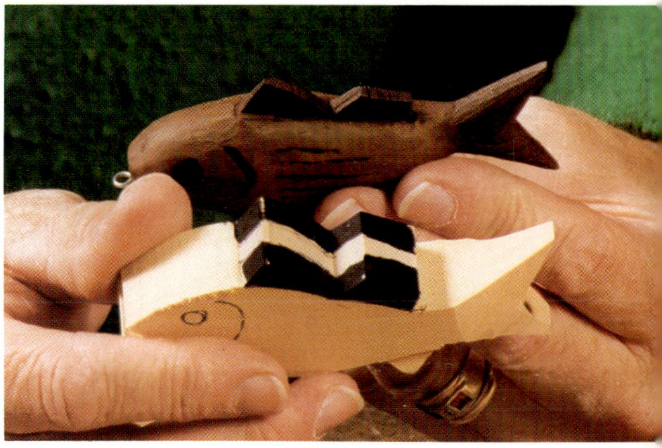

I've blackened the area on the top of the fish to be removed.

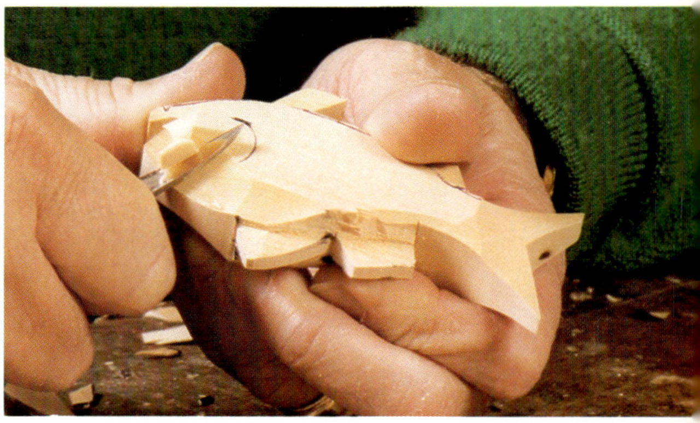

Shape and carefully remove the waste. I should wear the glove but the fish is so small it's hard to handle.

For the fish you will need a piece of basswood 4¼" long, 2" wide, and ¾" thick.

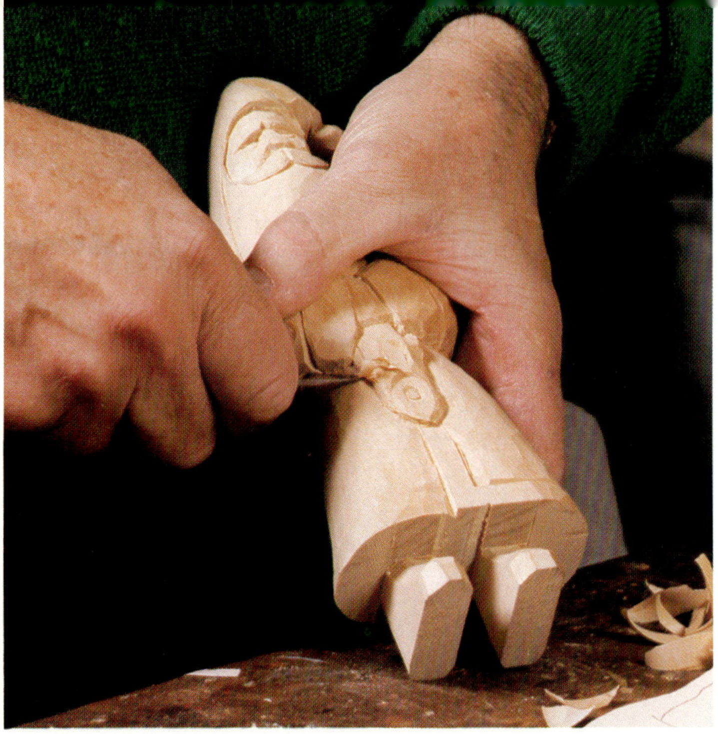

After shaping as you learned on previous patterns, incise and shape the generic fish.

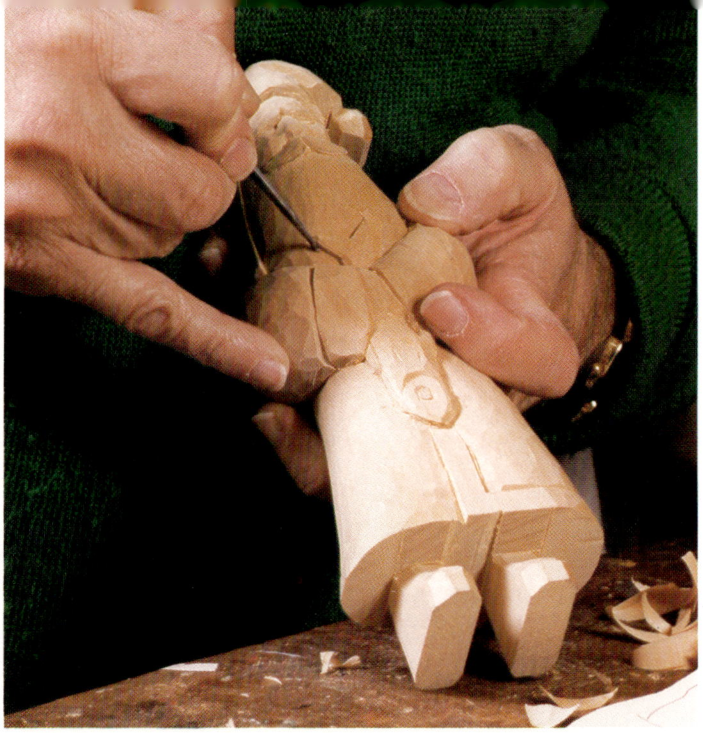

Blend the beard into the fish tail.

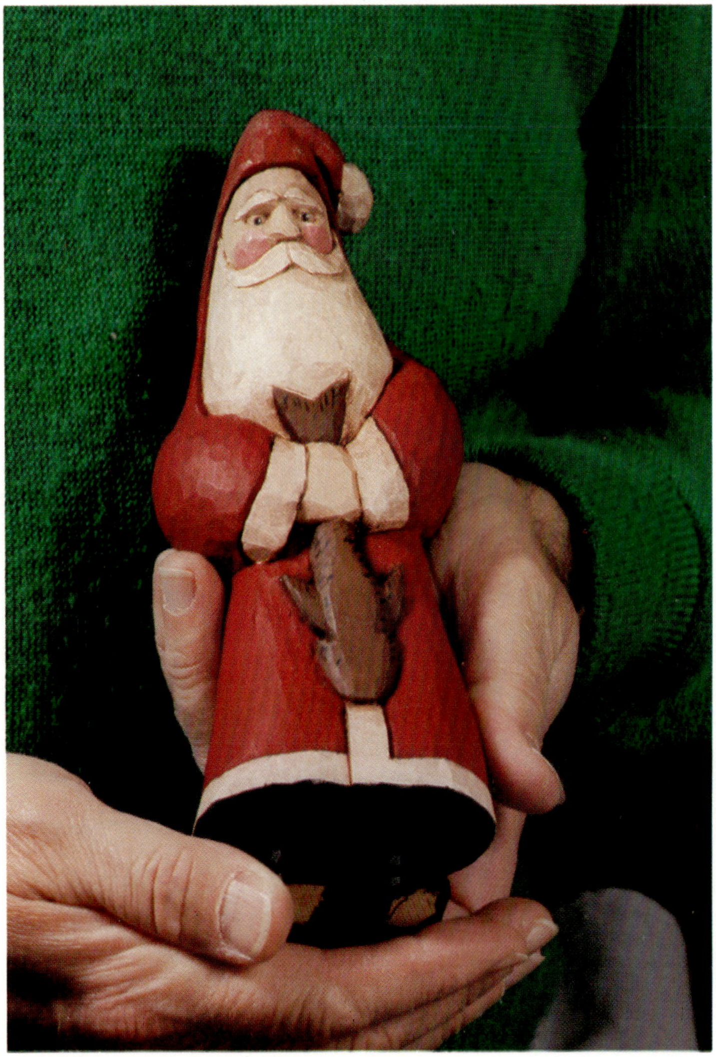

Completed Santa with fish.

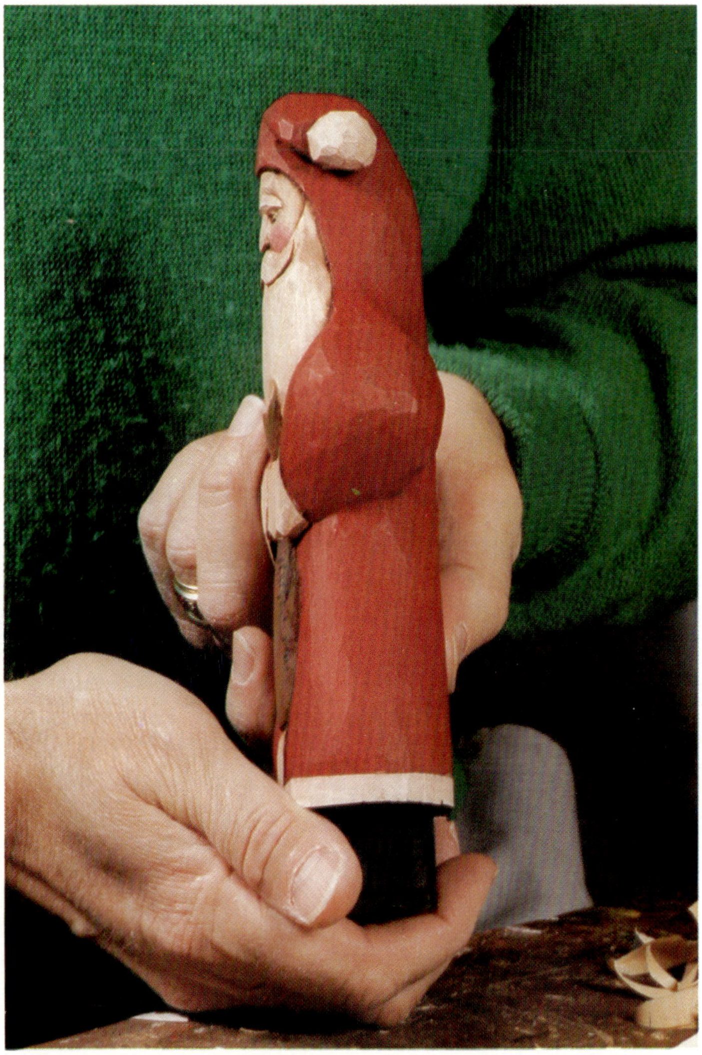

Left side showing placement of the ball on the cap.

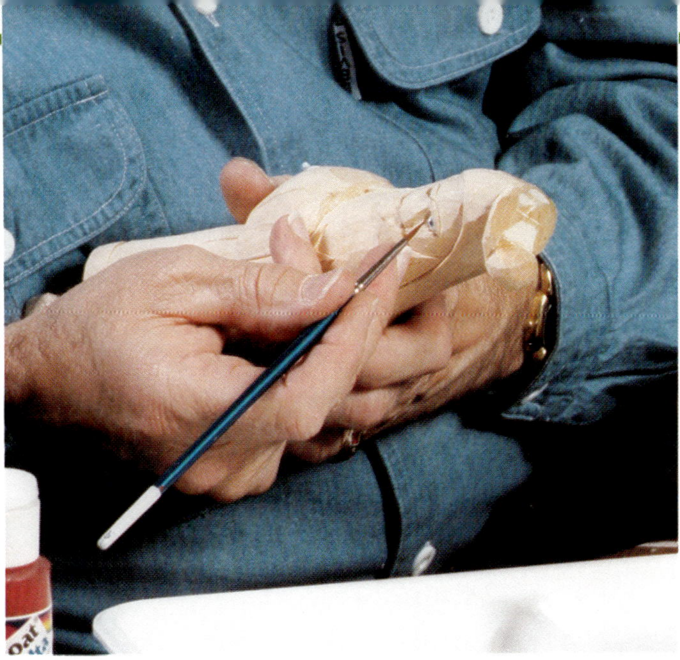

I am trying to demonstrate the painting of an eye. If you have trouble carving one, a painted one looks O.K.

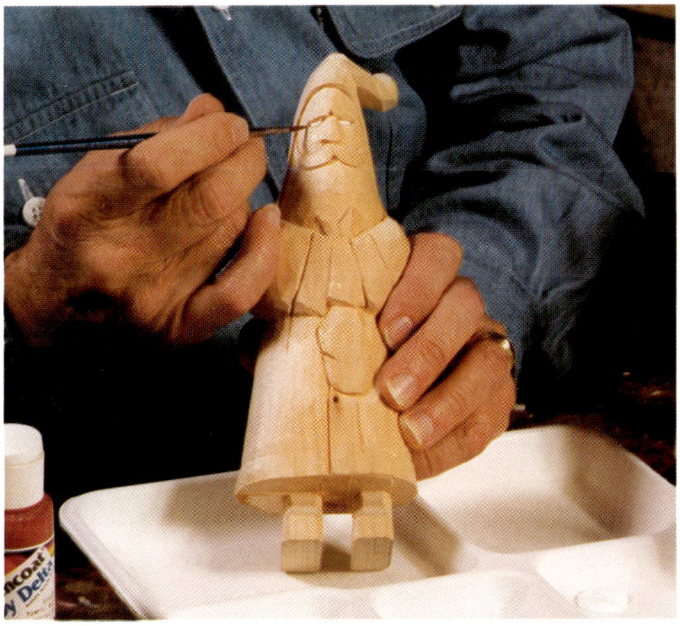

I can look in a mirror and see that my eye is white, blue, and black with little red lines.

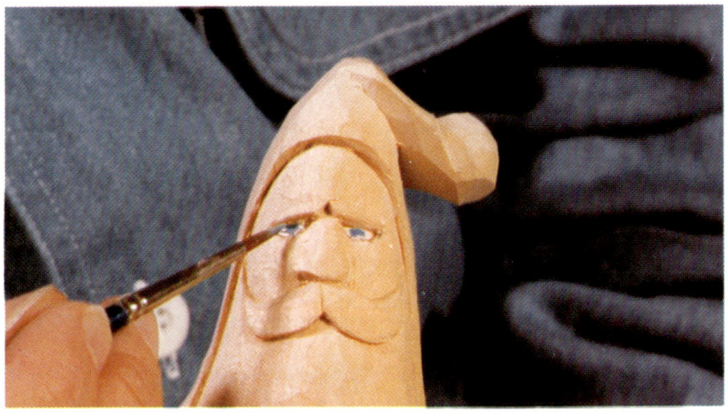

I'm going to leave out the little red lines.

Maybe this will help with painting the eye. Of course, each eye is the same.

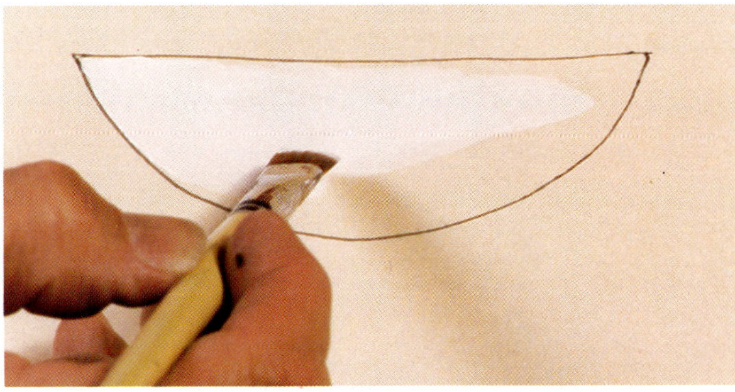

A. Paint the eye area white.

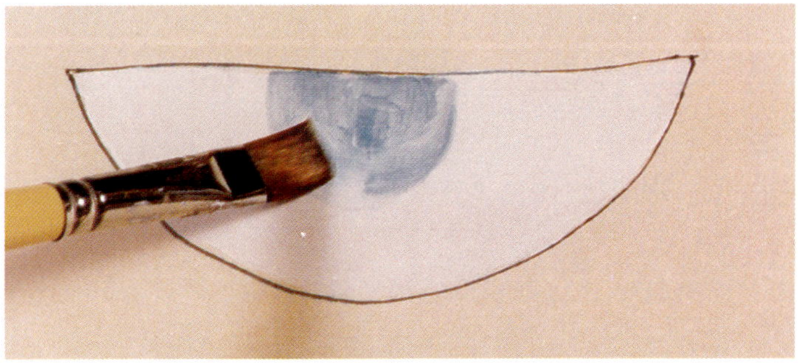

B. A blue semi-circle for the iris. Don't make it round unless you want the Santa to look surprised.

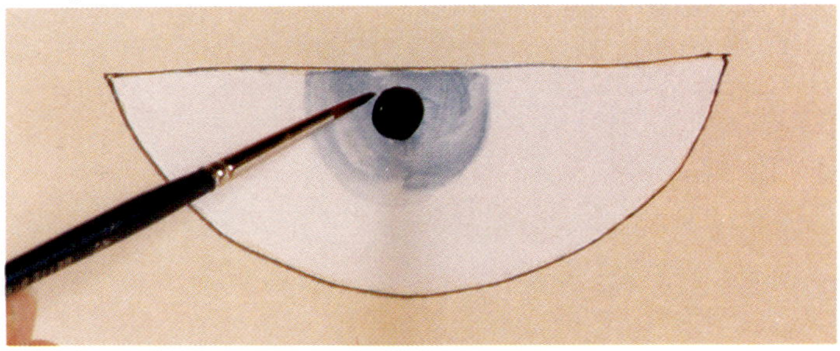

C. Make the pupil black.

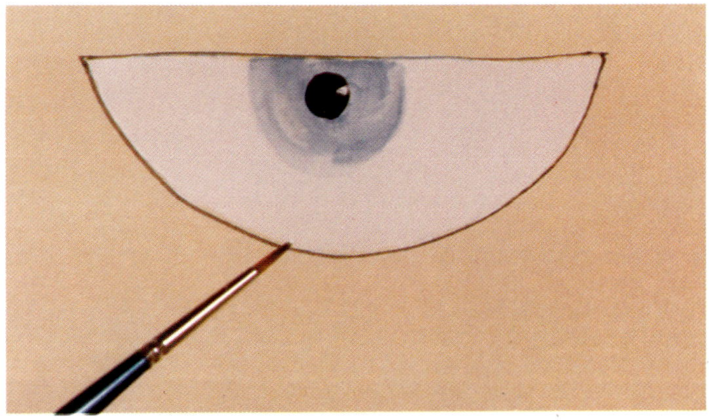

D. Put the white highlight in the same place on each eye. Imagine the pupil is a clock. On this eye I have put the highlight at 2:00 o'clock.

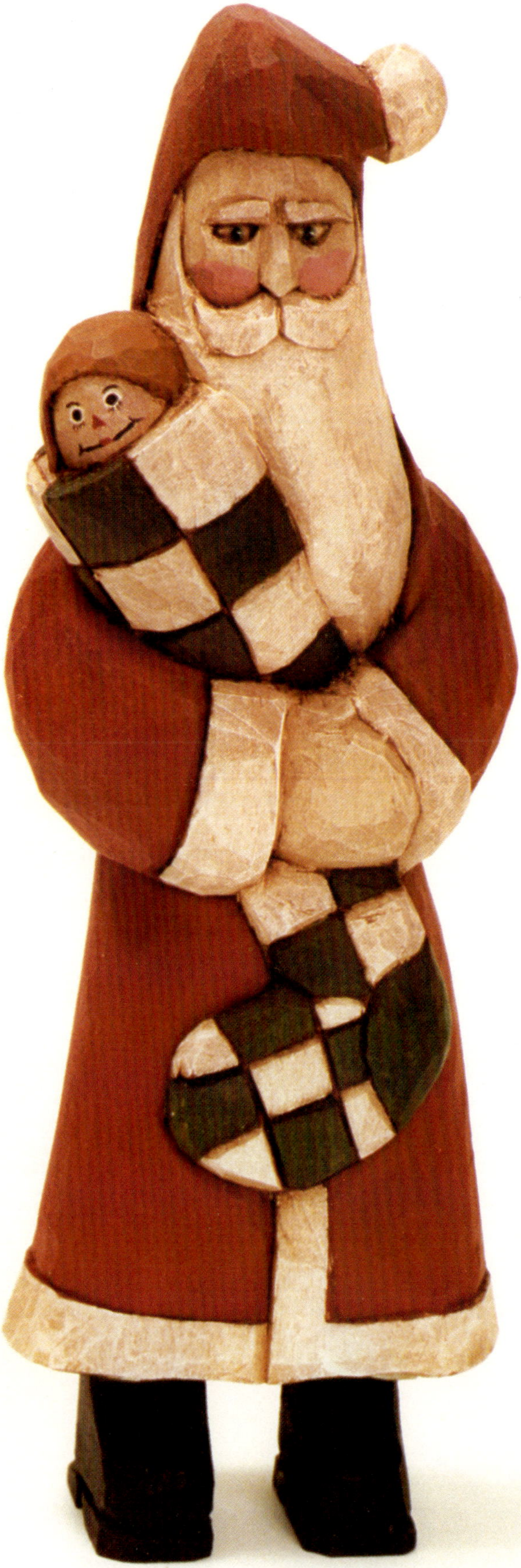

Gallery of Santas

Stocking Santa

One of the few lines of poetry I remember is "The stockings were hung by the chimney with care." The cloak is tompte red, the beard and trim are white, the hands and face are fleshtone, the cheeks are red mixed with the fleshtone to give a pink, healthy look, the boots are black, and the baby has brown hair and whatever type of face you want. I like green and white checked stockings. If you paint Santa's robe a different color, then paint the stocking a compatible color. I will only point out different colors on the other Santas.

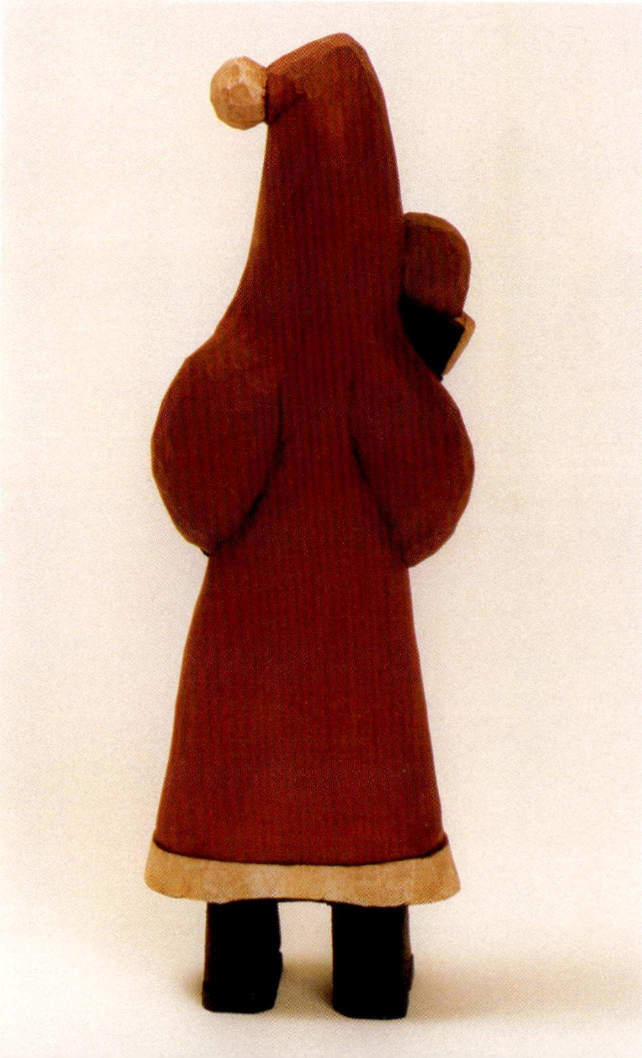

Golfer Santa

This Santa is painted with tompte red. I think Christmas green would look good. The bag is brown and white, but can be done in any color. You may personalize the bag by manufacturer or with the person's name ordering the Santa. The iron club may be painted silver or grey.

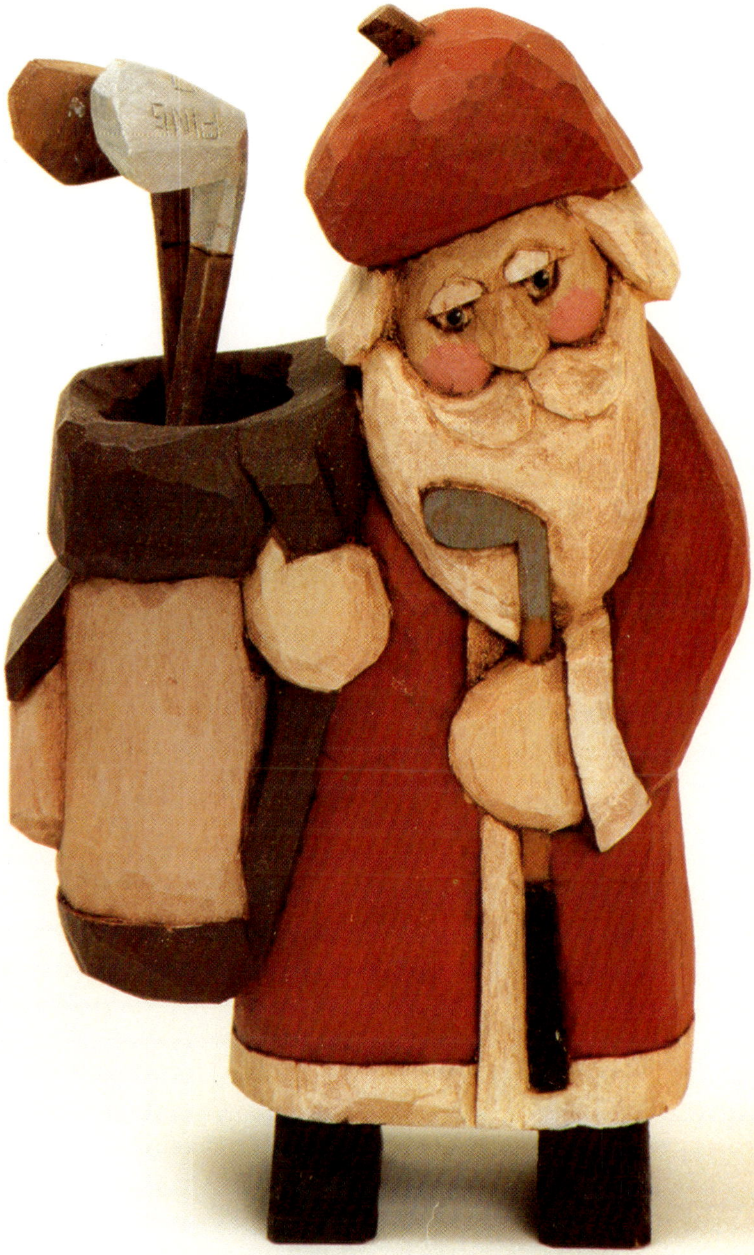

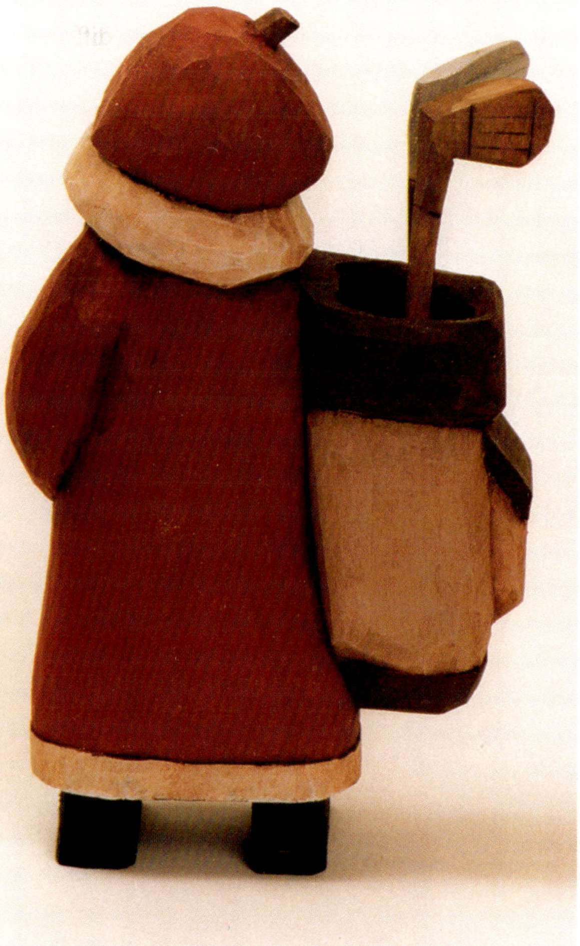

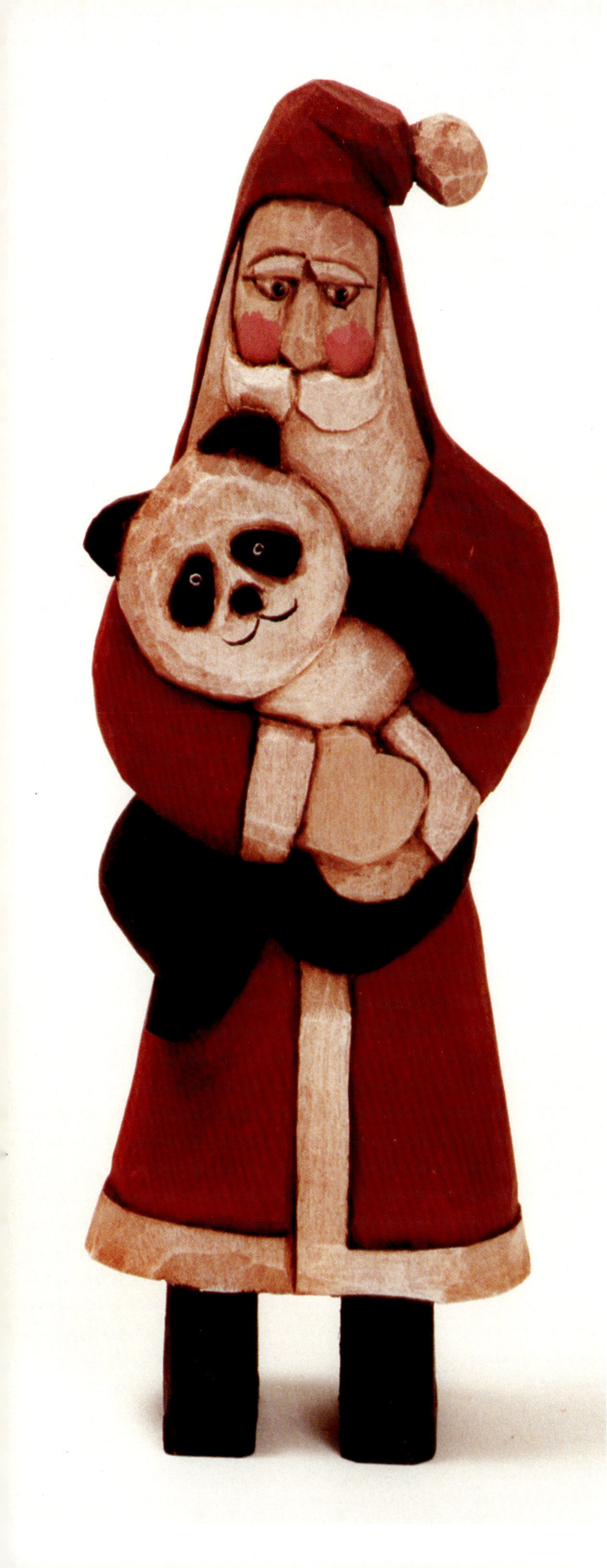

Panda Santa

The Panda is black and white and the Santa is painted the same as the previous ones.

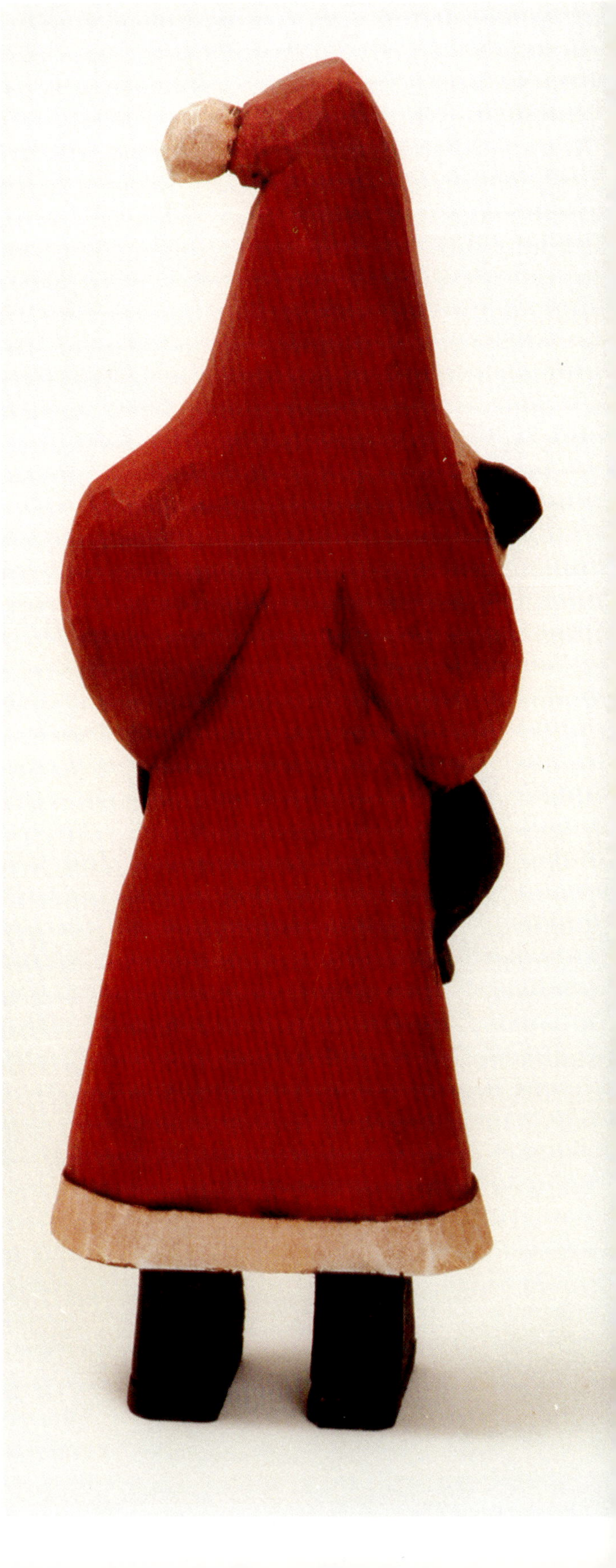

Skiing Santa

The skis and ski poles are brown because they are antiques. You can make them any color you wish. This pattern can easily be a non-Santa skier by leaving off the beard and painting the clothes differently. I don't think your non-Santa would have the big gut.

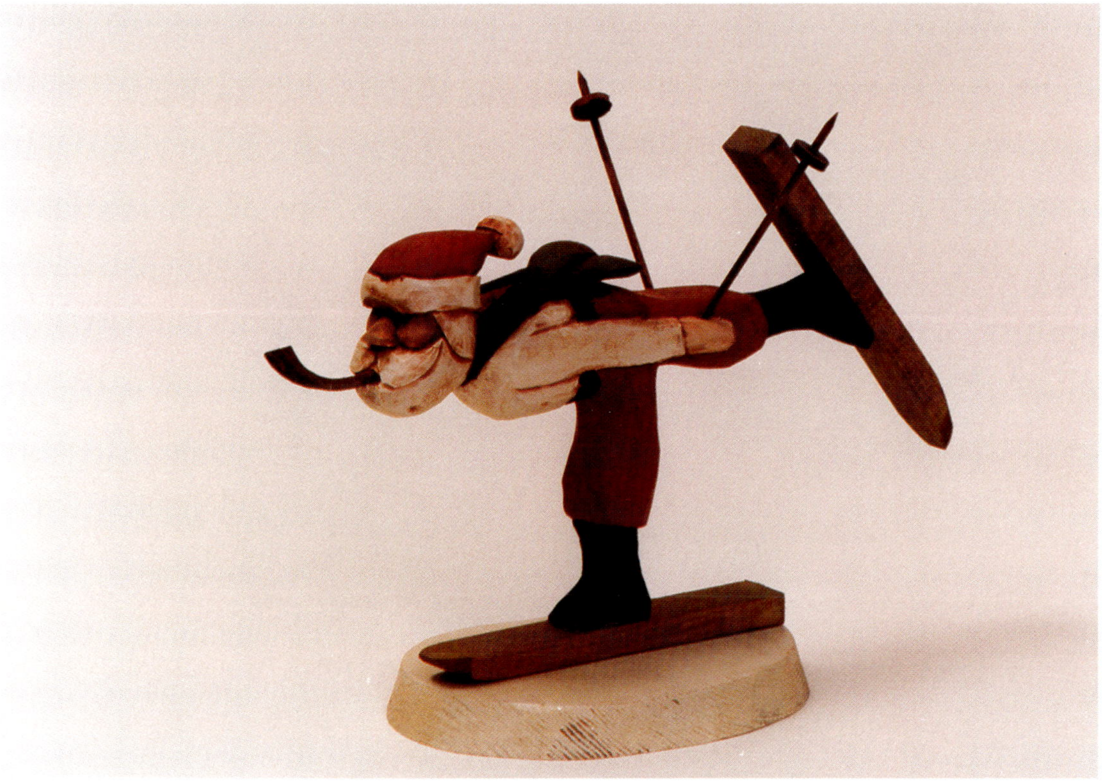

Old Fashioned Skater—Uncle Sam Skater

These are the only non-Santa patterns. I've included these to show how patterns my be interchanged. Paint the old-fashioned skater any color you wish, obviously, the Uncle Sam should be red, white, and blue.

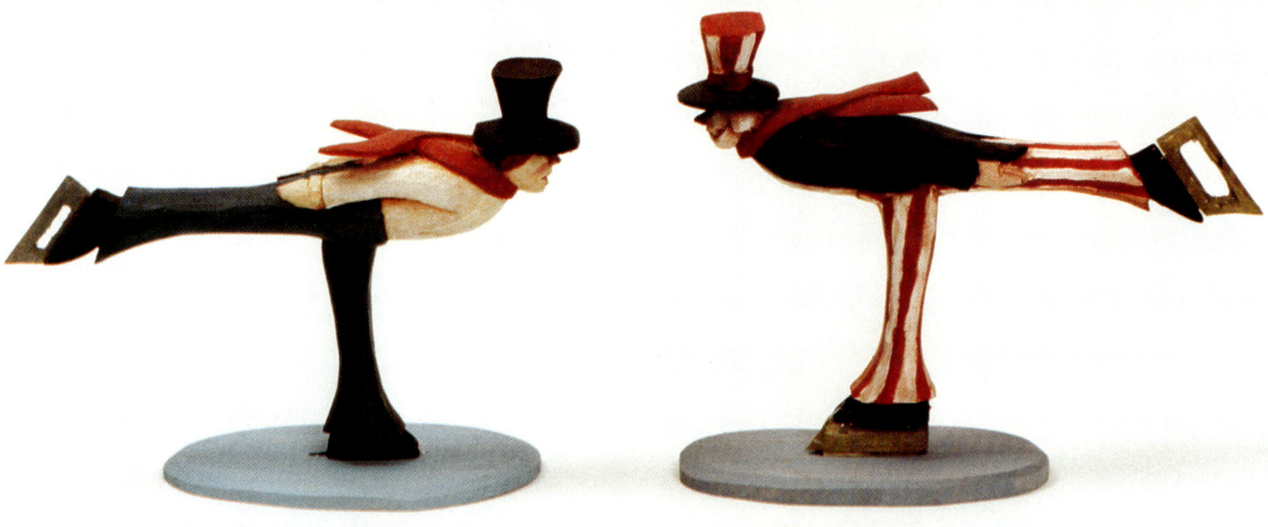

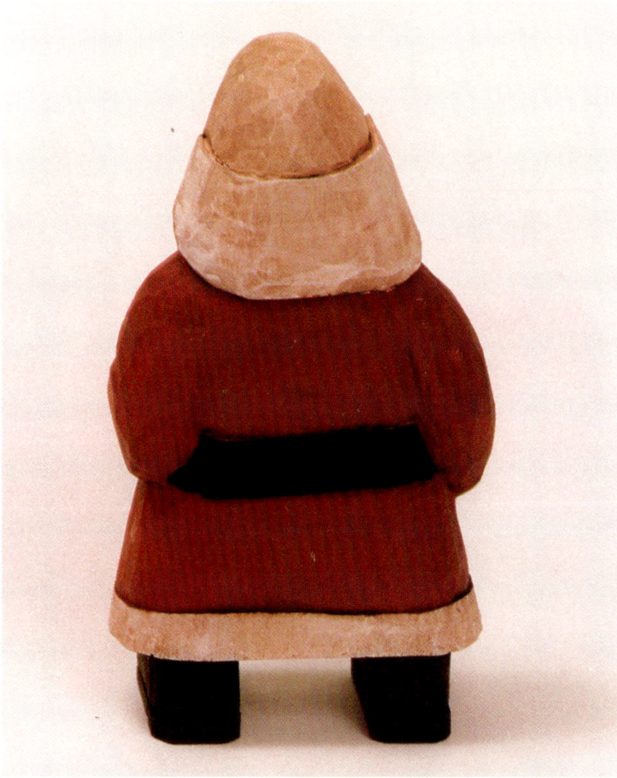

Decoy Santa

You are on your own to paint the decoy. There is a good photo of the decoy at the beginning of the Decoy Santa section. I have painted the area where the robe flares Christmas green.

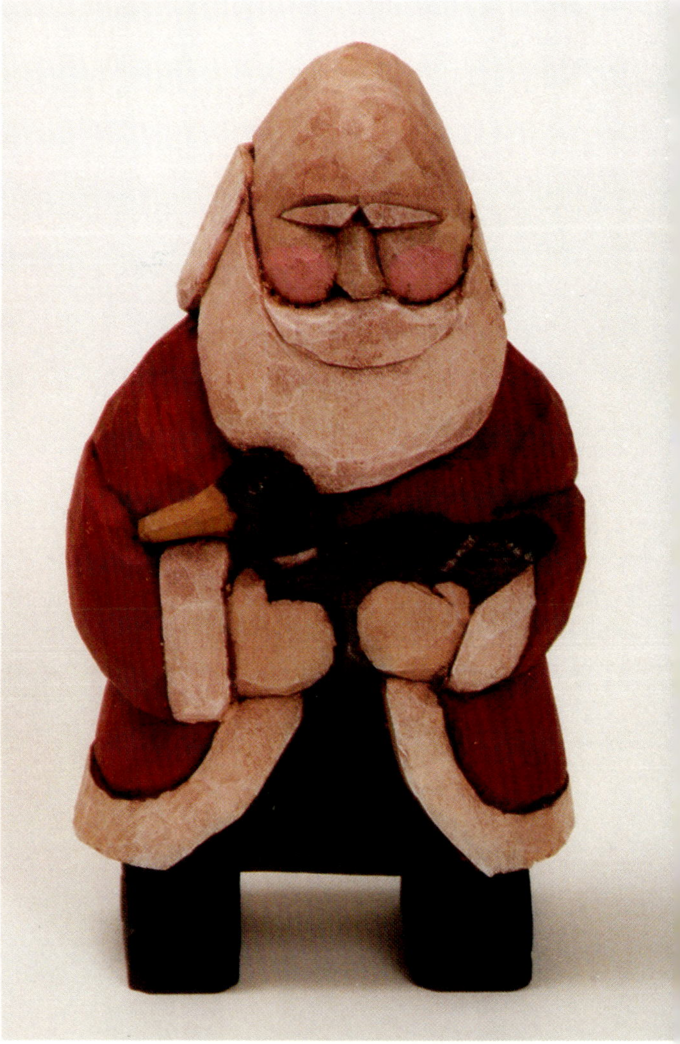

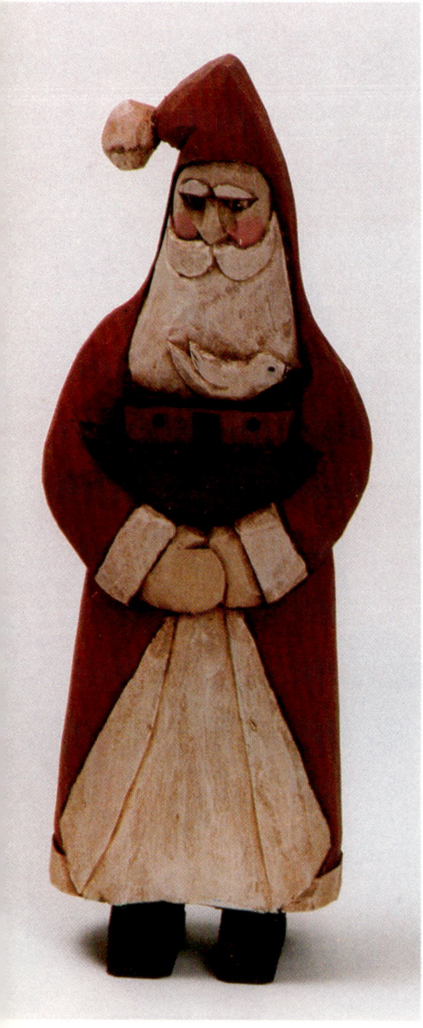

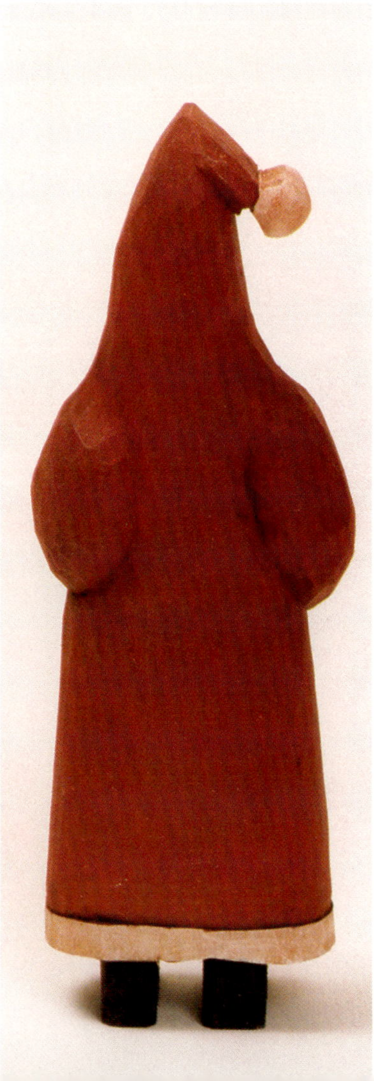

Noah's Ark Santa

The dove is white and the ark is two shades of brown. I use my woodburner to put the detail on the ark. Santa's colors are the same as those of previous Santas.

Santa with Catch

This one was really fun to do but if you are a new carver, I would suggest doing some of the others first. There are some good books on fish carving and you may want to try a few miniatures to go with the Santa.

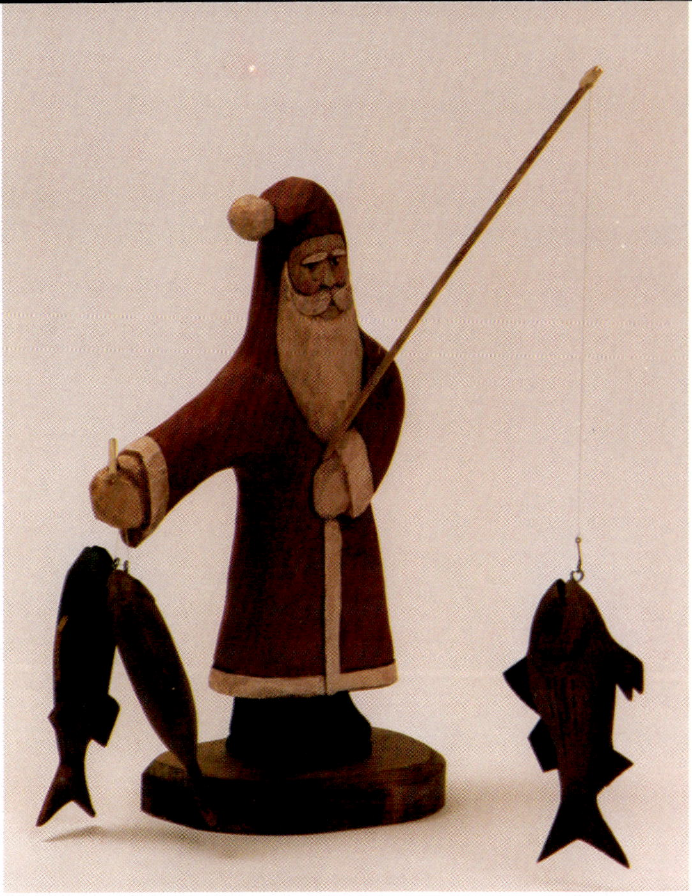

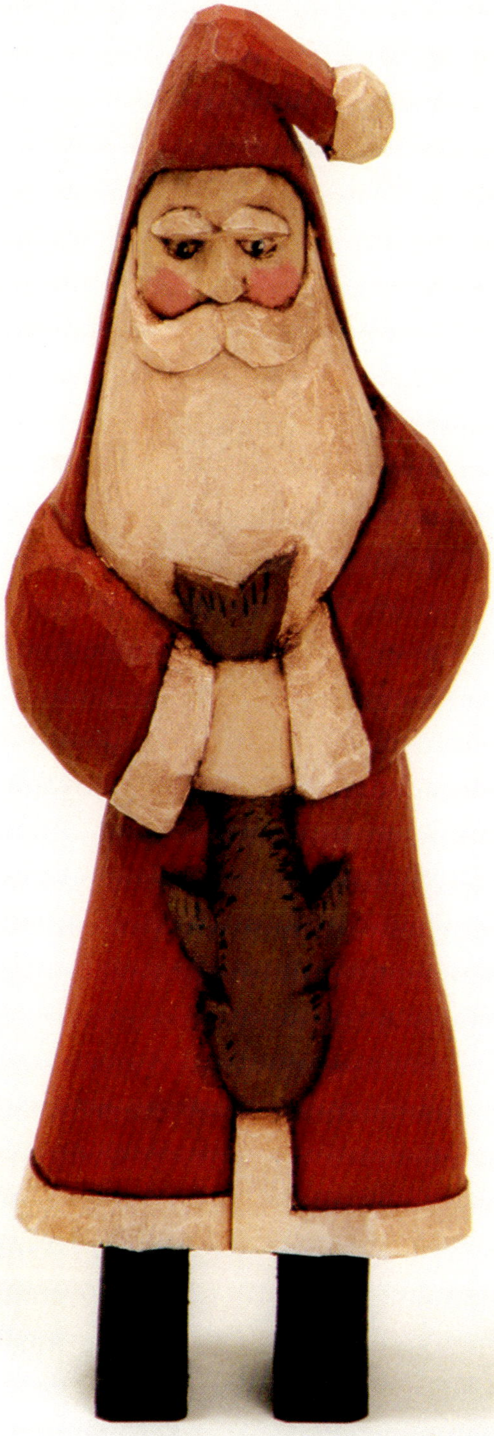

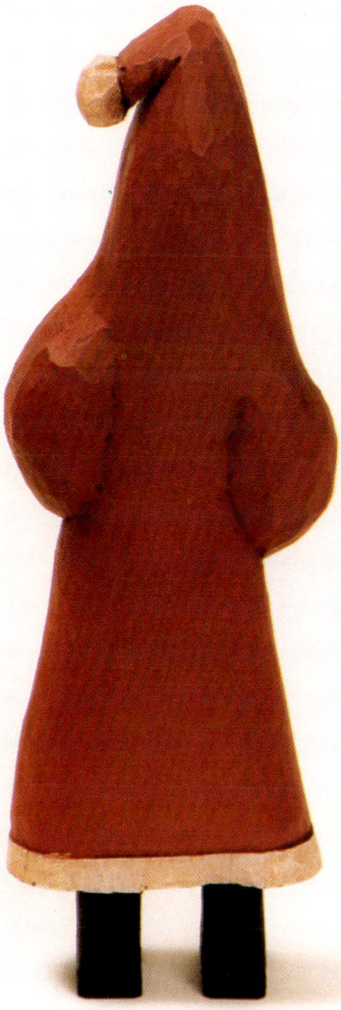

Study Santas

The photo below should help with carving detail as well as painting. I still prefer Ceramcoat Acrylic Paint by Delta. Thank goodness Griffin Bark Brown Show Polish, that I use for antiquing, is available from Woodcraft, if you are unable to find it at other sources. Call them toll free at 1-800-225-1153.

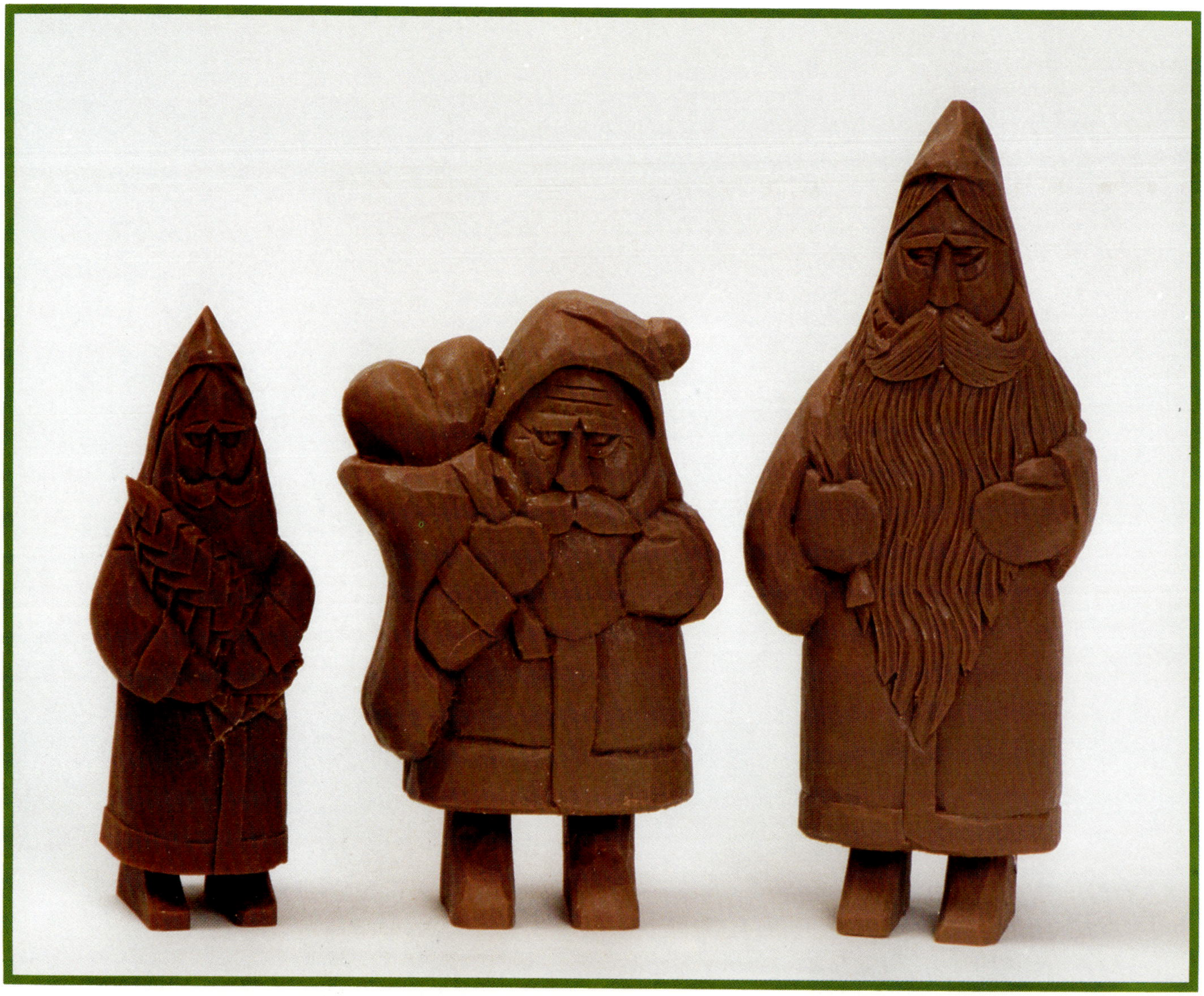